VISUAL QUICKSTART GUIDE

WORD X

FOR MAC OS X

Maria Langer

 Peachpit Press

Visual QuickStart Guide
Word X for Mac OS X
Maria Langer

Peachpit Press
1249 Eighth Street
Berkeley, CA 94710
510-524-2178 • 800-283-9444
510-524-2221 (fax)

Find us on the World Wide Web at: www.peachpit.com
To report errors, please send a note to errata@peachpit.com
Peachpit Press is a division of Pearson Education

Copyright © 2002 by Maria Langer

Editor: Nancy Davis
Indexer: Emily Glossbrenner
Cover Design: The Visual Group
Production: Maria Langer, Connie Jeung-Mills

Colophon

This book was produced with Adobe PageMaker 6.5 on a Power Macintosh G3/300. The fonts used were Kepler Multiple Master, Meta Plus, and PIXymbols Command. Screenshots were created using Snapz Pro X on a Strawberry iMac/266.

Notice of Rights

Notice of Liability

The information in this book is distributed on an "As Is" basis, without warranty. While every precaution has been taken in the preparation of the book, neither the author nor Peachpit Press shall have any liability to any person or entity with respect to any loss or damage caused or alleged to be caused directly or indirectly by the instructions contained in this book or by the computer software and hardware products described in it.

Trademarks

Visual QuickStart Guide is a registered trademark of Peachpit Press, a division of Pearson Education. Microsoft, Windows, PowerPoint, Entourage, and Visual Basic are either trademarks or registered trademarks of Microsoft Corporation in the United States and/or other countries. Apple, Macintosh, iMac, Mac OS, Finder, LaserWriter, and QuickTime are either trademarks or registered trademarks of Apple Computer, Inc. in the United States and/or other countries. PostScript is a trademark of Adobe Systems Incorporated. FileMaker Pro is a registered trademark of FileMaker, Inc. in the United States and other countries. Other product names used in this book may be trademarks or registered trademarks of their respective owners.

Throughout this book trademarked names are used. Rather than put a trademark symbol in every occurrence of a trademarked name, we state we are using the names only in an editorial fashion and to the benefit of the trademark owner with no intention of infringement of copyright.

ISBN 0-201-75843-1

9 8 7 6 5 4 3 2 1

Printed and bound in the United States of America.

Dedication

To Jimbo Norrena,
for all those great hugs

Thanks!

To Nancy Davis, for her patience, perseverance, and incredible editing skills. Even though I often push Nancy to the limit by forcing her to keep up with my last-minute manuscript preparation pace, she continuously finds even the tiniest mistakes without showing any sign of getting burned out. I hope Peachpit realizes how lucky they are to have Nancy on staff—I certainly feel lucky to have her as an editor!

To Nancy Ruenzel, Marjorie Baer, and the other powers-that-be at Peachpit Press, for allowing me to update my Word VQS for Word X.

To Connie Jeung-Mills, for her sharp eyes and gentle layout editing. And to the rest of the folks at Peachpit Press, for doing what they do so well.

To Erik Ryan and Irving Kwong at Microsoft and Danica Smith at Waggener Edstrom, for helping me get the software I needed to complete this book. To Bart Chellis at Microsoft for providing some additional information I needed to make Chapter 15 a bit more accurate. And to Microsoft Corporation for supporting Mac OS X and continuing to improve the best word processing program on earth.

And to Mike, for the usual reasons.

http://www.theflyingm.com/
http://www.marialanger.com/

TABLE OF CONTENTS

TABLE OF CONTENTS

TABLE OF CONTENTS

TABLE OF CONTENTS

INTRODUCTION TO WORD X

Figure 1 Word X is built for Mac OS X and has all the interface elements of Aqua.

Introduction

Microsoft Word X, a component of Microsoft Office v. X, is the latest version of Microsoft's powerful word processing application for Macintosh users. Now built for Mac OS X (**Figure 1**) and more powerful than ever, Word enables users to create a wide range of documents, ranging in complexity from simple, one-page letters to complex, multi-file reports with figures, table of contents, and index.

This Visual QuickStart Guide will help you learn Word X by providing step-by-step instructions, plenty of illustrations, and a generous helping of tips. On these pages, you'll find everything you need to know to get up and running quickly with Word—and more!

This book was designed for page flipping. Use the thumb tabs, index, or table of contents to find the topics for which you need help. If you're brand new to Word or word processing, however, I recommend that you begin by reading at least the first two chapters. **Chapter 1** provides basic information about Word's interface, while **Chapter 2** introduces word processing concepts and explains exactly how they work in Word.

If you've used other versions of Word and are interested in information about new Word X features, be sure to browse through this **Introduction**. It'll give you a good idea of the new things Word has in store for you.

New & Improved Features in Word X

Word X includes several brand new features, as well as improvements to some existing features. Here's a list.

Built for Mac OS X

Word X is built for Mac OS X and takes full advantage of the features of this new operating system. It also utilizes the Mac OS X Aqua interface throughout its interface elements (**Figure 1**).

Multi-selection

You can now select multiple non-contiguous blocks of text (**Figure 2**), both manually and with the improved Find and Replace dialog (**Figure 3**).

Clear Formatting

The Clear Formatting option on the Formatting Palette's Style pop-up menu (**Figure 4**) enables you to remove all manually applied formatting from a selection.

True transparency for graphics

The Quartz 2-D drawing technology that is part of Mac OS X makes it possible to set image transparency (**Figure 5**) and lay images on top of text or other images.

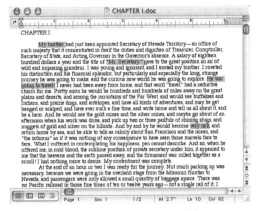

Figure 2 The Multi-selection feature enables you to select multiple non-contiguous blocks of text.

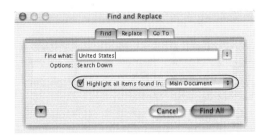

Figure 3 The Multi-selection feature is even supported in the Find and Replace dialog.

Figure 4 Removing formatting from a selection is as easy as choosing a command from the Formatting Palette's Style pop-up menu.

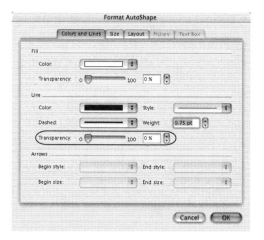

Figure 5 You can now set transparency for graphics.

International printing

Word X support more paper sizes for printing, including paper sizes common in countries other than the United States.

Compatibility

Word X is compatible with Word 2001 and Word 98 for Macintosh and Word 2002 (XP), Word 2000, and Word 97 for Windows.

NEW & IMPROVED FEATURES IN WORD X

THE WORD WORKPLACE

Meet Microsoft Word

Microsoft Word is a full-featured word processing application that you can use to create all kinds of text-based documents—letters, reports, form letters, mailing labels, envelopes, flyers, and even Web pages.

Word's interface combines common Mac OS X screen elements with buttons, commands, and controls that are specific to Word. To use Word effectively, you must have at least a basic understanding of these elements.

This chapter introduces the Word workplace by illustrating and describing the following elements:

◆ The Word screen, including window elements.

◆ Menus, shortcut keys, toolbars, palettes, and dialogs.

◆ Views and document navigation techniques.

◆ Word's Help feature, including the Office Assistant.

✔ Tips

■ If you're brand new to Mac OS X, don't skip this chapter. Many of the interface elements discussed in this chapter apply to all Mac OS X programs, not just Word.

■ If you've used previous versions of Word or Mac OS X, browse through this chapter to learn about some of the interface elements that are new to this version of Word.

The Word Screen

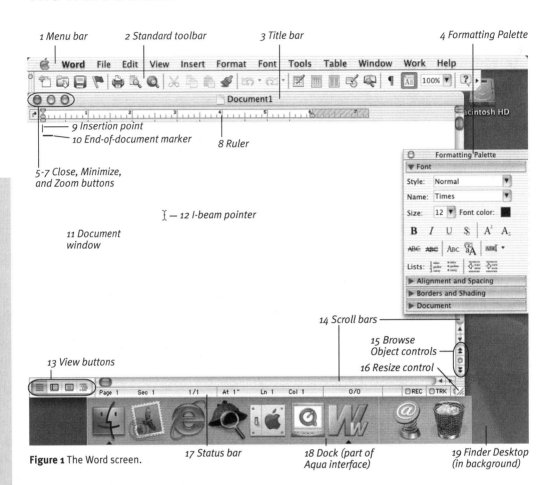

Figure 1 The Word screen.

1 Menu bar · **2 Standard toolbar** · **3 Title bar** · **4 Formatting Palette** · **9 Insertion point** · **10 End-of-document marker** · **8 Ruler** · **5-7 Close, Minimize, and Zoom buttons** · **12 I-beam pointer** · **11 Document window** · **14 Scroll bars** · **15 Browse Object controls** · **16 Resize control** · **13 View buttons** · **17 Status bar** · **18 Dock (part of Aqua interface)** · **19 Finder Desktop (in background)**

Key to the Word screen

1 Menu bar

The menu bar appears at the top of the screen and offers access to Word's commands.

2 Standard toolbar

The Standard toolbar offers buttons for basic Word commands. This toolbar is very similar in other Microsoft Office v. X applications.

3 Title bar

The title bar displays the document's title. You can drag the title bar to move the window.

4 Formatting Palette

The Formatting Palette offers buttons and other controls for applying formatting to document contents.

5 Close button

The close button offers one way to close the window.

6 Minimize button

The minimize button enables you to collapse the window into the Dock. To display the window again, click its icon in the Dock.

7 Zoom button

The zoom button enables you to toggle the window's size from full size to a custom size that you create with the resize control.

8 Ruler

Word's ruler enables you to set paragraph formatting options such as tabs and indentation.

9 Insertion point

The blinking insertion point indicates where text will appear when typed or inserted with the Paste command.

10 End-of-document marker

The end-of-document marker indicates the end of the document.

11 Document window

The document window is where you create, edit, and view Word documents.

12 I-beam pointer

The I-beam pointer enables you to position the insertion point or select text. This pointer, which is controlled by the mouse, turns into other pointer shapes depending on its position on the screen and over objects.

13 View buttons

View buttons enable you to switch between various Word views.

14 Scroll bars

Scroll bars enable you to shift the window's contents to view different parts of the document.

15 Browse Object controls

These buttons enable you to navigate among various document elements.

16 Resize control

The resize control enables you to resize the window to a custom size.

17 Status bar

The status bar displays information about the document, such as the current page number and section, insertion point location, and word counts.

18 Dock

The Dock, which is part of the Aqua interface, offers quick access to commonly used programs and minimized windows.

19 Finder Desktop

The Finder Desktop appears in the background as you work with Word. Clicking the Desktop switches you to the Finder.

THE WORD SCREEN

The Mouse

As with most Mac OS programs, you use the mouse to select text, activate buttons, and choose menu commands.

Mouse pointer appearance

The appearance of the mouse pointer varies depending on its location and the item to which it is pointing. Here are some examples:

◆ In the document window, the mouse pointer usually looks like an I-beam pointer (**Figure 1**).

◆ On a menu name, the mouse pointer appears as an arrow pointing up and to the left (**Figure 2**).

◆ In the selection bar between the left edge of the document window and the text, the mouse pointer appears as an arrow pointing up and to the right (**Figure 3**).

◆ On selected text, the mouse pointer appears as an arrow pointing up and to the left (**Figure 4**).

To use the mouse

There are four basic mouse techniques:

◆ *Pointing* means to position the mouse pointer so that its tip is on the item to which you are pointing (**Figure 2**).

◆ *Clicking* means to press the mouse button once and release it. You click to position the insertion point or to activate a button.

◆ *Double-clicking* means to press the mouse button twice in rapid succession. You double-click to open an item or to select a word.

◆ *Dragging* means to press the mouse button down and hold it while moving the mouse. You drag to resize windows, select text, choose menu commands, or draw shapes.

Figure 2
Pointing to a menu name.

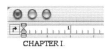

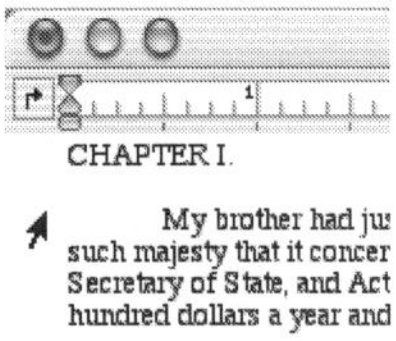

Figure 3
The mouse pointer in the selection bar.

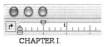

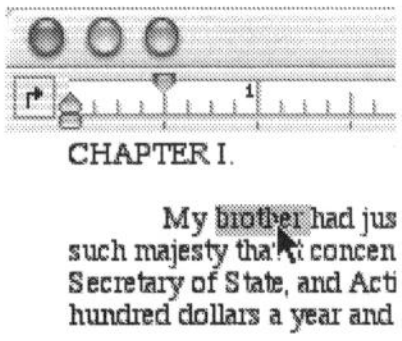

Figure 4
The mouse pointer pointing to a selected word.

Figure 5
The Edit menu.

Figure 6
The Toolbars
submenu under
the View menu.

Menus

All of Word's commands are accessible through its menus. Word has two types of menus:

◆ Standard menus appear on the menu bar at the top of the screen. **Figures 5** and **6** show examples of standard Word menus.

◆ Shortcut or contextual menus appear at the mouse pointer. **Figure 9** on the next page shows an example of a shortcut menu.

Here are some rules to keep in mind when working with menus:

◆ A menu command that appears in gray cannot be selected.

◆ A menu command followed by an ellipsis (...) displays a dialog.

◆ A menu command followed by a triangle has a submenu. The submenu displays additional commands when the main command is highlighted.

◆ A menu command followed by the Command or Option key symbol and a letter or number can be chosen with a shortcut key.

◆ A menu command preceded by a check mark has been "turned on." To toggle the command from on to off or off to on, choose it from the menu.

✔ Tips

■ The above menu rules apply to the menus of most Mac OS applications, not just Word.

■ I discuss dialogs and shortcut keys later in this chapter.

■ In Mac OS X, menus are translucent—you can see right through them. Although I try to minimize menu backgrounds in screen-shots throughout this book, **Figure 9** shows an example of Mac OS X menu translucency.

MENUS

To choose a menu command

1. Click on the name of the menu from which you want to choose the command. The menu appears (**Figure 5**).

2. Click the command you want (**Figure 7**).

   or

   If the command is on a submenu, click on the submenu to display it (**Figure 6**) and then click on the command you want (**Figure 8**).

   The command may blink before the menu disappears, confirming that it has been successfully selected.

To use a shortcut menu

1. Point to the item on which you want to use the shortcut menu.

2. Hold down Control and press the mouse button down. The shortcut menu appears (**Figure 9**).

3. Choose the command that you want.

✔ Tip

■ The shortcut menu only displays the commands that can be applied to the item to which you are pointing.

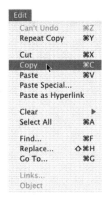

Figure 7
Choosing the Copy command from the Edit menu.

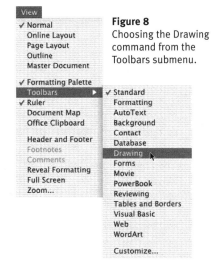

Figure 8
Choosing the Drawing command from the Toolbars submenu.

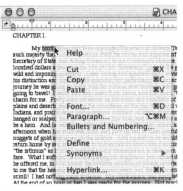

Figure 9 A shortcut menu for selected text.

Shortcut Keys

Shortcut keys are combinations of keyboard keys that, when pressed, choose a menu command without displaying the menu. For example, the shortcut key for the Copy command under the Edit menu (**Figure 7**) is ⌘C. Pressing this key combination chooses the command.

✔ Tips

- All shortcut keys use at least one of the following modifier keys:

Key Name	Keyboard Key
Command	⌘
Option	Option
Shift	Shift
Control	Control

- A menu command's shortcut key is displayed to its right on the menu (**Figure 7**).

- Many shortcut keys are standardized from one application to another. The Save, Print, and Quit commands are three good examples; they're usually ⌘S, ⌘P, and ⌘Q.

- Mac OS X introduced several new standard shortcut keys, including ⌘H (Hide application) and ⌘M (Minimize Window). Keep this in mind if you're a longtime Word user and used these shortcuts to access the Change and Indent commands.

- **Appendix A** includes a complete list of Word's shortcut keys.

To use a shortcut key

1. Hold down the modifier key for the shortcut (normally ⌘).

2. Press the letter or number key for the shortcut.

For example, to choose the Copy command, hold down the Command key and press the C key.

Toolbars & Palettes

Word includes a number of toolbars and palettes for various purposes. Each one includes buttons or menus that activate menu commands or set options.

Figure 10 The Standard toolbar.

By default, Word automatically displays a toolbar and a palette when you launch it:

◆ The Standard toolbar (**Figure 10**) offers buttons for a wide range of commonly used commands.

◆ The Formatting Palette (**Figure 11**) offers buttons and menus for formatting selected items.

Figure 11
The Formatting Palette.

✔ Tips

■ The options that appear in the Formatting Palette (**Figure 11**) vary depending on what is selected.

■ You can expand the Formatting Palette by clicking a triangle beside a tool category heading (**Figure 12**).

■ Other toolbars may appear automatically depending on the task you are performing with Word.

■ Buttons with faint icon images cannot be selected.

■ A button that appears in a gray box with rounded edges is "turned on."

■ You can identify a button by its ScreenTip (**Figure 13**).

■ A toolbar can be docked or floating. A *docked* toolbar (**Figure 10**) is positioned against the top or bottom of the screen and the document window automatically resizes and repositions around it. A *floating* toolbar can be moved anywhere onscreen and, when positioned on top of the document window, floats above the window's contents.

Click here to view tools in this category.

Figure 12
Clicking the triangles beside each tool category heading expands the Formatting Palette to display more options.

Figure 13
A ScreenTip appears when you point to a button.

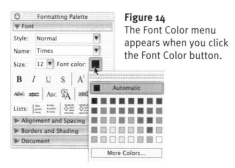

Figure 14
The Font Color menu appears when you click the Font Color button.

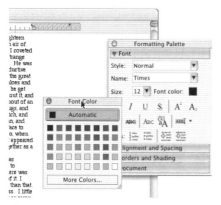

Figure 15 Drag the menu away from the toolbar.

Figure 16
The menu appears as a floating menu or palette.

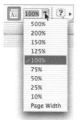

Figure 17
Click the triangle beside the menu to display the menu.

Figure 18 Enter a new value and press [Return].

To view ScreenTips

Point to a toolbar or palette button. A tiny yellow box containing the name of the button appears (**Figure 13**).

✔ Tip

- This feature was known as *ToolTips* in previous versions of Word.

To use a toolbar or palette button

1. Click once on the button for the command or option that you want to activate to select it (**Figure 13**).

2. If the button displays a menu (**Figure 14**), click once on a menu option to select it.

✔ Tip

- Button menus that display a dotted move handle along the top edge (**Figure 14**) can be "torn off" and used as floating menus or palettes. Simply display the menu and drag it away from the toolbar. When the palette appears (**Figure 15**), release the mouse button. The menu is displayed as a floating menu with a title bar that displays its name (**Figure 16**).

To use a toolbar or palette menu

1. Click on the triangle beside the menu to display the menu and its commands (**Figure 17**).

2. Click a command or option to select it.

✔ Tip

- Menus that display text boxes (**Figure 17**) can be changed by typing a new value into the text box. Just click the contents of the text box to select it, then type in the new value and press [Return] (**Figure 18**).

To display or hide a toolbar

Choose the name of the toolbar that you want to display or hide from the Toolbars submenu under the View menu (**Figure 6**).

If the toolbar name has a check mark to its left, it is displayed and will be hidden.

or

If the toolbar name does not have a check mark to its left, it is hidden and will be displayed.

✔ Tip

■ You can also hide a toolbar by clicking its close button.

To display or hide the Formatting Palette

Choose View > Formatting Palette (**Figure 19**).

If the Formatting Palette has a check mark to its left, it is displayed and will be hidden.

or

If the Formatting Palette does not have a check mark to its left, it is hidden and will be displayed.

✔ Tips

■ You can also display or hide the Formatting Palette by clicking the Formatting Palette button on the Standard toolbar.

■ You can also hide the Formatting Palette by clicking its close button.

To move a toolbar or palette

Drag the move handle (**Figure 20**) or title bar for the toolbar or palette to reposition it on screen.

To resize a toolbar

Drag the resize control in the lower-right corner of the toolbar. As you drag, the size and shape of the toolbar changes (**Figure 21**). Release the mouse button (**Figure 22**).

Figure 19
Display or hide the Formatting Palette by choosing its command from the View menu.

Move handle

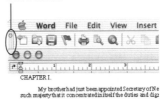

Figure 20 The move handle for a toolbar is like a tiny vertical title bar without a title.

Figure 21 Drag the lower-right corner of a toolbar to resize it...

Figure 22
...to almost any dimensions.

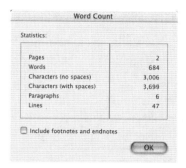

Figure 23 The Word Count dialog just displays information.

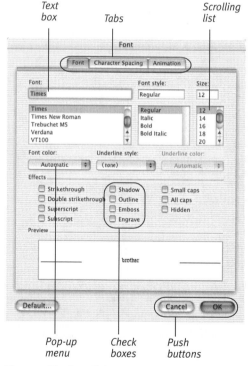

Text box   *Tabs*   *Scrolling list*

Pop-up menu   *Check boxes*   *Push buttons*

Figure 24 The Font dialog.

Dialogs

Like most other Mac OS applications, Word uses dialogs to communicate with you.

Word can display many different dialogs, each with its own purpose. There are two basic types of dialogs:

◆ Dialogs that simply provide information (**Figure 23**).

◆ Dialogs that offer options to select (**Figure 24**) before Word completes the execution of a command.

✔ Tip

■ Often, when a dialog appears, you must dismiss it by clicking OK or Cancel before you can continue working with Word.

Anatomy of a Word dialog

Here are the components of many Word dialogs, along with information about how they work.

◆ **Tabs** (**Figure 24**), which appear at the top of some dialogs, let you move from one group of dialog options to another. To switch to another group of options, click its tab.

◆ **Text boxes** (**Figures 24** and **25**) let you enter information from the keyboard. You can press the Tab key to move from one text box to the next or click in a text box to position the insertion point within it. Then enter a new value.

◆ **Scrolling lists** (**Figure 24**) offer a number of options to choose from. Use the scroll bar to view options that don't fit in the list window. Click an option to select it; it becomes highlighted and appears in the text box.

Continued on next page...

DIALOGS

Continued from previous page.

- ◆ **Check boxes (Figure 24)** let you turn options on or off. Click a check box to toggle it. When a **✔** or **X** appears in the check box, its option is turned on.

- ◆ **Radio buttons (Figure 25)** let you select only one option from a group. Click an option to select it; the option that was selected before you clicked is deselected.

- ◆ **Pop-up menus (Figure 24)** also let you select one option from a group. Display a pop-up menu as you would any other menu **(Figure 26)**, then choose the option that you want.

- ◆ **Preview areas (Figures 24 and 25)**, when available, illustrate the effects of your changes before you finalize them by clicking the OK button.

- ◆ **Push buttons (Figures 23, 24 and 25)** let you access other dialogs, accept the changes and close the dialog (OK), or close the dialog without making changes (Cancel). To choose a button, click it once.

✔ Tips

- ■ When the contents of an text box are selected, whatever you type will replace the selection.

- ■ Word often uses text boxes and scrolling lists together **(Figure 24)**. You can use either one to make a selection.

- ■ If a pair of tiny triangles appears to the right of a text box **(Figure 25)**, you can click a triangle to increase or decrease the value in the text box.

- ■ In some scrolling lists, double-clicking an option selects it and dismisses the dialog.

- ■ You can turn on any number of check boxes in a group, but you can select only one radio button in a group.

Radio buttons

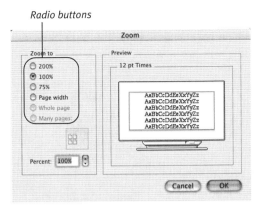

Figure 25 The Zoom dialog.

Figure 26
Displaying a
pop-up menu.

- ■ The Word onscreen help system sometimes refers to pop-up menus as *drop-down* lists.

- ■ Mac OS X documentation sometimes refers to text boxes as *entry fields*.

- ■ A pulsating blue push button is the default button; you can "click" it by pressing (Enter).

- ■ You can usually "click" the Cancel button by pressing (Esc) or (⌘ ⌘ .).

- ■ A *dialog sheet* is a dialog that is attached to a specific document window. Dialog sheets are new in Mac OS X.

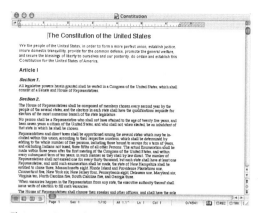

Figure 27 Normal view.

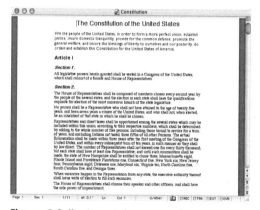

Figure 28 Online Layout view.

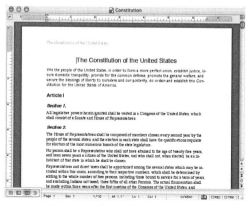

Figure 29 Page Layout view.

Views

Word offers several different ways to view the contents of a document window.

◆ **Normal view (Figure 27)**, which is the default view, shows continuously scrolling text. It is the fastest view for entering and editing text but does not show page layout elements.

◆ **Online Layout view (Figure 28)** displays the contents of a document so they are easier to read on screen. Text appears in a larger font size and wraps to fit the window rather than margins or indentations.

◆ **Page Layout view (Figure 29)** displays the objects on a page positioned as they will be when the document is printed. This is a good view for working with documents that include multiple column text or positioned graphics, such as a newsletter or flyer.

◆ **Outline view (Figure 30)** displays the document's structure—headings and body text—in a way that makes it easy to rearrange the document. Headings can be collapsed to hide detail and simplify the view. I discuss working with Outline view in **Chapter 8**.

◆ **Master Document view** displays the structure of a master document that includes several Word documents. It is useful for working with very long documents that consist of multiple smaller documents, such as chapters in a book.

Continued on next page...

VIEWS

Continued from previous page.

✔ Tips

■ Although each view is designed for a specific purpose, you can use almost any view to work with a document.

■ The illustrations throughout this book display windows in Normal view, unless otherwise indicated.

To switch to another view

Choose the desired option from the View menu (**Figure 31**).

or

Click the appropriate view button at the bottom of the window (**Figure 32**). (There is no button for Master Document view.)

✔ Tip

■ View buttons do not appear at the bottom of the document window in Online layout view (**Figure 28**). You must use the View menu to switch to another view from that view.

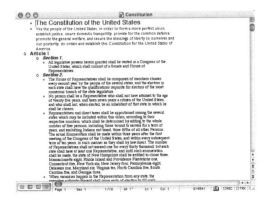

Figure 30 Outline view.

Figure 31
The View menu.

Normal   Page layout

Figure 32 View buttons at the bottom of the document window.

Online layout   Outline

VIEWS

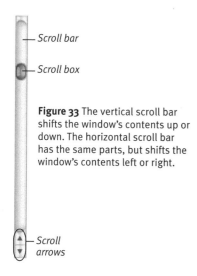

Scroll bar

Scroll box

Figure 33 The vertical scroll bar shifts the window's contents up or down. The horizontal scroll bar has the same parts, but shifts the window's contents left or right.

Scroll arrows

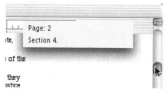

Figure 34 When you drag the scroll box, a yellow box with the page number and heading appears.

Document Navigation

Word offers a variety of ways to view different parts of a document.

◆ Use **scroll bars** to shift the contents of the document window.

◆ Use the **Go To command** to view a specific document element, such as a certain page.

◆ Use **Browse Object buttons** to browse a document by its elements.

◆ Use the **Document Map** to move quickly to a specific heading.

✔ Tip

■ Although some keyboard keys change the portion of the document being viewed, they also move the insertion point. I tell you about these keys in **Chapter 2**.

To scroll the contents of the document window

Click the scroll arrow (**Figure 33**) for the direction that you want to view. For example, to scroll down to view the end of a document, click the down arrow.

or

Drag the scroll box (**Figure 33**) in the direction that you want to view. As you drag, a yellow box appears on screen (**Figure 34**). It indicates the page and, if applicable, the heading that you are scrolling to.

or

Click in the scroll bar above or below the scroll box (**Figure 33**). This shifts the window contents one screenful at a time.

✔ Tips

■ Having trouble remembering which scroll arrow to click? Just remember this: click up to see up, click down to see down, click left to see left, and click right to see right.

■ You can use the Mac OS X General preferences pane to change the way scroll arrows appear on the scroll bar. **Figure 33** illustrates the default configuration.

To use the Go To command

1. Choose Edit > Go To (**Figure 5**) or press ⌃ ⌘G or F5 . The Find and Replace dialog appears with its Go To tab displayed (**Figure 35**).

2. In the Go to what scrolling list, select the type of document element that you want to view.

3. Enter the appropriate reference in the text box in the middle of the dialog.

4. Click the Next button to go to the next reference.

5. Click the dialog's close button to dismiss it.

For example, to go to page 5 of a document, select Page in step 2 and enter the number 5 in step 3.

To browse a document by its elements

1. Point to the Select Browse Object button (**Figure 36**).

2. Click to display the Select Browse Object pop-up menu.

3. Choose the element by which you want to browse (**Figure 37**).

4. Use the Next and Previous navigation buttons to view the next or previous element.

✔ Tips

■ The name of the object that a button represents appears at the top of the Select Browse Object pop-up menu when you point to the button (**Figure 37**).

■ Some of the buttons on the Select Browse Object pop-up menu (**Figure 37**) display dialogs that you can use for browsing.

Figure 35 The Go To tab of the Find and Replace dialog.

Figure 36 The Browse Object buttons at the bottom of the vertical scroll bar.

Figure 37
This menu pops up when you click the Select Browse Object button.

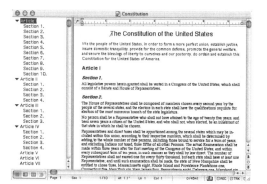

Figure 38 The Document Map in Normal view.

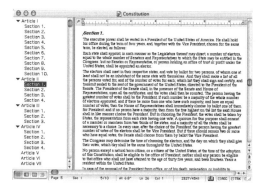

Figure 39 Clicking a heading in the Document Map shifts the document view to display that part of the document.

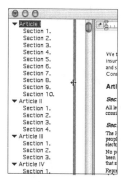

Figure 40 You can resize the Document Map's pane by dragging its right border.

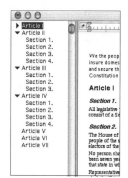

Figure 41 Click a heading's triangle to hide its subheadings.

To use the Document Map

1. Choose View > Document Map (**Figure 31**).

   The Document Map appears in a narrow pane on the left side of the window (**Figure 38**).

2. Click the heading that you want to view. The main window pane's view shifts to show the heading that you clicked (**Figure 39**).

✔ Tips

- The Document Map is a good way to navigate documents that use Word's heading styles. I explain how to use headings in **Chapter 8** and styles in **Chapter 5**.

- Navigating with the Document Map also moves the insertion point. I tell you more about moving the insertion point in **Chapter 2**.

- You can change the width of the Document Map's pane by dragging the blue border between it and the main window pane (**Figure 40**). When you release the border, both panes resize.

- You can collapse and expand the headings displayed in the Document Map by clicking the triangles to the left of the heading names (**Figure 41**).

- To hide the Document Map when you are finished using it, choose View > Document Map or double-click the blue border between the Document Map and the main window pane.

USING THE DOCUMENT MAP

Windows

Word allows you to open more than one document window at a time (**Figure 42**).

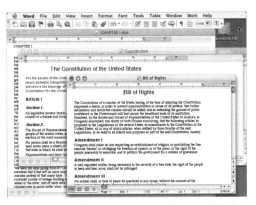

✔ Tips

- The active window appears "on top" of the stack of windows and has a striped title bar (**Figure 42**). The other title bars are translucent.

- I explain how to create and open documents in **Chapter 2**.

Figure 42 Multiple open document windows; Bill of Rights is the active document.

To activate a different window

Choose the name of the window that you want to view from the list at the bottom of the Window menu (**Figure 43**).

or

Click on any visible part of the window that you want to view.

The window you selected or clicked comes to the front and becomes the active window.

Figure 43
The Window menu.

To neatly arrange windows

Choose Window > Arrange All (**Figure 43**).

The windows are resized and repositioned so you can see into each one (**Figure 44**).

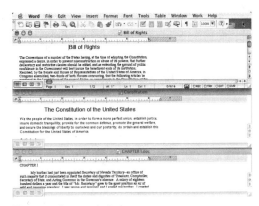

Figure 44 Arranged windows.

Figure 45 A minimized document window appears in the Dock.

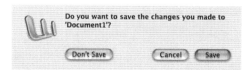

Figure 46 The dialog that appears when you close a window that contains unsaved changes.

To minimize a window

1. If necessary, activate the window that you want to minimize.

2. Choose Window > Minimize Window (**Figure 43**) or press ⌃⌘M.

   or

   Click the window's minimize button.

   The window shrinks into the Dock (**Figure 45**).

To display a minimized window

Click the icon for the window in the Dock (**Figure 45**).

The window expands from the Dock and becomes the active window.

To close a window

1. If necessary, activate the window that you want to close.

2. Choose File > Close or press ⌃⌘W.

   or

   Click the window's close button.

✔ Tip

- If the document contains unsaved changes, Word warns you by displaying a dialog sheet like the one in **Figure 46**. I tell you about saving documents in **Chapter 2**.

WORKING WITH DOCUMENT WINDOWS

The Office Assistant

The Office Assistant displays an animated character (**Figure 47**) that can provide tips and assistance while you work. While enabled, the Office Assistant is the main interface for working with Word's onscreen Help feature.

Figure 47
The Office Assistant.

To enable or disable the Office Assistant

Choose Help > Use the Office Assistant (**Figure 48**).

If a check mark appears to the left of the command, the Office Assistant is enabled and choosing the command will disable it.

or

If a check mark does not appear to the left of the command, the Office Assistant is not enabled and choosing the command will enable (and display) it.

Figure 48
Word's Help menu.

To display the Office Assistant

Click the Office Assistant button 🔘 on the Standard toolbar. The Office Assistant appears.

To hide the Office Assistant

Click the close button on the Office Assistant window (**Figure 47**). The Office Assistant will wave goodbye before disappearing.

Figure 49 An Office Assistant tip.

To move the Office Assistant

Drag the Office Assistant's move handle to reposition it on screen.

To get tips

1. Click the light bulb that appears in the Office Assistant window (**Figure 47**) when the Office Assistant has a tip for you. The tip appears, along with a prompt to get more information (**Figure 49**).

2. Click Cancel to close the tip.

Figure 50 Get the Office Assistant's attention,...

Figure 51 ...then enter a description of what you want to do.

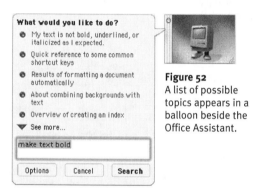

Figure 52
A list of possible topics appears in a balloon beside the Office Assistant.

To ask the Office Assistant a question

1. Click the Office Assistant to get its attention. A balloon with instructions appears (**Figures 49** and **50**).

2. Type a brief description of what you want to do into the text box (**Figure 51**) and click the Search button. A list of possible topics appears in another balloon (**Figure 52**).

3. Click a topic that interests you. A Microsoft Office Help window like the one in (**Figure 53**) appears. Information about the topic appears in the right side of the window.

4. When you are finished reading help information, click the Microsoft Office Help window's close button.

Figure 53 When you click the button beside a topic, the Microsoft Office Help window appears with information about that topic.

USING THE OFFICE ASSISTANT

Word Help

Word has an extensive onscreen Help feature that provides information about using Word to complete specific tasks. You access Word Help via the Office Assistant (as discussed on the previous page) or commands under the Help menu (**Figure 48**).

To browse Help

1. Choose Help > Word Help Contents (**Figure 48**). The Microsoft Office Help contents window appears (**Figure 54**).

2. Navigate through topics and information as follows:

    ▲ To expand a topic in the left side of the window, click the triangle beside it. Subtopics appear beneath it.

    ▲ Click underlined links to display information and subtopics in the right side of the window.

    Figure 55 shows an example of expanded help topics with subtopic links, along with step-by-step instructions for completing a task.

✔ Tips

- You can click the left arrow button at the top of the Help window to browse topics you browsed earlier in the help session.

- You can also display help contents (**Figure 54**) by clicking the Contents button in any Microsoft Office Help window.

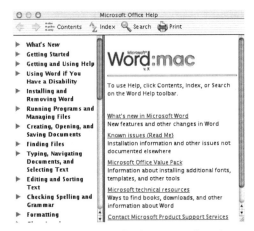

Figure 54 Choosing Word Help Contents from the Help menu with the Office Assistant turned off displays Help contents.

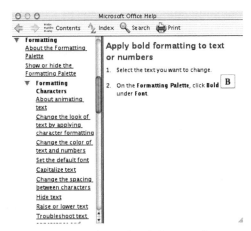

Figure 55 Navigate through Help by expanding topic outlines and clicking underlined links.

USING WORD HELP

Figure 56 Clicking the Index button in the Microsoft Office Help window displays a link for each letter of the alphabet.

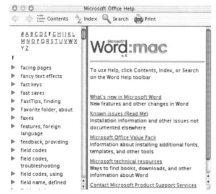

Figure 57 Click a letter to display topics beginning with that letter.

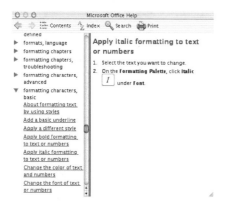

Figure 58 Continue clicking topics and links until the information you want appears on the right side of the window.

To use the Help Index

1. Choose Help > Word Help Contents (**Figure 48**). The Microsoft Office Help contents window appears (**Figure 54**).

2. Click the Index button. A link for each letter of the alphabet appears on the left side of the screen (**Figure 56**).

3. Click the letter for the topic that interests you. A list of main topics beginning with that letter appears beneath the letter links (**Figure 57**).

4. Navigate through topics and information as follows:

   ▲ To expand a topic in the left side of the window, click it. Subtopics appear beneath it.

   ▲ Click underlined links to display information and subtopics in the right side of the window.

   Figure 58 shows an example of subtopic links, along with step-by-step instructions for completing a task.

USING WORD HELP

WORD BASICS

Word Processing Basics

Word processing software has revolutionized the way we create text-based documents. Rather than committing each character to paper as you type—as you would do with a typewriter—word processing enables you to enter documents on screen, edit and format them as you work, and save them for future reference or revision. Nothing appears on paper until you use the Print command.

If you're brand new to word processing, here are a few concepts you should understand before you begin working with Word or any other word processing software:

- ◆ Words that you type that do not fit at the end of a line automatically appear on the next line. This feature is called *word wrap*.

- ◆ Do not press Return at the end of each line as you type. Doing so inserts a Return character, which signals the end of a paragraph, not the end of a line. Press Return only at the end of a paragraph or to skip a line between paragraphs.

- ◆ Do not use Spacebar to indent text or position text in simple tables. Instead, use Tab in conjunction with tab settings on the ruler.

- ◆ Text can be inserted or deleted anywhere in the document.

✔ Tip

- ■ I tell you more about all of these concepts in this chapter and throughout this book.

Launching Word

To use Word, you must open the Word application. This loads Word into RAM (Random Access Memory), so your computer can work with it.

To launch Word by opening its application icon

1. In the Finder, locate the Microsoft Word application icon (**Figure 1**). It should be in the Microsoft Office X or Microsoft Word X folder on your hard disk.

2. Click the icon once to select it, then choose File > Open or press ⌃ ⌘ O.

   or

   Double-click the icon.

   The Word splash screen appears briefly (**Figure 2**), then the Project Gallery window appears (**Figure 3**).

✔ Tip

- You can disable the display of the Project Gallery window at startup by turning off the check box at the bottom of its window (**Figure 3**). When disabled, a blank document window appears instead. I tell you about the Project Gallery later in this chapter.

To launch Word by opening a Word document icon

1. In the Finder, locate the icon for the document that you want to open (**Figure 4**).

2. Click the icon once to select it, then choose File > Open or press ⌃ ⌘ O.

   or

   Double-click the icon.

   The Word splash screen appears briefly (**Figure 2**), then a document window containing the document you opened appears (**Figure 5**).

Figure 1
The Microsoft Word application icon.

Microsoft Word

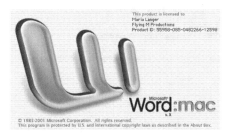

Figure 2 The Word X splash screen.

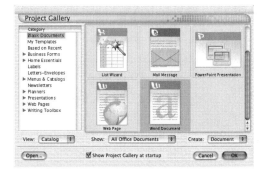

Figure 3 When you launch Word by opening the Word application icon, it displays the Project Gallery window.

Figure 4
A Word document icon.

CHAPTER I.doc

Figure 5 When you launch Word by opening a Word document icon, it displays the document you opened.

Figure 6
The Word menu.

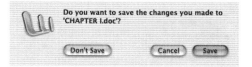

Figure 7 A dialog like this appears when a document with unsaved changes is open when you quit Word.

Quitting Word

When you're finished using Word, you should use the Quit command to close the application. This completely clears Word out of RAM, freeing up RAM for other applications.

✔ Tips

- Closing all document windows is not the same as quitting. The only way to remove Word from RAM is to quit. I tell you about closing document windows in **Chapter 1**.

- Quitting Word also instructs Word to save preference settings and any changes to the Normal template.

To quit Word

Choose Word > Quit Word (**Figure 6**) or press ⌃⌘Q. Here's what happens:

- ◆ If any documents are open, they close.

- ◆ If an open document contains unsaved changes, a dialog appears (**Figure 7**) so you can save the changes. I explain how to save documents later in this chapter.

- ◆ The Word application quits.

✔ Tip

- As you've probably guessed, Word automatically quits when you restart or shut down your computer.

Word Documents, Templates, & Wizards

The documents you create and save using Word are Word document files. These files contain all the information necessary to display the contents of the document as formatted using Microsoft Word.

All Word document files are based on *templates*. A template is a collection of styles and other formatting features that determines the appearance of a document. Templates can also include default text, macros, and custom toolbars.

For example, you can create a letterhead template that includes your company's logo and contact information or is designed to be printed on special paper. The template can include styles that utilize specific fonts. It can also include custom toolbars with buttons for commands commonly used when writing letters.

Wizards take templates a step further. They are special Word document files that include Microsoft Visual Basic commands to automate the creation of specific types of documents. Word comes with many wizards, some of which are covered in this book.

Figure 8
A Word
Dental Record   template icon.

Figure 9
A Word
Label Wizard   wizard icon.

Figure 10
Word's File menu.

✔ Tips

- A Word document icon (**Figure 4**), template icon (**Figure 8**), and wizard icon (**Figure 9**) have the same big *W* found on the Word application icon (**Figure 1**).

- Word can open and save files in formats other than Word document format. I tell you more about file formats later in this chapter.

- When no other template is specified for a document, Word applies the default template, Normal.

- I cover styles in **Chapter 4**. Macros, custom toolbars, and Visual Basic, however, are advanced features that are beyond the scope of this book.

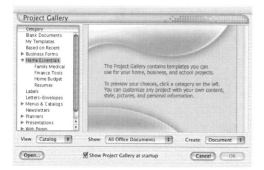

Figure 11 Click the triangle beside a category you want to view to display subcategories within it.

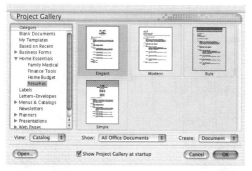

Figure 12 When you click a subcategory, previews of the items within it appear.

Figure 13 Use the View pop-up menu...

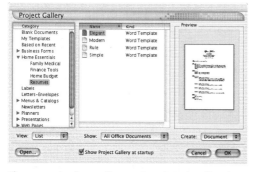

Figure 14 ...to change the way templates are listed.

The Project Gallery

The Project Gallery (**Figure 3**) offers an easy way to create documents with Microsoft Office applications.

To open the Project Gallery

Choose File > Project Gallery (**Figure 10**) or press Shift ⌃ ⌘ P.

✔ Tip

■ By default, the Project Gallery automatically appears when you launch Word by opening its application icon.

To display templates & wizards in a specific category

1. On the left side of the window, click the triangle beside a category you want to view. A list of subcategories appears beneath it (**Figure 11**).

2. Click on the name of a subcategory to display previews of the templates or wizards within it (**Figure 12**).

To customize the Project Gallery's display

Use the pop-up menus at the bottom of the Project Gallery window to set options:

◆ View menu options (**Figure 13**) let you switch between Catalog view (**Figure 3**) and List view (**Figure 14**).

◆ Show menu options (**Figure 15**) let you specify the type of documents you want to show.

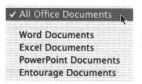

Figure 15 The Show pop-up menu enables you to show a specific type of Office document.

THE PROJECT GALLERY

29

Creating Documents

You can create a new document with the Project Gallery or with the New Blank Document command.

To create a blank document

1. Choose File > Project Gallery (**Figure 10**) to display the Project Gallery window (**Figure 3**).

2. In the Category list, select Blank Documents.

3. In the preview area, select Word Document.

4. Click OK.

or

Choose File > New Blank Document (**Figure 10**) or press ⌃ ⌘ N.

or

Click the New Blank Document button on the Standard toolbar.

A blank document based on the Normal template appears (**Figure 16**).

To create a document based on a template other than Normal

1. Choose File > Project Gallery (**Figure 10**) to display the Project Gallery window (**Figure 3**).

2. In the Category list, select the category for the template you want to use.

3. In the preview area, select the preview for the template you want to use (**Figure 12**).

4. Click OK.

A document based on the template that you selected appears (**Figure 17**). Follow the instructions in the template to replace place-holder text with your text.

Figure 16 A blank document window based on the Normal template.

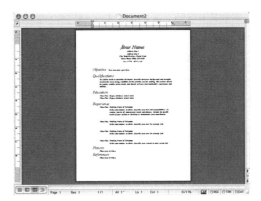

Figure 17 A document based on a template.

CREATING DOCUMENTS

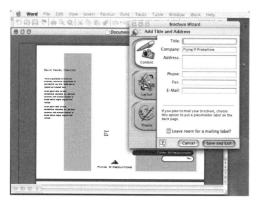

Figure 18 A template with a wizard.

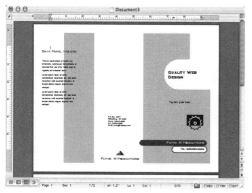

Figure 19 A document created with a template and wizard.

To create a document with a wizard

1. Choose File > Project Gallery (**Figure 10**) to display the Project Gallery window (**Figure 3**).

2. In the Category list, select the category for the template or wizard you want to use.

3. In the preview area, select the preview for the template or wizard you want to use.

4. Click OK.

5. A document window appears, along with a Wizard window (**Figure 18**). Enter appropriate information in each tab of the Wizard window to create the document. (The tabs are along the left side of the Wizard's window.)

6. When you've finished entering information, click Save and Exit to dismiss the Wizard. The document you created remains open (**Figure 19**) so you can continue to work with it.

✔ Tips

- Many templates automatically launch wizards. The brochure template in **Figure 18** is a good example. So even if you think you're creating a document based on a template, a wizard may appear to guide you through the creation process.

- When the wizard is finished, you can customize the document it creates to meet your specific needs.

To create a document based on a recently accessed document

1. Choose File > Project Gallery (**Figure 10**) to display the Project Gallery window (**Figure 3**).

2. Select Based on Recent in the Category list.

3. Select a document in the preview area (**Figure 20**).

4. Click OK.

5. A copy of the recent document you selected in step 3 appears. Modify the document as discussed throughout this book to create the new document.

To create a template

1. Choose File > Project Gallery (**Figure 10**) to display the Project Gallery window (**Figure 3**).

2. Use the Category list and preview area to select a template on which to base the new template.

   or

   Select Blank Documents in the Category list and Word Document in the preview area to create a document based on the Normal template.

3. Choose Template from the Create pop-up menu (**Figure 21**) at the bottom of the Project Gallery window.

4. Click OK.

5. A new document window appears. Add text, styles, or other features to the document as discussed throughout this book.

✔ Tip

■ When you save the document, it is automatically saved as a template. I tell you how to save documents and templates later in this chapter.

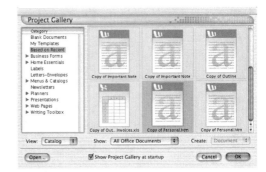

Figure 20 The Based on Recent category lists documents you recently opened.

Figure 21 Use the Create pop-up menu to specify whether you want to create a regular document or a template.

CREATING TEMPLATES

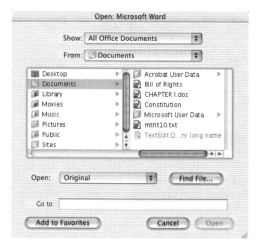

Figure 22 The Open dialog.

Figure 23
The From pop-up menu near the top of the Open dialog. This is the same menu that appears as the Where pop-up menu in the Save As dialog.

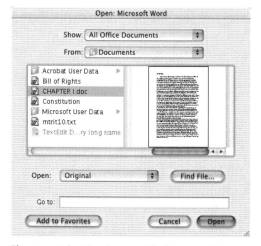

Figure 24 Select the document that you want to open.

Opening Existing Documents

Once a document has been saved, you can reopen it to read it, modify it, or print it.

To open an existing document

1. Choose File > Open (**Figure 10**) or press ⌃ ⌘ O .

   or

   Click the Open button on the Standard toolbar.

2. Use the Open dialog that appears (**Figure 22**) to locate the file that you want to open:

   ▲ Use the From pop-up menu near the top of the dialog (**Figure 23**) to go to a different location.

   ▲ Double-click a folder to open it.

3. Select the file that you want to open (**Figure 24**) and click the Open button.

   or

   Double-click the file that you want to open.

✔ Tips

- To view only specific types of files in the Open dialog, select a format from the Show pop-up menu at the top of the dialog (**Figure 25**).

- If you select All Documents from the Show pop-up menu (**Figure 25**), you can open just about any kind of file. Be aware, however, that a document in an incompatible format may not appear the way you expect when opened.

Continued on next page...

OPENING EXISTING DOCUMENTS

Continued from previous page.

■ If a preview is available for a file, it will appear in the dialog when you select the file's name (**Figure 24**). Normally, documents you create with Word do not include previews; the templates that come with Word, however, do.

■ You can use the Find File button in the Open dialog to search for a file based on criteria you specify.

■ To open a copy of a file rather than the original, choose Copy from the Open pop-up menu (**Figure 26**).

■ You can open a recent file by selecting it from the list of recently opened files at the bottom of the File menu (**Figure 10**).

■ To add a folder to your Favorite Places list, select it in the Open dialog and click the Add to Favorites button.

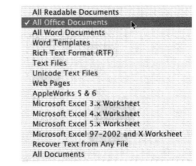

Figure 25 The Show pop-up menu lists file formats that can be read by Word.

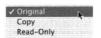

Figure 26 You can open a copy of a document rather than the original by choosing Copy from the Open pop-up menu.

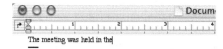

Figure 27 Text characters appear at the insertion point as you type.

Figure 28 Word wrap automatically occurs when the text you type won't fit on the current line.

Figure 29 Press Return to start a new paragraph.

Figure 30 Press Shift Return to start a new line in the same paragraph.

✔ Tip

- Use a line break instead of a paragraph break if you want to begin a new line without beginning a new paragraph. This makes it easy to apply paragraph formatting to a group of lines that belong together. I tell you more about paragraph formatting in **Chapters 4** and **5**.

Entering Text

In most cases, you will enter text into a Word document using the keyboard.

✔ Tip

- A jagged red or green line appearing beneath the text you type indicates that the text has a possible spelling or grammar error. I tell you about the spelling and grammar checking features of Word in **Chapter 5**.

To type text

Type the characters, words, or sentences that you want to enter into the document. Text appears at the blinking insertion point as you type it (**Figure 27**).

✔ Tips

- I explain how to move the insertion point a little later in this chapter.

- Do not press Return at the end of a line. A new line automatically begins when a word can't fit on the current line (**Figure 28**).

To start a new paragraph

At the end of a paragraph, press Return. This inserts a paragraph break or return character that ends the current paragraph and begins a new one (**Figure 29**).

To start a new line

To end a line without ending the current paragraph, press Shift Return. This inserts a line break character within the current paragraph (**Figure 30**).

Nonprinting Characters

Every character you type is entered into a Word document—even characters that normally can't be seen, such as space, tab, return, line break, and optional hyphen characters.

Word enables you to display these *nonprinting characters* as gray marks (**Figure 31**), making it easy to see all the characters in a document.

✔ Tips

- By displaying invisible characters, you can get a better understanding of the structure of a document. For example, **Figure 31** clearly shows the difference between the return and line break characters entered in **Figure 30**.

- Nonprinting characters are sometimes referred to as *invisible characters*.

To show or hide nonprinting characters

Click the Show/Hide ¶ button ¶ on the Standard toolbar. This toggles the display of nonprinting characters.

To specify which nonprinting characters should be displayed

1. Choose Word > Preferences (**Figure 6**).

2. Click View in the list on the left side of the Preferences dialog that appears (**Figure 32**).

3. Turn on the check boxes in the Nonprinting characters area of the dialog to specify which characters should appear.

4. Click OK.

✔ Tips

- To display all nonprinting characters, turn on the All check box in step 3.

- I tell you more about Word's preferences in **Chapter 15**.

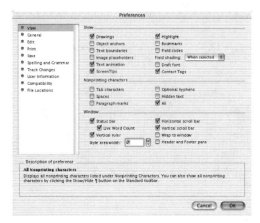

Figure 31 Text with nonprinting characters displayed. This example shows space, return, line break, and tab characters.

Figure 32 The View options of the Preferences dialog.

Table 1

Keystrokes for Moving the Insertion Point	
PRESS:	**TO MOVE THE INSERTION POINT:**
→	one character to the right
←	one character to the left
↑	one line up
↓	one line down
⌃ ⌘ →	one word to the right
⌃ ⌘ ←	one word to the left
⌃ ⌘ ↑	one paragraph up
⌃ ⌘ ↓	one paragraph down
End	to the end of the line
Home	to the beginning of the line
⌃ ⌘ End	to the end of the document
⌃ ⌘ Home	to the beginning of the document
Page Up	up one screen
Page Down	down one screen
⌃ ⌘ Page Up	to the top of the previous page
⌃ ⌘ Page Down	to the top of the next page
⌃ ⌘ Option Page Up	to the top of the window
⌃ ⌘ Option Page Down	to the bottom of the window
Shift F5	to the previous edit

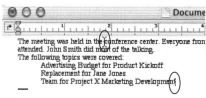

Figure 33 Position the mouse pointer where you want the insertion point to move.

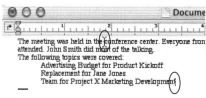

Figure 34 Click to move the insertion point.

The Insertion Point

The blinking insertion point indicates where the information you type or paste will be inserted. There are two main ways to move the insertion point: with the keyboard and with the mouse.

✔ Tip

■ The insertion point also moves when you use the Document Map to navigate within a document. I tell you about the Document Map in **Chapter 1**.

To move the insertion point with the keyboard

Press the appropriate keyboard key(s) (**Table 1**).

✔ Tip

■ There are additional keystrokes that work within cell tables. I tell you about them in **Chapter 9**, where I discuss tables.

To move the insertion point with the mouse

1. Position the mouse's I-beam pointer where you want to move the insertion point (**Figure 33**).

2. Click the mouse button once. The insertion point moves (**Figure 34**).

✔ Tips

■ Simply moving the I-beam pointer is not enough. You must click to move the insertion point.

■ Do not move the mouse while clicking. Doing so will select text.

MOVING THE INSERTION POINT

Inserting & Deleting Text

You can insert or delete characters at the insertion point at any time.

◆ When you insert characters, any text to the right of the insertion point shifts to the right to make room for new characters (**Figures 35** and **36**).

◆ When you delete text, any text to the right of the insertion point shifts to the left to close up space left by deleted characters (**Figures 37** and **38**).

◆ When you insert or delete text, word wrap adjusts if necessary to comfortably fit characters on each line (**Figures 36** and **38**).

To insert text

1. Position the insertion point where you want to insert the text (**Figure 35**).

2. Type the text you want to insert (**Figure 36**).

✔ Tip

■ You can also insert text by pasting the contents of the Clipboard at the insertion point. I tell you about using the Clipboard to copy and paste text later in this chapter.

To delete text

1. Position the insertion point to the right of the character(s) you want to delete (**Figure 37**).

2. Press [Delete] to delete the character to the left of the insertion point (**Figure 38**).

or

1. Position the insertion point to the left of the character(s) you want to delete.

2. Press [Del] or [Clear] to delete the character to the right of the insertion point.

Figure 35 Position the insertion point.

Figure 36 Type the text that you want to insert.

Figure 37 Position the insertion point to the right of the character(s) you want to delete.

Figure 38 Press [Delete] to delete the characters, one at a time.

✔ Tip

■ You can also delete text by selecting it and pressing [Delete] or [Del]. I tell you how to select text a little later in this chapter.

Figure 39
The Click and Type pointer.

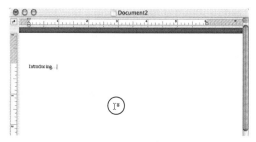

Figure 40 Position the Click and Type pointer where you want to enter text.

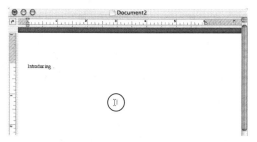

Figure 41 Double-click to position the insertion point.

Figure 42 Type the text you want to appear.

Click and Type

Word's Click and Type feature makes it easier to position text in a blank area of a page. You simply double-click with the Click and Type pointer (**Figure 39**) and enter the text you want to appear there. Word automatically applies necessary formatting to the text to position it where you want it.

✔ Tip

■ Click and Type works only in Page Layout and Online Layout views. I tell you more about Word's views in **Chapter 1**.

To enter text with Click and Type

1. If necessary, switch to Page Layout or Online Layout view.

2. Position the mouse pointer in an empty area of the document window. The mouse pointer should turn into a Click and Type pointer (**Figure 40**).

3. Double-click. The insertion point appears at the mouse pointer (**Figure 41**).

4. Type the text you want to enter (**Figure 42**).

✔ Tips

■ The appearance of the Click and Type pointer indicates how it will align text at the insertion point. For example, the pointer shown in **Figures 39** and **40** indicates that text will be centered (**Figure 42**). I tell you more about alignment, including how to change it, in **Chapter 3**.

■ There are some limitations to where you can use the Click and Type feature. Generally speaking, if the Click and Type pointer does not appear, you cannot use it to position text.

Selecting Text

You can select one or more characters to delete, replace, copy, cut, or format. Selected text appears with a colored background or in inverse type.

✔ Tip

- There are many ways to select text. This section provides just a few of the most useful methods.

To select text by dragging

1. Position the mouse I-beam pointer at the beginning of the text.

2. Press the mouse button down and drag to the end of the text you want to select (**Figure 43**).

3. Release the mouse button.

All characters between the starting and ending points are selected.

✔ Tips

- This is the most basic text selection technique. It works for any amount of text.

- By default, Word automatically selects entire words when you drag through more than one word. To disable this feature, choose Word > Preferences (**Figure 6**), click Edit in the list on the left side of the Preferences dialog that appears (**Figure 44**), and turn off the check box for When selecting, automatically select entire word.

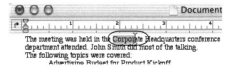

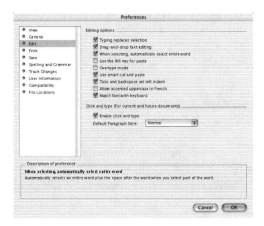

Figure 43 Drag over text to select it.

Figure 44 The Edit options of the Preferences dialog.

Table 2

Techniques for Selecting Text by Clicking	
To select:	**Do this:**
a word	double-click the word
a sentence	hold down ⌘ and click in the sentence
a line	click in the selection bar to the left of the line (**Figure 45**)
a paragraph	triple-click in the paragraph or double-click in the selection bar to the left of the paragraph
the document	hold down ⌘ and click in the selection bar to the left of any line
any text	position the insertion point at the beginning of the text, then hold down (Shift) and click at the end of the text

SELECTING TEXT

Figure 45 Click in the selection bar beside a line to select the line.

Figure 46 Hold down ⌃⌘ to make a second selection.

Figure 47 This example shows four separate selections.

Figure 48
The Edit menu.

To select text by clicking

Click as instructed in **Table 2** to select specific amounts of text.

✔ Tips

■ You can combine techniques in **Table 2** with dragging to select multiple lines and paragraphs.

■ When you select an entire word by double-clicking it, Word also selects any spaces after it.

To make multiple selections

1. Use any technique to select text.

2. Hold down ⌃⌘ while making another selection (**Figure 46**).

3. Repeat step 2 until all selections are made (**Figure 47**).

✔ Tip

■ This ability to select *non-contiguous* blocks of text, which is new to Word X, makes it easy to format multiple blocks of text at once.

To select the contents of a document

Choose Edit > Select All (**Figure 48**) or press ⌃⌘A.

Editing Selected Text

Once you select text, you can delete it or replace it with other text.

To delete selected text

Press Delete, Del, or Clear. The selected text disappears.

To replace selected text

With text selected, type the replacement text. The selected text disappears and the replacement text is inserted in its place.

Copying & Moving Text

Word offers two ways to copy or move text:

- ◆ Use the Copy, Cut, and Paste commands (or their shortcut keys) to place text on the Clipboard and then copy it from the Clipboard to another location.

- ◆ Use drag-and-drop editing to copy or move selected text.

You can copy or move text to the following locations:

- ◆ To a different location within the same document.

- ◆ To a different document.

- ◆ To a document created with a program other than Word.

✔ Tips

- ■ Copying and moving text make it possible to reuse text and reorganize a document without a lot of retyping.

- ■ The Clipboard is a place in RAM that is used to temporarily store selected items that are copied or cut.

- ■ Text copied or cut to the Clipboard remains on the Clipboard until you use the Copy or Cut command again or restart your computer. This makes it possible to use Clipboard contents over and over in any document created with Word or another application.

- ■ Word isn't the only program that supports the Copy, Cut, and Paste commands or drag-and-drop text editing. Most Mac OS programs do. That means you can copy and move text in non-Word documents into a Word document.

- ■ These techniques also work with objects such as graphics and QuickTime movies. I tell you more about working with objects in **Chapter 7**.

Figure 49 Select the text that you want to copy.

Figure 50
Position the insertion point where you want the copied text to appear.

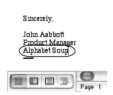

Figure 51
When you use the Paste command, the contents of the Clipboard appear at the insertion point.

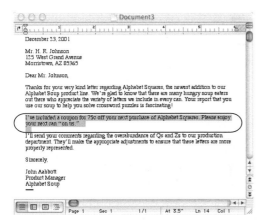

Figure 52 Select the text that you want to move.

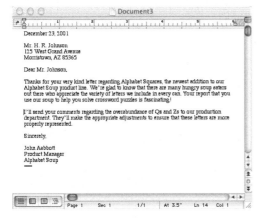

Figure 53 The text you cut disappears.

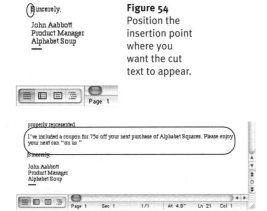

Figure 54
Position the
insertion point
where you
want the cut
text to appear.

Figure 55 The contents of the Clipboard appear at the insertion point.

To copy text with Copy & Paste

1. Select the text that you want to copy (**Figure 49**).

2. Choose Edit > Copy (**Figure 48**), press ⌃⌘C, or click the Copy button on the Standard toolbar.

   The selected text is copied to the Clipboard. The document does not change (**Figure 49**).

3. Position the insertion point where you want the text copied (**Figure 50**).

4. Choose Edit > Paste (**Figure 48**), press ⌃⌘V, or click the Paste button on the Standard toolbar.

   The text in the Clipboard is copied into the document at the insertion point (**Figure 51**).

To move text with Cut & Paste

1. Select the text that you want to move (**Figure 52**).

2. Choose Edit > Cut (**Figure 48**), press ⌃⌘X, or click the Cut button on the Standard toolbar.

   The selected text is copied to the Clipboard and removed from the document (**Figure 53**).

3. Position the insertion point where you want the cut text to appear (**Figure 54**).

4. Choose Edit > Paste (**Figure 48**), press ⌃⌘V, or click the Paste button on the Standard toolbar.

   The text in the Clipboard is copied into the document at the insertion point (**Figure 55**).

To copy text with drag-and-drop editing

1. Select the text that you want to copy (**Figure 49**).

2. Position the mouse pointer on the selected text (**Figure 56**).

3. Hold down Option, press the mouse button down, and drag. As you drag, the shadow text and vertical line move with the mouse pointer, which has a plus sign beside it to indicate that it is copying (**Figure 57**).

4. When the vertical line at the mouse pointer is where you want the text copied to, release the mouse button and Option. The selected text is copied (**Figure 51**).

To move text with drag-and-drop editing

1. Select the text that you want to move (**Figure 52**).

2. Position the mouse pointer on the selected text (**Figure 58**).

3. Press the mouse button down and drag. As you drag, the shadow text and vertical line move with the mouse pointer (**Figure 59**).

4. When the vertical line at the mouse pointer is where you want the text moved to, release the mouse button. The selected text is moved (**Figure 55**).

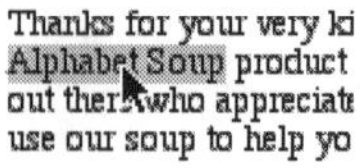

Thanks for your very ki
Alphabet Soup product
out there who appreciate
use our soup to help yo

Figure 56 Point to the selection.

John Aabbott
Product Manager
Alphabet Soup

Figure 57 Hold down Option and drag to copy the selection.

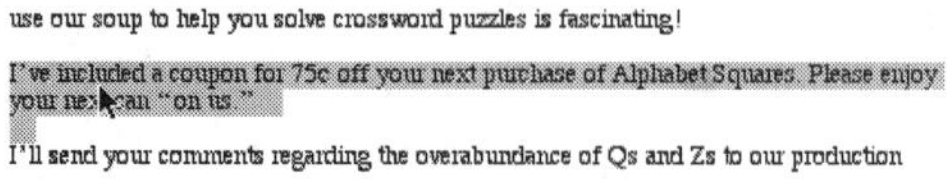

use our soup to help you solve crossword puzzles is fascinating!

I've included a coupon for 75¢ off your next purchase of Alphabet Squares. Please enjoy your next can "on us."

I'll send your comments regarding the overabundance of Qs and Zs to our production

Figure 58 Point to the selection.

properly represented.

I've included a coupon for 75¢ off your next purchase of Alphabet Squares. Please enjoy your next can "on us."
Sincerely,
John Aabbott
Product Manager

Figure 59 Drag to move the selection.

Figure 60
Choose Office
Clipboard from
the View menu.

Figure 61
The Office
Clipboard, with
nothing on it.

Figure 62
The Office Clipboard
with three items on it:
two selections of text
and a picture.

The Office Clipboard

The Office Clipboard enables you to "collect
and paste" multiple items. You simply display
the Office Clipboard, then copy or cut text or
objects as usual. But instead of the Clipboard
contents being replaced each time you use the
Copy or Cut command, all items are stored on
the Office Clipboard (**Figure 62**). You can then
paste any of the items on the Office Clipboard
into your Word document.

✔ Tips

- The Office Clipboard works with all Microsoft Office applications—not just Word—
  so you can store items from different types
  of Office documents.

- This feature is also known as *Collect and
  Paste*.

To add items to the Office Clipboard

1. If necessary, choose View > Office Clipboard (**Figure 60**) to display the Office
   Clipboard (**Figure 61**).

2. Select the text or object you want to copy.

3. Choose Edit > Copy (**Figure 48**), press
   ⌃⌘C, or click the Copy button on
   the Standard toolbar.

   The selection is added to the Office
   Clipboard.

4. Repeat steps 2 and 3 for each item you
   want to add to the Office Clipboard.
   Figure 62 shows what it might look like
   with multiple items added.

ADDING ITEMS TO THE OFFICE CLIPBOARD

To use Office Clipboard items

1. If necessary, choose View > Office Clipboard (**Figure 60**) to display the Office Clipboard.

Then:

2. Drag the item you want to use from the Office Clipboard window into the document window.

Or then:

2. In the document window, position the insertion point where you want to place the Office Clipboard item (**Figure 54**).

3. In the Office Clipboard window, click the item you want to paste into the document (**Figure 62**).

4. Click the Paste button at the bottom of the Office Clipboard (**Figure 62**).

The item you pasted or dragged appears in the document window (**Figure 55**).

✔ Tips

- You can select multiple Office Clipboard items by holding down Shift while clicking each one.

- If more than one item in the Office Clipboard is selected, clicking the Paste button pastes them all in, in the order they were selected.

- Choosing Paste All from the Paste All & Clear All pop-up menu at the bottom of the Office Clipboard window (**Figure 63**) pastes all items into the document.

To remove Office Clipboard items

1. In the Office Clipboard window, select the item(s) you want to remove.

2. Click the Clear button at the bottom of the Office Clipboard (**Figure 62**).

or

Choose Clear All from the Paste All & Clear All pop-up menu at the bottom of the Office Clipboard (**Figure 63**) to remove all items.

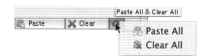

Figure 63 Use the Paste All & Clear All pop-up menu at the bottom of the Office Clipboard to either paste or remove all Office Clipboard items.

Figures 64, 65, & 66
Some examples of how the Undo, Redo, and Repeat commands can appear under the Edit menu.

Undoing, Redoing, & Repeating Actions

Word offers a trio of commands that enable you to undo, redo, or repeat the last thing you did.

◆ **Undo** reverses your last action. Word supports multiple levels of undo, enabling you to reverse more than just the very last action.

◆ **Redo** reverses the Undo command. This command is only available if the last thing you did was use the Undo command.

◆ **Repeat** performs your last action again. This command is only available after you perform any action other than using the Undo or Redo command.

✔ Tips

■ The exact wording of these commands on the Edit menu (**Figure 48**) varies depending on the last action performed. The Undo command is always the first command under the Edit menu; the Redo or Repeat command (whichever appears on the menu) is always the second command under the Edit menu. **Figures 64, 65**, and **66** show some examples.

■ The Redo and Repeat commands are never both available at the same time.

■ Think of the Undo command as the Oops command—anytime you say "Oops," you'll probably want to use it.

■ The Repeat command is especially useful for applying formatting to text scattered throughout your document. I tell you more about formatting in **Chapters 3** and **4**.

To undo the last action

Choose Edit > Undo (**Figures 64**, **65**, or **66**), press ⌃⌘Z, or click the Undo button ↺⁝ on the Standard toolbar.

To undo multiple actions

Choose Edit > Undo (**Figures 64**, **65**, or **66**) or press ⌃⌘Z repeatedly.

or

Click the triangle beside the Undo button on the Standard toolbar to display a pop-up menu of recent actions. Drag down to select all the actions that you want to undo (**Figure 67**). Release the mouse button to undo all selected actions.

To reverse the last undo

Choose Edit > Redo (**Figure 64**), press ⌃⌘Y, or click the Redo button ↻⁝ on the Standard toolbar.

To reverse multiple undos

Choose Edit > Redo (**Figure 64**) or press ⌃⌘Y repeatedly.

or

Click the triangle beside the Redo button on the Standard toolbar to display a pop-up menu of recently undone actions. Drag down to select all the actions that you want to redo (**Figure 68**). Release the mouse button to reverse all selected undos.

To repeat the last action

Choose Edit > Repeat (**Figures 65** and **66**) or press ⌃⌘Y.

Figure 67 Use the Undo pop-up menu to select actions to undo.

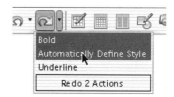

Figure 68 Use the Redo pop-up menu to select actions to redo.

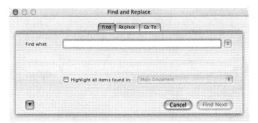

Figure 69 The Find tab of the Find and Replace dialog.

Figure 70 Word selects each occurrence of the text that it finds.

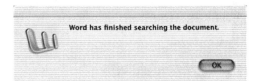

Figure 71 When Word has finished showing all occurrences of the search text, it tells you.

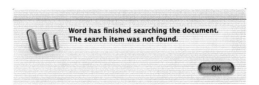

Figure 72 Word also tells you when it can't find the search text at all.

Find & Replace

Word has a very powerful find and replace feature. With it, you can search a document for specific text strings and, if desired, replace them with other text.

✔ Tip

- By default, the Find and Replace commands search the entire document, beginning at the insertion point.

To find text

1. Choose Edit > Find (**Figure 48**) or press ⌃ ⌘ F.

2. In the Find tab of the Find and Replace dialog that appears (**Figure 69**), enter the text that you want to find.

3. Click the Find Next button. One of two things happens:

   ▲ If Word finds the search text, it selects the first occurrence that it finds (**Figure 70**). Repeat step 3 to find all occurrences, one at a time. When the last occurrence has been found, Word tells you (**Figure 71**).

   ▲ If Word does not find the search text, it tells you (**Figure 72**). Repeat steps 2 and 3 to search for different text.

4. When you're finished, dismiss the Find and Replace dialog by clicking its close button.

✔ Tips

- To search only part of a document, select the text you want to search, then follow the above instructions.

- If desired, you can fine-tune search criteria. I tell you how a little later in this chapter.

FINDING TEXT

To select all occurrences of a text string

1. Choose Edit > Find (**Figure 48**) or press ⌘ F.

2. In the Find tab of the Find and Replace dialog that appears (**Figure 69**), enter the text that you want to find.

3. Turn on the Highlight all items found in check box and select Main Document from the pop-up menu beside it (**Figure 73**).

4. Click the Find All button. One of two things happens:

   ▲ If Word finds the search text, it selects all occurrences (**Figure 74**).

   ▲ If Word does not find the search text, it tells you (**Figure 72**).

5. When you're finished, dismiss the Find and Replace dialog by clicking its Close button.

✔ Tips

■ The ability to use the Find dialog to select all occurrences of a text string is a great way to apply special formatting to multiple blocks of text all at once.

■ You can also use this technique to select all occurrences of a text string in selected text—for example, to select all occurrences of the words *Alphabet Soup* in the body of the letter in **Figure 74**. Before starting, select the text you want to search. Then, in step 3, choose Current Selection from the pop-up menu (**Figure 75**).

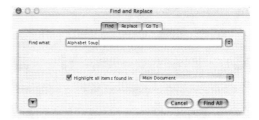

Figure 73 Use the check box and pop-up menu beside it to select all occurrences of a text string.

Figure 74 The text you are searching for is selected throughout the document.

Figure 75 When text is selected, you can use the pop-up menu to specify what should be searched.

Figure 76 The Replace tab of the Find and Replace dialog.

Figure 77 Word selects each occurrence of the search text that it finds.

Figure 78 Clicking the Replace button replaces the selected occurrence and finds the next one.

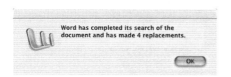

Figure 79 Clicking the Replace All button replaces all occurrences. Word tells you how many replacements it made.

To replace text

1. Choose Edit > Replace (**Figure 48**) or press ⇧ ⌘ H. The Replace tab of the Find and Replace dialog appears (**Figure 76**).

2. Enter the text that you want to find in the Find what text box.

3. Enter the text that you want to replace the found text with in the Replace with text box.

4. Click the Find Next button to start the search. One of two things happens:

   ▲ If Word finds the search text, it selects the first occurrence that it finds (**Figure 77**). Continue with step 5.

   ▲ If Word does not find the search text, it tells you (**Figure 72**). You can repeat steps 2 and 4 to search for different text.

5. Do one of the following:

   ▲ To replace the selected occurrence and automatically find the next occurrence, click the Replace button (**Figure 78**). You can repeat this step until Word has found all occurrences (**Figure 71**).

   ▲ To replace all occurrences, click the Replace All button. Word tells you how many changes it made (**Figure 79**).

   ▲ To skip the current occurrence and move on to the next one, click the Find Next button. You can repeat this step until Word has found all occurrences (**Figure 71**).

6. When you're finished, dismiss the Find and Replace dialog by clicking its Close button.

✔ Tip

■ If desired, you can fine-tune search criteria. I tell you how on the next page.

To fine-tune criteria

1. In the Find or Replace tab of the Find and Replace dialog, click the triangle button in the lower-left corner. The dialog expands to show additional search criteria options (**Figure 80**).

2. Click in the Find what or Replace with text box to indicate which criterion you want to fine-tune.

3. Set search criteria options as desired:

   ▲ **Search** (**Figure 81**) lets you specify whether you want to search the current document or all open documents and which direction you want to search.

   ▲ **Match case** exactly matches capitalization of the Find what text.

   ▲ **Find whole words only** finds the search text only when it is a separate word or phrase.

   ▲ **Use wildcards** lets you include wildcard characters (such as ? for a single character and * for multiple characters).

   ▲ **Sounds like** finds homonyms—words that sound alike but are spelled differently.

   ▲ **Find all word forms** searches for all verb, noun, or adjective forms of the search text.

4. Set search or replace critera options as desired:

   ▲ **Format** (**Figure 82**) lets you specify formatting options. Choosing one of these options displays the corresponding dialog. I explain how to use these dialogs in **Chapters 3** and **4**.

   ▲ **Special** (**Figure 83**) lets you find and replace special characters.

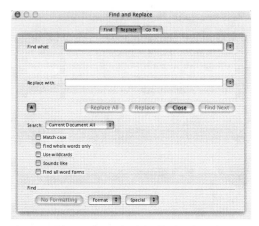

Figure 80 The Replace tab of the Find and Replace dialog expanded to show additional criteria options.

Figure 81
The Search pop-up menu in the Find and Replace dialog.

Figure 82
The Format pop-up menu in the Find and Replace dialog.

Figure 83
The Special pop-up menu in the Find and Replace dialog.

FINE-TUNING CRITERIA

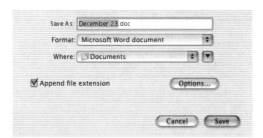

Figure 84 The Save As dialog sheet with a file name suggested by Word. This is the collapsed version of this dialog.

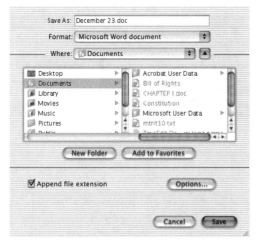

Figure 85 Clicking the triangle beside the Where pop-up menu expands the dialog to show the file hierarchy.

Figure 86
The New Folder dialog.

Figure 87 The name you give a document appears in its title bar after you save it.

Saving Documents

When you save a document, you put a copy of it on disk. You can then open it at a later time to edit or print it.

✔ Tips

- Until you save a document, its information is stored only in your computer's RAM. Your work on the document could be lost in the event of a power outage or system crash.

- It's a good idea to save documents frequently as you work. This ensures that the most recent versions are always saved to disk.

- I explain how to open files near the beginning of this chapter.

To save a document for the first time

1. Choose File > Save or File > Save As (**Figure 10**), press ⌃ ⌘ S, or click the Save button 💾 on the Standard toolbar to display the Save As dialog sheet (**Figure 84**).

2. Click the triangle beside the Where pop-up menu to expand the dialog so it shows the file hierarchy (**Figure 85**).

3. Navigate to the folder in which you want to save the file:
   - ▲ Use the Where pop-up menu near the top of the dialog (**Figure 23**) to select a different location.
   - ▲ Double-click a folder to open it.
   - ▲ Click the New Folder button to create a new folder within the current folder. Enter the name for the folder in the New Folder dialog (**Figure 86**) and click the Create button.

4. Enter a name for the file in the Save As text box.

5. Click Save.

The file is saved to disk. Its name appears on the document window's title bar (**Figure 87**).

To save changes to a document

Choose File > Save (**Figure 10**), press ⌃⌘S, or click the Save button 🖫 on the Standard toolbar. The document is saved with the same name in the same location on disk.

To save a document with a different name or in a different disk location

1. Choose File > Save As (**Figure 10**).

2. Follow steps 2 through 4 on the previous page to select a new disk location and/or enter a different name for the file.

3. Click the Save button.

✔ Tips

■ You can use the Format pop-up menu at the bottom of the Save As dialog (**Figure 88**) to specify a different format for the file. This enables you to save the document in a format that can be opened and read by other versions of Word or other applications.

■ If you know the file you're saving may be opened by a Word for Windows user, turn on the Append file extension check box (**Figures 84** and **85**). This automatically adds the correct three-character extension to the file name (**Figure 87**), making it easier for a Windows user to open it.

■ If you save a file with the same name and same disk location as another file, a dialog appears, asking if you want to replace the file (**Figure 89**).

   ▲ Click the Replace button to replace the file on disk with the file you are saving.

   ▲ Click the Cancel button to return to the Save As dialog where you can enter a new name or specify a new disk location.

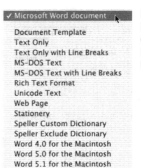

Figure 88
File formats offered on the Format pop-up menu.

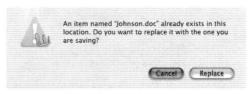

Figure 89 This dialog appears when you attempt to save a file with the same name and same disk location as another file.

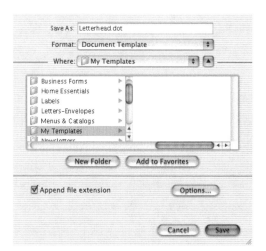

Figure 90 The Save As dialog when you save a document as a template.

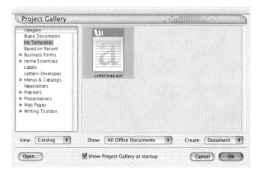

Figure 91 When a file has been saved as a template, it appears in the Project Gallery dialog.

To save a document as a template

1. Choose File > Save As (**Figure 10**).

2. Enter a name for the file in the Save As text box.

3. Choose Document Template from the Format pop-up menu (**Figure 88**). The dialog automatically displays the contents of the My Templates folder (**Figure 90**).

4. To store the template in a different folder, click the name of the folder to open it.

5. Click the Save button.

The file is saved as a template. Its name appears in the document title bar.

✔ Tips

- To begin using a template right after you created it, close it, then follow the instructions near the beginning of the chapter to open a new file based on a template. The template appears in the Project Gallery dialog in the My Templates tab (**Figure 91**).

- I tell you more about templates in the beginning of this chapter.

FORMATTING BASICS

Figure 1 A document with no formatting.

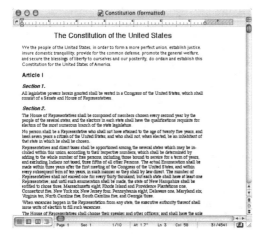

Figure 2 The same document with font and paragraph formatting applied.

Formatting Basics

Word offers a wide range of formatting options that you can use to make your documents more interesting and readable. Most formatting can be broken down into three types:

◆ **Font** or **character formatting** applies to individual characters of text. Examples include bold, italic, underline, and font color. The actual font or typeface used to display characters is also a part of font formatting.

◆ **Paragraph formatting** applies to entire paragraphs of text. Examples are indentation, justification, and line spacing.

◆ **Document formatting** applies to entire documents or sections of documents. Examples include margins and vertical alignment of text on the page.

In this chapter, I introduce you to the most basic kinds of formatting—the formatting you'll probably use most often.

✔ Tips

■ When properly applied, formatting can make the document easier to read, as illustrated in **Figures 1** and **2**.

■ Don't get carried away with formatting—especially font formatting. Too much formatting distracts the reader, making the document difficult to read.

Revealing Formatting

Word offers an easy way to see what kind of formatting is applied to text: the Reveal Formatting command (**Figure 3**). This enables you to display a window that tells you exactly what kind of formatting is applied to the text characters on which you click (**Figures 5** and **6**).

To reveal formatting

1. Choose View > Reveal Formatting (**Figure 3**). The mouse pointer turns into a little cartoon balloon icon (**Figure 4**).

2. Click on a character for which you want to reveal formatting. A box appears around the character you clicked. A window indicating the formatting applied to the character appears (**Figures 5** and **6**).

3. Repeat step 2 for each character for which you want to reveal formatting.

✔ Tips

- Reveal Formatting shows the formatting applied to the paragraph in which a character resides as well as the character itself.

- Reveal Formatting distinguishes between formatting applied as part of a style and formatting that is directly applied. I cover styles in **Chapter 4**.

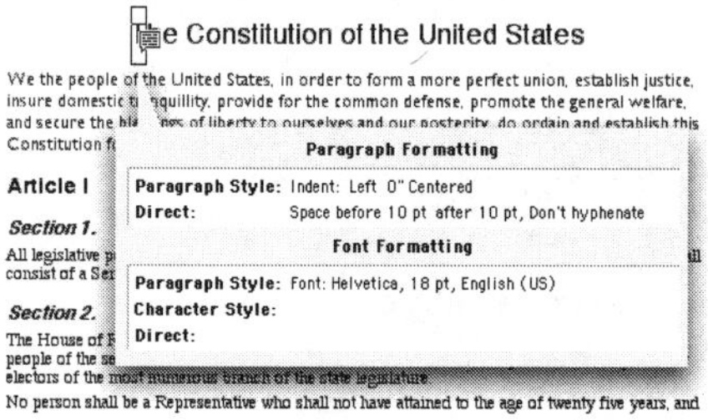

To stop revealing formatting

Press Esc or ⌘ . .

or

Choose View > Reveal Formatting again to turn it off.

The mouse pointer returns to normal and you can continue working with the document.

Figure 3
Choosing Reveal Formatting from the View menu.

Figure 4 The Reveal Formatting pointer.

Figure 5 One example of revealing formatting.

Figure 6 Another example of revealing formatting.

American Typewriter
Andale Mono
Apple Chancery
Arial
Baskerville
Big Caslon
Century Gothic
Charcoal
Chicago
Comic Sans MS
COPPERPLATE
Courier

Figure 7
Some font examples using the fonts installed on my system. Your system's fonts may differ.

Regular
Bold
Italic
Bold Italic

Figure 8
The font styles offered by Word.

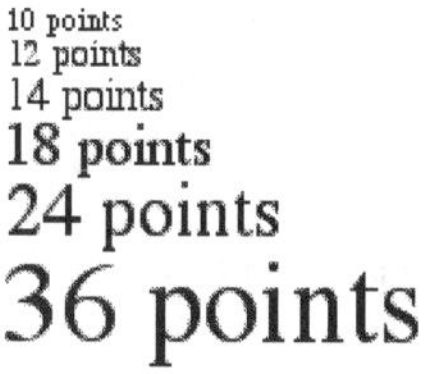

10 points
12 points
14 points
18 points
24 points
36 points

Figure 9
Examples of font sizes. This illustration is not at actual size.

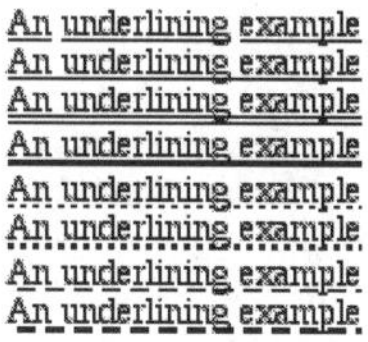

An underlining example
An underlining example
An underlining example
An underlining example
An underlining example
An underlining example
An underlining example
An underlining example

Figure 10
Examples of underlines offered by Word.

Strikethrough
Double Strikethrough
Superscript
Subscript
Shadow
Outline
Emboss
Engrave
SMALL CAPS
ALL CAPS

Figure 11
Examples of effects.

Font Formatting

Font formatting, which is sometimes referred to as *character formatting*, can be applied to individual characters of text. Word offers a wide variety of options.

- **Font** (**Figure 7**) is the typeface used to display characters.

- **Font style** (**Figure 8**) is the appearance of font characters: regular, italic, bold, or bold italic.

- **Size** (**Figure 9**) is the size of characters, expressed in points.

- **Font Color** is the color applied to text characters.

- **Underline style** (**Figure 10**) options allow you to apply a variety of underlines to characters.

- **Underline color** is the color of the applied underline.

- **Effects** (**Figure 11**) are special effects that change the appearance of characters. Options include strikethrough, double strikethrough, superscript, subscript, shadow, outline, emboss, engrave, small caps, all caps, or hidden.

✔ Tips

- Although some fonts come with Microsoft Office, Word enables you to apply any font that is properly installed in your system.

- A *point* is approximately 1/72 inch. The larger the point size, the larger the characters.

- Hidden characters do not show on screen unless nonprinting characters are displayed. I tell you about nonprinting characters in **Chapter 2**.

- Word offers additional font formatting options not covered here; I tell you about them in **Chapter 4**.

FONT FORMATTING

Applying Font Formatting

Font formatting is applied to selected characters or, if no characters are selected, to the characters you type at the insertion point after applying formatting. Here are two examples:

- To apply a bold font style to text that you have already typed, select the text (**Figure 12**), then apply the formatting. The appearance of the text changes immediately (**Figure 13**).

- To apply a bold font style to text that you have not yet typed, position the insertion point where the text will be typed (**Figure 14**), apply the bold formatting, and type the text. The text appears in bold (**Figure 15**). You must remember, however, to "turn off" bold formatting before you continue to type (**Figure 16**).

Word offers several methods of applying font formatting:

- The Font menu enables you to apply font formatting.

- The Formatting Palette enables you to apply font, size, some font styles, and font color formatting.

- Shortcut keys enable you to apply some font formatting.

- The Font dialog enables you to apply all kinds of font formatting.

✔ Tips

- In my opinion, it's easier to type text and apply formatting later than to format as you type.

- I explain how to select text in **Chapter 2**.

To apply a font with the Font menu

Choose the font that you want to apply from the Font menu (**Figure 17**).

The Constitution of the United States
We the people of the United States, in order
domestic tranquillity, provide for the commo
blessings of liberty to ourselves and our pos
United States of America.

Figure 12 Select the text that you want to format,...

The Constitution of the United States
We the people of the United States, in orde
domestic tranquillity, provide for the commo
blessings of liberty to ourselves and our pos
United States of America.

Figure 13 ...then apply the formatting.

We the people of the|

Figure 14 Position the insertion point where you want the formatted text to appear,...

We the people of the **United States**|

Figure 15 ...then "turn on" the formatting and type the text.

We the people of the **United States**, in order to|

Figure 16 Be sure to "turn off" the formatting before continuing to type.

Font
American Typewriter
American Typewriter Condensed
American Typewriter Condensed Light
American Typewriter Light
Andale Mono
Apple Chancery
Arial
Arial Black
Arial Narrow
Arial Rounded MT Bold
Baskerville
Baskerville Semibold
Big Caslon
Brush Script MT
CAPITALS
Century Gothic
Charcoal
Chicago
Comic Sans MS
COPPERPLATE
COPPERPLATE GOTHIC BOLD
COPPERPLATE GOTHIC LIGHT
COPPERPLATE LIGHT
Courier
Courier New
Curlz MT
Didot
Futura
Futura Condensed
Gadget
Geneva

Figure 17
The first bunch of fonts on the Font menu on my Mac. (Your Font menu may list different fonts.) Font names appear on the menu with the font applied, so you can see what a font looks like before you apply it.

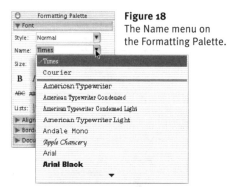

Figure 18
The Name menu on the Formatting Palette.

Figure 19
The Size menu on the Formatting Palette.

Figure 20 Select the contents of the Name text box.

Figure 21 Type in the name of the font that you want to apply.

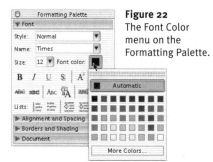

Figure 22
The Font Color menu on the Formatting Palette.

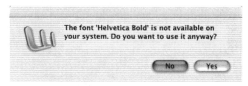

Figure 23 Word tells you when you've entered a font that isn't installed.

To apply font formatting with the Formatting Palette

Choose the font or size that you want to apply from the Name or Size menu (**Figures 18** and **19**).

or

1. Click the Name (**Figure 20**) or Size text box to select it.

2. Enter the name of the font (**Figure 21**) or the size that you want to apply.

3. Press ⌐Return⌐.

or

Click the button for the effect you want to apply: Bold B, Italic I, Underline U, Shadow S, Superscript A^2, Subscript A_2, Strikethrough ABC, Double Strikethrough ABC, Small Caps ABC, All Caps ^A_A, or Highlight ABC.

or

1. Click the Font Color button ▣ to display a menu of colors (**Figure 22**).

2. Click the color you want to apply.

or

1. Click the arrow beside the Highlight button ABC to display a menu of colors.

2. Click the color you want to apply.

✔ Tips

- Font names appear on the Name menu in their typefaces (**Figure 18**).

- Recently applied fonts appear at the top of the Formatting Palette's Name menu (**Figure 18**).

- If you enter the name of a font that is not installed on your system, Word warns you (**Figure 23**). If you use the font anyway, the text appears in the document in the default paragraph font. The text will appear in the applied font when the document is opened on a system on which the font is installed.

APPLYING FONT FORMATTING

61

To apply font formatting with shortcut keys

Press the shortcut key combination (**Table 1**) for the formatting that you want to apply.

✔ Tip

- The shortcut key to change the font requires that you press the first key combination, enter the name of the desired font, and then press [Return]. This shortcut key activates the Name text box on the Formatting Palette.

To apply font formatting with the Font dialog

1. Choose Format > Font (**Figure 24**) or press ⌃ ⌘ D.

2. Set formatting options as desired in the Font tab of the Font dialog that appears (**Figure 25**).

3. Click OK.

✔ Tip

- The Preview area of the Font dialog illustrates what text will look like with the selected formatting applied.

Table 1

Shortcut Keys for Font Formatting	
FORMATTING	KEYSTROKE
Font	⌃ ⌘ Shift F
	Font Name [Return]
Grow font	⌃ ⌘ Shift .
Grow font 1 point	⌃ ⌘]
Shrink font	⌃ ⌘ Shift ,
Shrink font 1 point	⌃ ⌘ [
Bold	⌃ ⌘ B or ⌃ ⌘ Shift B
Italic	⌃ ⌘ I or ⌃ ⌘ Shift I
Underline	⌃ ⌘ U or ⌃ ⌘ Shift U
Word underline	⌃ ⌘ Shift W
Double underline	⌃ ⌘ Shift D
Superscript	⌃ ⌘ Shift =
Subscript	⌃ ⌘ =
All caps	⌃ ⌘ Shift A
Small caps	⌃ ⌘ Shift K

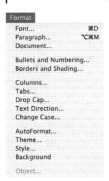

Figure 24
The Format menu.

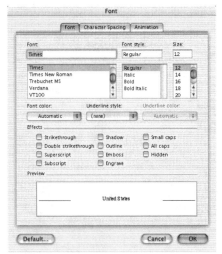

Figure 25 The Font dialog.

Figure 26 Examples of alignment options.

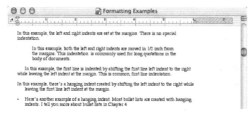

Figure 27 Examples of indentation options. The ruler in this illustration shows the indent markers set for the first sample paragraph.

Figure 28 Examples of line spacing options.

Figure 29 Paragraph spacing options.

Paragraph Formatting

Paragraph formatting is applied to entire paragraphs of text. Word offers a variety of paragraph formatting options:

◆ **Alignment** (**Figure 26**) is the way lines of text line up between the indents.

◆ **Indentation** (**Figure 27**) is the spacing between text and margins. Word allows you to set left and right margins, as well as special indentations for first line and hanging indents.

◆ **Line spacing** (**Figure 28**) is the amount of space between lines. Spacing can be set as single, 1.5 lines, double, at least a certain amount, exactly a certain amount, or multiple lines.

◆ **Paragraph spacing** (**Figure 29**) is the amount of space before and after the paragraph.

✔ Tip

■ Word offers additional paragraph formatting options that are not covered here. I tell you about tabs later in this chapter and about other paragraph formatting options in **Chapter 4**.

Applying Paragraph Formatting

Paragraph formatting is applied to selected paragraphs (**Figure 30**) or, if no paragraphs are selected, to the paragraph in which the insertion point is blinking (**Figure 31**).

Word offers several methods of applying paragraph formatting:

- The Formatting Palette enables you to apply some paragraph formatting.
- Shortcut keys enable you to apply some paragraph formatting.
- The ruler enables you to apply indentation formatting.
- The Paragraph dialog enables you to apply most kinds of paragraph formatting.

✔ Tips

- Paragraph formatting applies to the entire paragraph, even if only part of the paragraph is selected (**Figure 32**).
- A paragraph is the text that appears between paragraph marks. You can see paragraph marks when you display nonprinting characters (**Figures 30**, **31**, and **32**). I tell you about nonprinting characters in **Chapter 2**.
- If you press Return, the paragraph formatting of the current paragraph is carried forward to the new paragraph.
- I explain how to select paragraphs in **Chapter 2**.

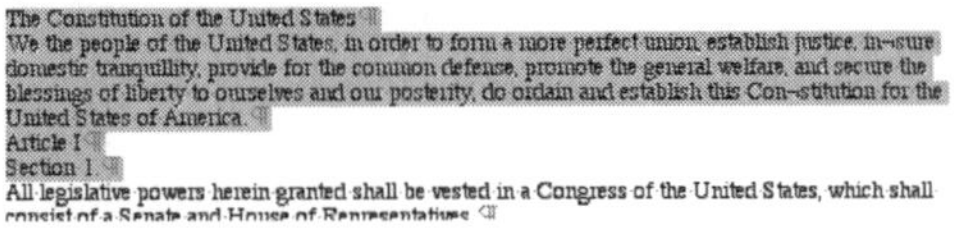
The Constitution of the United States ¶
We the people of the United States, in order to form a more perfect union, establish justice, in-sure domestic tranquillity, provide for the common defense, promote the general welfare, and secure the blessings of liberty to ourselves and our posterity, do ordain and establish this Con-stitution for the United States of America. ¶
Article I ¶
Section 1. ¶
All legislative powers herein granted shall be vested in a Congress of the United States, which shall consist of a Senate and House of Representatives. ¶

Figure 30 In this example, the first four paragraphs are completely selected and will be affected by any paragraph formatting applied.

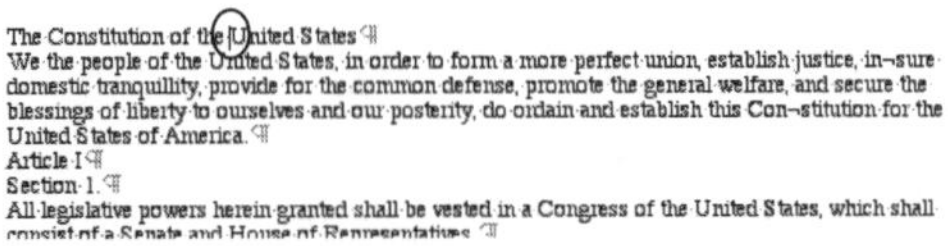
The Constitution of the United States ¶
We the people of the United States, in order to form a more perfect union, establish justice, in-sure domestic tranquillity, provide for the common defense, promote the general welfare, and secure the blessings of liberty to ourselves and our posterity, do ordain and establish this Con-stitution for the United States of America. ¶
Article I ¶
Section 1. ¶
All legislative powers herein granted shall be vested in a Congress of the United States, which shall consist of a Senate and House of Representatives. ¶

Figure 31 In this example, the insertion point is in the first paragraph. That entire paragraph will be affected by any paragraph formatting applied.

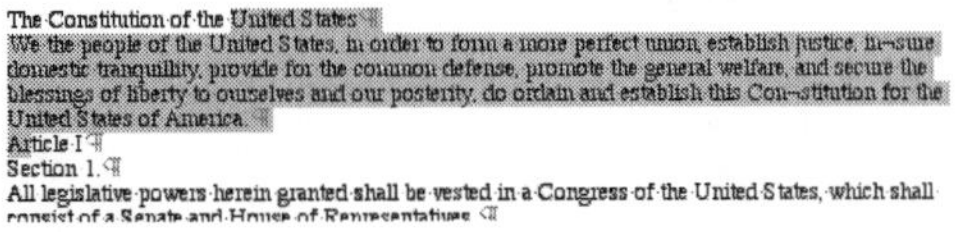
The Constitution of the United States ¶
We the people of the United States, in order to form a more perfect union, establish justice, in-sure domestic tranquillity, provide for the common defense, promote the general welfare, and secure the blessings of liberty to ourselves and our posterity, do ordain and establish this Con-stitution for the United States of America. ¶
Article I ¶
Section 1. ¶
All legislative powers herein granted shall be vested in a Congress of the United States, which shall consist of a Senate and House of Representatives. ¶

Figure 32 In this example, only part of the first paragraph and part of the third paragraph are selected, along with all of the second paragraph. All three paragraphs will be affected by any paragraph formatting applied.

Figure 33
Some paragraph formatting options are in the Font area of the Formatting Palette, while others are in the Alignment and Spacing area.

Table 2

Shortcut Keys for Paragraph Formatting	
FORMATTING	KEYSTROKE
Align left	⌃⌘L
Center	⌃⌘E
Align right	⌃⌘R
Justify	⌃⌘J
Indent	⌃⌘M
Unindent	⌃⌘Shift M
Hanging indent	⌃⌘T
Unhang indent	⌃⌘Shift T
Single line space	⌃⌘1
1.5 line space	⌃⌘5
Double line space	⌃⌘2
Open/Close Up Paragraph	⌃⌘0 (zero)

To apply paragraph formatting with Formatting Palette buttons

To set alignment, click one of the Horizontal buttons (**Figure 33**): Align Left ▤, Align Center ▤, Align Right ▤, or Justify ▤.

or

To set left indentation, click one of the Lists buttons (**Figure 33**): Decrease Indent ▤ or Increase Indent ▤.

or

To set left, right, or first line indentation, enter values in the Left, Right, or First line text boxes (**Figure 33**).

or

To set line spacing, click one of the Line spacing buttons (**Figure 33**): Single Space ▤, 1.5 Space ▤, or Double Space ▤.

or

To set Paragraph Spacing, enter values in the Before or After text boxes (**Figure 33**).

✔ Tip

■ Remember, you can show or hide groups of options on the Formatting Palette by clicking the triangle to the left of a section heading (**Figure 33**).

To apply paragraph formatting with shortcut keys

Press the shortcut key combination (**Table 2**) for the formatting that you want to apply.

APPLYING PARAGRAPH FORMATTING

To set indentation with the ruler

Drag the indent markers (**Figure 34**) to set indentation as desired:

- ◆ **First Line Indent** sets the left boundary for the first line of a paragraph.

- ◆ **Hanging Indent** sets the left boundary for all lines of a paragraph other than the first line.

- ◆ **Left Indent** sets the left boundary for all lines of a paragraph. (Dragging this marker moves the First Line Indent and Hanging Indent markers.)

- ◆ **Right Indent** sets the right boundary for all lines of a paragraph.

✔ Tips

- ▪ If the ruler is not showing, choose View > Ruler to display it.

- ▪ Dragging the First Line Indent marker to the right creates a standard indent.

- ▪ Dragging the Hanging Indent marker to the right creates a hanging indent.

To apply paragraph formatting with the Paragraph dialog

1. Choose Format > Paragraph (**Figure 24**) or press (Option) ⌃ ⌘ (M).

2. Set formatting options as desired in the Indents and Spacing tab of the Paragraph dialog that appears (**Figure 35**).

3. Click OK.

✔ Tip

- ▪ The Preview area of the Paragraph dialog illustrates what text will look like with formatting applied.

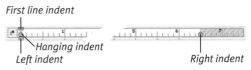

First line indent

Hanging indent
Left indent

Right indent

Figure 34 Indent markers on the ruler.

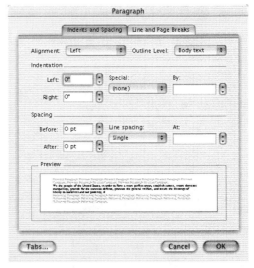

Figure 35 The Indents and Spacing tab of the Paragraph dialog.

Tab marker icon

Figure 36 Default tab stops appear as tiny gray lines on the ruler.

Substance	Date Tested	Tested By	Results
MSG	5/18/98	Maria Langer	452.6589
Magnesium	6/4/98	John Aabbott	51.84
Sulfur	6/15/98	Mary Johannesburg	14596.25489
Aspirin	10/17/98	Tim Jones	1.1

Figure 37 Word's five tab stops in action. In order, they are: right, bar, left, center, decimal. Examine the ruler to see how they're set.

Here's an example without a tab leader	Page 1
Here's an example with a dotted tab leader	14
Here's an example with a dashed tab leader	140
Here's an example with an underscore tab leader	Section 51

Figure 38 Word's tab leader options: none, dotted, dashed, and underscore.

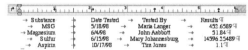

Substance	Date Tested	Tested By	Results
MSG	5/18/98	Maria Langer	452.6589
Magnesium	6/4/98	John Aabbott	51.84
Sulfur	6/15/98	Mary Johannesburg	14596.25489
Aspirin	10/17/98	Tim Jones	1.1

Figure 39 Displaying nonprinting characters enables you to see the tab characters.

Tabs

Tab stops determine the position of the insertion point when you press (Tab).

By default, a blank document includes tab stops every half inch. They appear as gray marks on the bottom of the ruler (**Figure 36**). You can use the ruler or Tabs dialog to set tabs that override the defaults.

Word supports five kinds of tabs (**Figure 37**):

◆ **Left tab** aligns tabbed text to the left against the tab stop.

◆ **Center tab** centers tabbed text beneath the tab stop.

◆ **Right tab** aligns tabbed text to the right against the tab stop.

◆ **Decimal tab** aligns the decimal point of tabbed numbers beneath the tab stop. When used with text, a decimal tab works just like a right tab.

◆ **Bar tab** is a vertical line that appears beneath the tab stop.

Word also supports four types of tab leaders (**Figure 38**)—characters that appear in the space otherwise left by a tab: none, periods, dashes, and underscores.

✔ Tips

■ Tabs are a type of paragraph formatting; when set, they apply to an entire paragraph.

■ Tabs are often used to create simple tables.

■ When trying to align text in a simple table, use tabs, not spaces. Tabs always align to tab stops while text positioned with space characters may not align properly due to the size and spacing of characters in a font.

■ It's a good idea to display nonprinting characters when working with tabs (**Figure 39**) so you can distinguish tabs from spaces. I tell you about nonprinting characters in **Chapter 2**.

To set tab stops with the ruler

1. Click the tab marker icon at the far-left end of the ruler (**Figure 36**) until it displays the icon for the type of tab stop that you want to set (**Figure 40**).

2. Click on the ruler where you want to position the tab stop to set it there.

3. Repeat steps 1 and 2 until all desired tab stops have been set (**Figure 37**).

✔ Tip

■ When you set a tab stop, all default tab stops to its left disappear (**Figures 37** and **39**).

To move a tab stop with the ruler

1. Position the mouse pointer on the tab stop that you want to move.

2. Press the mouse button down and drag the tab stop to its new position.

✔ Tip

■ Don't click on the ruler anywhere except on the tab stop that you want to move. Doing so will set another tab stop.

To remove a tab stop from the ruler

1. Position the mouse pointer on the tab stop that you want to remove.

2. Press the mouse button down and drag the tab stop down into the document. When you release the mouse button, the tab stop disappears.

Figure 40 The tab marker icons for left, center, right, decimal, and bar tabs.

SETTING TAB STOPS WITH THE RULER

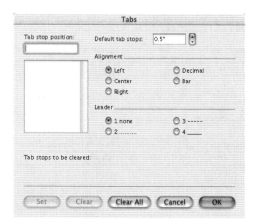

Figure 41 The Tabs dialog.

Figure 42
When you add a tab, it appears in the list in the Tabs dialog.

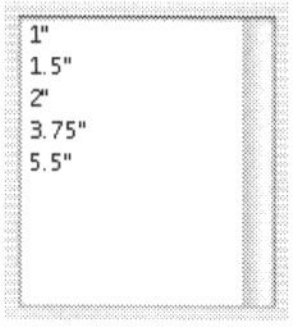

Figure 43
The tab stop settings for Figure 37.

Figure 44
When you click Clear to remove a tab stop, it is removed from the tab list.

To open the Tabs dialog

Choose Format > Tabs (**Figure 24**).

or

Click the Tabs button in the Paragraph dialog (**Figure 35**).

To set tab stops with the Tabs dialog

1. Open the Tabs dialog (**Figure 41**).

2. In the Alignment area, select the radio button for the type of tab that you want.

3. In the Leader area, select the radio button for the type of leader that you want the tab stop to have.

4. Enter a ruler location in the Tab stop position text box.

5. Click the Set button. The tab stop is added to the tab list (**Figure 42**).

6. Repeat steps 2 through 5 for each tab stop that you want to set (**Figure 43**).

7. Click OK.

To remove tab stops with the Tabs dialog

1. In the Tabs dialog, select the tab stop that you want to remove.

2. Click the Clear button. The tab stop is removed from the list and added to the list of Tab stops to be cleared near the bottom of the dialog (**Figure 44**).

3. Repeat steps 1 and 2 for each tab stop that you want to remove.

4. Click OK.

✔ Tip

■ To remove all tab stops, click the Clear All button in the Tabs dialog (**Figure 41**), then click OK.

To change the default tab stops

1. In the Tabs dialog (**Figure 41**), enter a new value in the Default tab stops text box.

2. Click OK.

✔ Tip

■ Remember, tab stops that you set manually on the ruler or with the Tabs dialog override default tab stops to their left.

To create a simple table with tab stops

1. Position the insertion point in the paragraph in which you set tabs (**Figure 45**).

2. To type at a tab stop, press ⌜Tab⌟, then type your text (**Figure 46**).

3. Repeat step 2 to type at each tab stop.

4. Press ⌜Return⌟ or ⌜Shift⌟⌜Return⌟ to end the paragraph or line and begin a new one. The tab stops in the paragraph are carried forward (**Figure 47**).

5. Repeat steps 2 through 4 to finish typing your table (**Figure 39**).

✔ Tips

■ You can move tabs at any time—even after you have begun using them. Be sure to select all the paragraphs that utilize the tabs before you move them. Otherwise, you may only adjust tabs for part of the table.

■ Another way to create tables is with Word's table feature, which is far more flexible than using tab stops. I tell you about it in **Chapter 9**.

Figure 45 Position the insertion point in the paragraph for which you have set tab stops.

Figure 46 Press tab to type at the first tab stop, then type. In this example, text is typed at a right-aligned tab stop.

Figure 47 When you are finished typing a line press ⌜Return⌟ to start a new paragraph with the same tab stops.

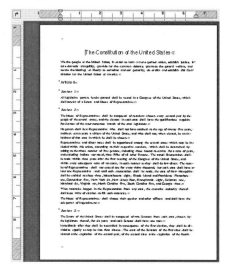

Figure 48 A margin is the space between the edge of the paper and the indent.

Figure 49 Examples of vertical alignment: top (left), center (middle), and justified (right).

Document Formatting

Document formatting is applied to an entire document or section of a document. Word offers several options for document formatting, two of which are covered in this chapter:

◆ **Margins** are the spacing between the edge of the paper and the indents (**Figure 48**). **Gutter** is the amount of extra space on the inside margin of a document (**Figure 52**), designed to account for space used in binding.

◆ **Vertical alignment** (**Figure 49**) is the vertical position of text on a page. Options include top, center, and justified.

✔ Tip

■ Word offers additional document formatting options that are not covered here. I tell you about working with header, footer, and section break options in **Chapter 4**.

DOCUMENT FORMATTING

Applying Document Formatting

Document formatting can be applied four ways:

♦ To the entire document.

♦ To the document from the insertion point forward. This creates a section break at the insertion point.

♦ To selected text. This creates a section break before and after the selected text.

♦ To selected document sections. This requires that section breaks already be in place and that you either select the sections or position the insertion point in a section.

You can format a document or section two ways:

♦ The Formatting Palette enables you to set margin and gutter options.

♦ The Document dialog enables you to apply all kinds of document formatting.

✔ Tip

■ I explain how to create and use section breaks in **Chapter 4**. Be sure to read about section breaks before using the Document dialog to format a section.

To set margin options with the Formatting Palette

In the Document area of the Formatting Palette, set options in the Left, Right, Top, or Bottom text boxes (**Figure 50**).

or

Enter a value in the Gutter text box (**Figure 50**).

or

Turn on the Mirror margins check box (**Figure 50**) to set up margins for double-sided pages.

Figure 50
To set document options, display the Document area of the Formatting Palette.

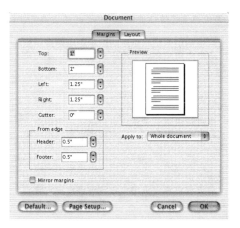

Figure 51 The Margins tab of the Document dialog.

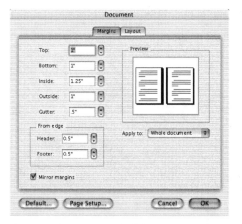

Figure 52 The Margins tab of the Document dialog with Mirror margins turned on and a half-inch gutter.

To set margin options with the Document dialog

1. Choose Format > Document (**Figure 24**) to display the Document dialog.

2. If necessary, click the Margins tab to display its options (**Figure 51**).

3. Enter values in the Top, Bottom, Left, and Right text boxes.

4. To set a gutter width, enter a value in the Gutter text box.

5. To apply your changes to the entire document, make sure Whole document is selected from the Apply to pop-up menu. Otherwise, choose the desired option from the Apply to pop-up menu; I tell you more about that in **Chapter 4**.

6. Click OK.

✔ Tips

■ If you turn on the Mirror margins check box, the dialog changes for double-sided pages (**Figure 52**).

■ The Preview area of the Document dialog illustrates margin and gutter settings (**Figures 51** and **52**).

To set vertical alignment

1. Choose Format > Document (**Figure 24**) to display the Document dialog.

2. If necessary, click the Layout tab to display its options (**Figure 53**).

3. Choose the alignment option that you want from the Vertical alignment pop-up menu (**Figure 54**).

4. To apply your changes to the entire document, make sure Whole document is selected from the Apply to pop-up menu. Otherwise, choose the desired option from the Apply to pop-up menu; I tell you more about that in **Chapter 4**.

5. Click OK.

✔ Tips

- Vertical alignment is only apparent on pages that are less than a full page in length.

- On screen, you can only view vertical alignment in Online Layout, Page Layout, and Print Preview views.

To set default document formatting

1. Choose Format > Document (**Figure 24**) to display the Document dialog.

2. Set options as desired in the Margins and Layout tabs (**Figures 51** and **53**).

3. Click the Default button.

4. Word asks if you want to change the default settings for the document (**Figure 55**). Click Yes only if you want the settings to apply to all new documents that you create based on the Normal (Blank Document) template.

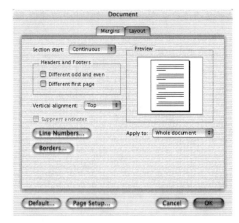

Figure 53 The Layout tab of the Document dialog.

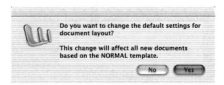

Figure 54
The Vertical alignment pop-up menu in the Layout tab of the Document dialog.

Figure 55 Word confirms that you really want to change the default document settings.

ADVANCED FORMATTING

Advanced Formatting

Word offers a number of formatting options and techniques in addition to those I discuss in **Chapter 3**:

- ◆ **Character spacing** includes the horizontal scale, spacing, position, and kerning of characters.

- ◆ **Drop Caps** enlarges the first character(s) of a paragraph and wraps text around it.

- ◆ **Change Case** changes the case of typed characters.

- ◆ **Bullets and numbering** instructs Word to automatically insert bullet characters or numbers at the beginning of paragraphs.

- ◆ **Borders and shading** enable you to place borders around text, and color or shades of gray within text areas.

- ◆ **Format Painter** enables you to copy font and paragraph formats from one selection to another.

- ◆ **Styles** enables you to define and apply named sets of formatting options for individual characters or paragraphs.

- ◆ **AutoFormat** instructs Word to automatically format text you type.

- ◆ **Breaks** determines the end of a page, section, or column.

- ◆ **Multiple-column text** enables you to use newspaper-like columns in documents.

- ◆ **Headers and footers** enables you to specify text to appear at the top and bottom of every page in the document.

✔ Tip

- ■ It's a good idea to have a solid understanding of the concepts covered in **Chapter 3** before you read this chapter.

Character Spacing

Chapter 3 omitted a few more advanced font formatting options:

◆ **Scale** determines the horizontal sizing of characters. Scale enables you to horizontally stretch or squeeze individual characters (**Figure 1**).

◆ **Spacing** determines the amount of space between each character of text. Spacing can be normal or can be expanded or condensed by the number of points you specify (**Figure 2**).

◆ **Position** determines whether text appears above or below the baseline. Position can be normal or can be raised or lowered by the number of points you specify (**Figure 3**).

◆ **Kerning** determines how certain combinations of letters "fit" together (**Figure 4**).

✔ Tips

■ Like other types of font formatting, you can apply character spacing to characters as you type them or to characters that have been typed. Check **Chapter 3** for details.

■ The *baseline* is the invisible line on which characters sit.

■ Don't confuse character position with superscript and subscript. Although all three of these font formatting options change the position of text in relation to the baseline, superscript and subscript also change the size of characters. I tell you about superscript and subscript in **Chapter 3**.

■ The effect of kerning varies based on the size and font applied to characters for which kerning is enabled. Kerning is more apparent at larger point sizes and requires that the font contain *kerning pairs*— predefined pairs of letters to kern. In many instances, you may not see a difference in spacing at all.

This is an example of horizontal scale.
This is an example of horizontal scale.
This is an example of horizontal scale.

Figure 1 Three examples of character scale: 100%, 150%, and 66%.

This is an example of character spacing.
This is an example of character spacing.
This is an example of character spacing.

Figure 2 Three examples of character spacing: normal (top), expanded by 1 point (middle), and condensed by 1 point (bottom).

This is an example of normal position.
This is an example of raised position.
This is an example of lowered position.

Figure 3 Three examples of character position: normal (top), raised 3 points (middle), and lowered 3 points (bottom).

To We
To We

Figure 4 Two common kerning pairs without kerning enabled (top) and with kerning enabled (bottom).

Figure 5
The Format menu.

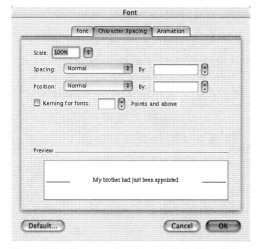

Figure 6 The Character Spacing tab of the Font dialog.

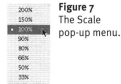

Figure 7
The Scale
pop-up menu.

Figure 8
The Spacing pop-up menu.

Figure 9
The Position pop-up menu.

To apply character spacing

1. Choose Format > Font (**Figure 5**), or press
   [⌃ ⌘ D].

2. In the Font dialog that appears, click the
   Character Spacing tab to display its options
   (**Figure 6**).

3. To change scale, enter a value in the Scale
   text box or choose an option from the
   Scale pop-up menu (**Figure 7**).

4. To change spacing, choose an option from
   the Spacing pop-up menu (**Figure 8**). Then
   enter a value in its By text box.

5. To change position, choose an option from
   the Position pop-up menu (**Figure 9**). Then
   enter a value in its By text box.

6. To enable kerning, turn on the Kerning for
   fonts check box. Then enter a value in the
   Points and above text box to specify the
   minimum point size of fonts to which
   kerning should be applied.

7. Click OK.

✔ Tip

■ The Preview area of the Font dialog (**Figure 6**) shows what selected characters
   will look like when you apply settings by
   clicking OK.

Drop Caps

A drop cap is an enlarged and/or repositioned character at the beginning of a paragraph. Word supports two types of drop caps (**Figure 10**):

◆ **Dropped** enlarges the character and wraps the rest of the text in the paragraph around it.

◆ **In Margin** enlarges the character and moves it into the margin.

✔ Tips

■ Word creates drop caps using frames, a feature that enables you to precisely position text on a page or in relation to a paragraph. Frames is an advanced feature of Word that is beyond the scope of this book.

■ To see drop caps, you must be in Page Layout view or Print Preview. A drop cap appears as an enlarged character in its own paragraph in Normal view (**Figure 11**).

My brother had just been appointed Secretary of Nevada Territory--an office of such majesty that it concentrated in itself the duties and dignities of Treasurer, Comptroller, Secretary of State, and Acting Governor in the Governor's absence. A salary of eighteen hundred dollars a year and the title of "Mr. Secretary," gave to the great position an air of wild and imposing grandeur. I was young and ignorant, and I envied my brother. I...

My brother had just been appointed Secretary of Nevada Territory--an office of such majesty that it concentrated in itself the duties and dignities of Treasurer, Comptroller, Secretary of State, and Acting Governor in the Governor's absence. A salary of eighteen hundred dollars a year and the title of "Mr. Secretary," gave to the great position an air of wild and imposing grandeur. I was young and ignorant, and I envied my brother. I...

My brother had just been appointed Secretary of Nevada Territory--an office of such majesty that it concentrated in itself the duties and dignities of Treasurer, Comptroller, Secretary of State, and Acting Governor in the Governor's absence. A salary of eighteen hundred dollars a year and the title of "Mr. Secretary," gave to the great position an air of wild and imposing grandeur. I was young and ignorant, and I envied my brother. I...

Figure 10 The same first lines of a paragraph three ways: without a drop cap (top), with a drop cap (middle), and with an in margin drop cap (bottom).

M
y brother had just been appointed Secretary of Nevada Territory--an office of such majesty that it concentrated in itself the duties and dignities of Treasurer, Comptroller, Secretary of State, and Acting Governor in the Governor's absence. A salary of eighteen hundred dollars a year and the title of "Mr. Secretary," gave to the great position an air of wild and imposing grandeur. I was young and ignorant and I envied my brother. I...

Figure 11 A paragraph with a drop cap when viewed in Normal view.

Figure 12
The Drop Cap
dialog.

To create a drop cap

1. Position the insertion point anywhere in the paragraph for which you want to create a drop cap.

2. Choose Format > Drop Cap (**Figure 5**).

3. In the Drop Cap dialog that appears (**Figure 12**), click the icon for the type of drop cap that you want to create.

4. Choose a font for the drop cap from the Font pop-up menu.

5. Enter the number of lines for the size of the drop cap character in the Lines to drop text box.

6. Enter a value for the amount of space between the drop cap character and the rest of the text in the paragraph in the Distance from text box.

7. Click OK.

If you are not in Page Layout view, Word switches to that view. You can then see that the first character of the paragraph appears as a drop cap (**Figure 10**).

To remove a drop cap

Follow the steps above, but select the icon for None in step 3.

CREATING & REMOVING DROP CAPS

Changing Case

You can use the Change Case dialog (**Figure 13**) to change the case of selected characters. There are five options (**Figure 14**):

◆ **Sentence case** capitalizes the first letter of a sentence.

◆ **lowercase** changes all characters to lowercase.

◆ **UPPERCASE** changes all characters to uppercase.

◆ **Title Case** capitalizes the first letter of every word.

◆ **tOGGLE cASE** changes uppercase characters to lowercase and lowercase characters to uppercase.

✔ Tips

■ · Technically speaking, changing the case of characters with the Change Case dialog (**Figure 13**) does not format the characters. Instead, it changes the actual characters that were originally entered into the document.

■ To change the case of characters without changing the characters themselves, use the All caps or Small caps option in the Font tab of the Font dialog (**Figure 15**). I tell you how in **Chapter 3**.

To change the case of characters

1. Select the characters whose case you want to change.

2. Choose Format > Change Case (**Figure 5**).

3. In the Change Case dialog that appears (**Figure 13**), select the radio button for the option that you want.

4. Click OK.

Figure 13
The Change Case dialog.

You can use the Change Case dialog to change the case of typed characters.
You can use the Change Case dialog to change the case of typed characters.
you can use the change case dialog to change the case of typed characters.
YOU CAN USE THE CHANGE CASE DIALOG TO CHANGE THE CASE OF TYPED CHARACTERS.
You Can Use The Change Case Dialog To Change The Case Of Typed Characters.
yOU CAN USE THE cHANGE cASE DIALOG TO CHANGE THE CASE OF TYPED CHARACTERS.

Figure 14 Change Case in action—from top to bottom: original text, Sentence case, lowercase, UPPERCASE, Title Case, and tOGGLE cASE.

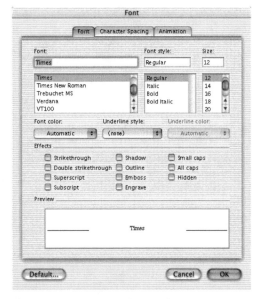

Figure 15 The Font tab of the Font dialog.

✔ Tip

■ If you use the Change Case dialog to change the case of characters and get unexpected results, use the Undo command to reverse the action, then try the Change Case dialog again. I cover the Undo command in **Chapter 2**.

The following topics were covered:
- Advertising budget for product kickoff
- Replacement for Jane Jones
- Team for Product X marketing development

The following topics were covered:
1. Advertising budget for product kickoff
2. Replacement for Jane Jones
3. Team for Product X marketing development

Figure 16 Three paragraphs with bullets (top) and numbering (bottom) formats applied.

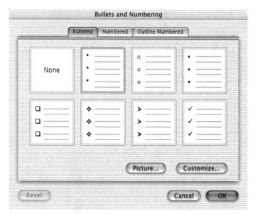

Figure 17 The Bulleted tab of the Bullets and Numbering dialog.

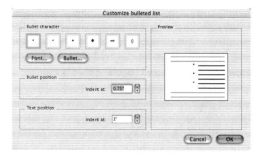

Figure 18 The Customize bulleted list dialog.

Bullets & Numbering

Word automatically includes bullets or numbers at the beginning of paragraphs to which you apply a bulleted or numbered list format (**Figure 16**).

✔ Tips

- You can apply list formats as you type or to paragraphs that have already been typed. Check **Chapter 3** for details.

- The bullet and number formats include hanging indents. I explain Word's indentation options in **Chapter 3**.

- If you use Word's numbering format, Word will automatically increment the number for each consecutive paragraph.

To apply bulleted list formatting

Click the Bullets button ⊞ on the Formatting palette.

or

1. Choose Format > Bullets and Numbering (**Figure 5**).

2. In the Bullets and Numbering dialog that appears, click the Bulleted tab to display its options (**Figure 17**).

3. Click the box that displays the type of bullet character that you want.

4. Click OK.

✔ Tips

- To further customize a bullet list, after step 3 above, click the Customize button in the Bullets and Numbering dialog (**Figure 17**). Set options in the Customize bulleted list dialog that appears (**Figure 18**), and click OK.

Continued on next page...

BULLETS & NUMBERING

Continued from previous page.

- Clicking the Bullets button on the Formatting Palette applies the last style of bullet set in the Bullets and Numbering dialog (**Figure 17**) or Customize bulleted list dialog (**Figure 18**).

- You can use pictures for bullets. Click the Picture button in the Bulleted tab of the Bullets and Numbering dialog (**Figure 17**). Then use the Choose a Picture dialog that appears (**Figure 19**) to locate and insert a picture file as a bullet. Word automatically uses the same picture for all bullets in the list.

To apply numbered list formatting

Click the Numbering button on the Formatting Palette.

or

1. Choose Format > Bullets and Numbering (**Figure 5**).

2. In the Bullets and Numbering dialog that appears, click the Numbered tab to display its options (**Figure 20**).

3. Click the box that displays the numbering format that you want.

4. Click OK.

✔ Tips

- To further customize a numbered list, after step 3 above, click the Customize button in the Bullets and Numbering dialog (**Figure 20**). Set options in the Customize numbered list dialog that appears (**Figure 21**), and click OK.

- Clicking the Numbering button on the Formatting Palette applies the last style of numbering set in the Bullets and Numbering dialog (**Figure 20**) or Customize numbered list dialog (**Figure 21**).

Figure 19 Use this dialog to locate and insert a picture to use as a bullet character.

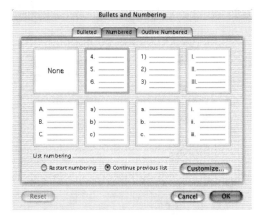

Figure 20 The Numbered tab of the Bullets and Numbering dialog.

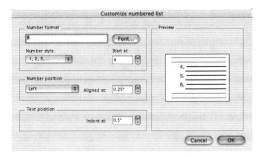

Figure 21 The Customize numbered list dialog.

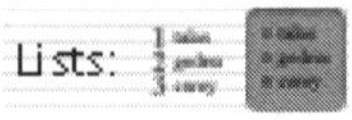

Figure 22 The Bullets button when a paragraph with a bulleted list format is selected.

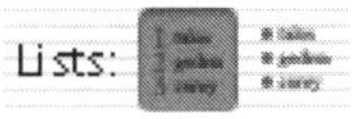

Figure 23 The Numbering button when a paragraph with a numbered list format is selected.

To remove bulleted or numbered list formatting

1. Choose Format > Bullets and Numbering (**Figure 5**).

2. In the Bullets and Numbering dialog (**Figure 17** or **20**), click the None box.

3. Click OK.

or

To remove bulleted list formatting, click the Bullets button on the Formatting Palette (**Figure 22**).

or

To remove numbered list formatting, click the Numbering button on the Formatting Palette (**Figure 23**).

BULLETS & NUMBERING

Borders & Shading

Borders and shading are two separate features that can work together to emphasize text:

◆ **Borders** enables you to place lines above, below, to the left, or to the right of selected characters or paragraphs (**Figure 24**).

◆ **Page borders** enables you to place simple or graphic borders at the top, bottom, left, or right sides of document pages (**Figure 25**).

◆ **Shading** enables you to add color or shades of gray to selected characters or paragraphs (**Figure 24**).

✔ Tips

■ How borders and shading are applied depends on how text is selected:

▲ To apply borders or shading to characters, select the characters.

▲ To apply borders or shading to a paragraph, click in the paragraph or select the entire paragraph.

▲ To apply borders or shading to multiple paragraphs, select the paragraphs.

▲ To apply page borders to all pages in a document, click anywhere in the document.

▲ To apply page borders to a specific document section, click anywhere in that section.

■ When applying borders to selected text characters (as opposed to selected paragraphs), you must place a border around each side, creating a box around the text.

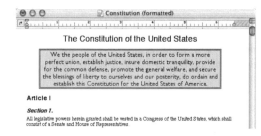

Figure 24 Borders and shading can emphasize text.

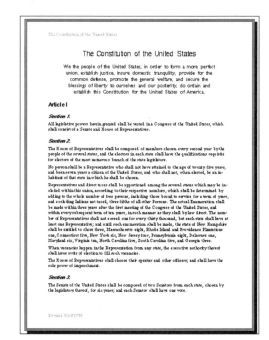

Figure 25 Page borders can make a page look fancy.

Figure 26
The Formatting
Palette with the
Borders and
Shading options
displayed.

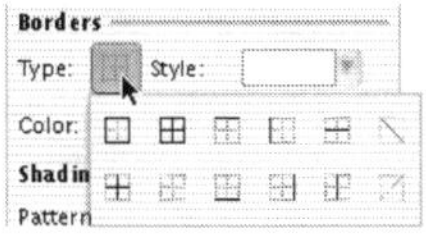

Figure 27
The Border Type
pop-up menu on the
Formatting Palette.

Figure 28
The Style pop-up
menu on the
Formatting Palette.

Figure 29
The Color pop-up
menu on the
Formatting Palette.

Figure 30
The Weight pop-up
menu on the
Formatting Palette.

To apply text borders with the Formatting Palette

1. Select the text to which you want to apply borders.

2. If necessary, display the Formatting Palette and its Borders and Shading options (**Figure 26**).

3. Choose a border type from the Border Type pop-up menu (**Figure 27**).

4. Choose a border style from the Style pop-up menu (**Figure 28**).

5. Choose a border color from the Color pop-up menu (**Figure 29**).

6. Choose a border weight from the Weight pop-up menu (**Figure 30**).

✔ Tips

- You can apply more than one border to selected paragraphs. For example, if you want a top and bottom border, choose the top border option and then choose the bottom border option. Both are applied.

- Some border options apply more than one border. For example, the outside border option (top left button) applies the outside border as well as the top, bottom, left, and right borders.

- Clicking the Border Type ⊞ or Border Color ■ button on the Formatting Palette applies the border type or border color that appears on the button, which is the last type or color chosen.

APPLYING TEXT BORDERS

To apply text borders with the Borders and Shading dialog

1. Select the text to which you want to apply borders.

2. Choose Format > Borders and Shading (**Figure 5**).

3. Click the Borders tab in the Borders and Shading dialog that appears to display its options (**Figure 31**).

4. Click a Setting icon to select the type of border. All options except None and Custom place borders around each side of the selected text.

5. Click a style in the Style scrolling list to select a line style.

6. Choose a line color from the Color pop-up menu (**Figure 32**). If you choose Automatic, Word applies the color specified in the paragraph style applied to the text.

7. Choose a line thickness from the Width pop-up menu (**Figure 33**).

8. If necessary, choose an option from the Apply to pop-up menu (**Figure 34**). The Preview area changes accordingly.

9. To apply custom borders, click the buttons in the Preview area to add or remove a line using the settings in the dialog.

10. When the Preview area illustrates the kind of border that you want to apply, click OK.

✔ Tips

■ You can repeat steps 5 through 7 and 9 to customize each border of a custom paragraph border.

■ You can further customize a paragraph border by clicking the Options button to display the Border and Shading Options dialog (**Figure 35**). Set options as desired and click OK to return to the Borders and Shading dialog.

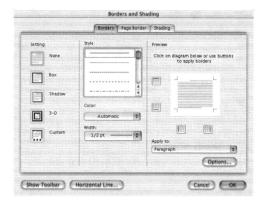

Figure 31 The Borders tab of the Borders and Shading dialog.

Figure 32 The Color pop-up menu.

Figure 33 The Width pop-up menu.

Figure 34 The Apply to pop-up menu.

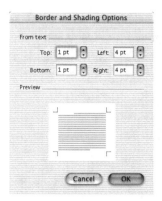

Figure 35 The Border and Shading Options dialog for text borders.

To remove text borders

1. Select the text from which you want to remove borders.

2. Click the No Borders button (the second button on the bottom row) on the Border Type pop-up menu on the Formatting Palette (**Figure 27**).

or

1. Select the text from which you want to remove borders.

2. Choose Format > Borders and Shading (**Figure 5**) and click the Borders tab in the Borders and Shading dialog that appears (**Figure 31**).

3. Click the None icon.

4. Click OK.

To apply page borders

1. If necessary, position the insertion point in the section of the document to which you want to apply page borders.

2. Choose Format > Borders and Shading (**Figure 5**).

3. Click the Page Border tab in the Borders and Shading dialog that appears to display its options (**Figure 36**).

4. Click a Setting icon to select the type of border. All options except None and Custom place borders around each side of the page.

5. Click a style in the Style scrolling list to select a line style. Then choose a line color from the Color pop-up menu (**Figure 32**) and a line thickness from the Width pop-up menu (**Figure 33**).

   or

   Select a graphic from the Art pop-up menu (**Figure 37**).

6. If necessary, choose an option from the Apply to pop-up menu (**Figure 38**).

7. To apply custom borders, click the buttons in the Preview area to add or remove a line using the settings in the dialog.

8. When the Preview area illustrates the kind of border that you want to apply, click OK.

✔ Tips

- You can repeat steps 5 and 7 to customize each border of a custom border.

- You can further customize a border by clicking the Options button in the Borders and Shading dialog to display the Border and Shading Options dialog (**Figure 39**). Set options as desired and click OK to return to the Borders and Shading dialog.

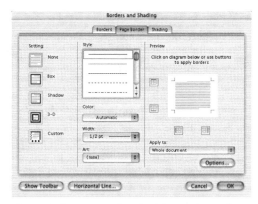

Figure 36 The Page Border tab of the Borders and Shading dialog.

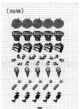

Figure 37 The Art pop-up menu.

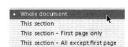

Figure 38 The Apply To pop-up menu.

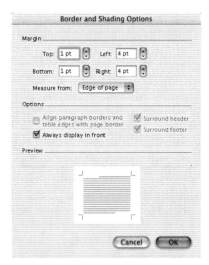

Figure 39 The Border and Shading Options dialog for page borders.

Figure 40
The Pattern pop-up menu on the Formatting Palette.

Figure 41
The Pattern Color pop-up menu on the Formatting Palette.

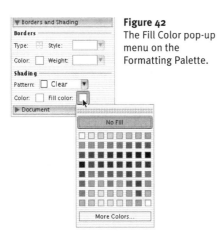

Figure 42
The Fill Color pop-up menu on the Formatting Palette.

To remove page borders

1. Position the insertion point in the section from which you want to remove borders.

2. Choose Format > Borders and Shading (**Figure 5**) and click the Page Border tab in the Borders and Shading dialog that appears (**Figure 36**).

3. Click the None icon.

4. Click OK.

To apply shading with the Formatting Palette

1. Select the text to which you want to apply shading.

2. If necessary, display the Formatting Palette and its Borders and Shading options (**Figure 26**).

3. Choose a shading percentage or pattern from the Pattern pop-up menu (**Figure 40**).

4. Choose a foreground color from the Pattern Color pop-up menu (**Figure 41**).

5. Choose a background color from the Fill Color pop-up menu (**Figure 42**).

✔ Tip

■ Use text shading with care. If overdone or if the pattern is too "busy," the text you have shaded may be impossible to read!

To apply shading with the Borders and Shading dialog

1. Select the text to which you want to apply shading.

2. Choose Format > Borders and Shading (**Figure 5**).

3. Click the Shading tab in the Borders and Shading dialog that appears to display its options (**Figure 43**).

4. Click a Fill color or shade to select it.

5. To create a pattern, choose an option from the Style pop-up menu (**Figure 44**) and then choose a color from the Color pop-up menu (**Figure 32**).

6. If necessary, choose an option from the Apply to pop-up menu (**Figure 34**). The Preview area changes accordingly.

7. When the Preview area illustrates the kind of shading that you want to apply, click OK.

To remove shading

1. Select the text from which you want to remove shading.

2. Choose Clear from the Pattern pop-up menu on the Formatting Palette (**Figure 40**). Then choose No Fill from both the Fill color and Pattern color pop-up menus (**Figures 41** and **42**).

or

1. Select the text from which you want to remove shading.

2. Choose Format > Borders and Shading (**Figure 5**) and click the Shading tab in the Borders and Shading dialog that appears (**Figure 43**).

3. Click the No Fill button in the Fill area.

4. Choose Clear from the Style pop-up menu (**Figure 44**).

5. Click OK.

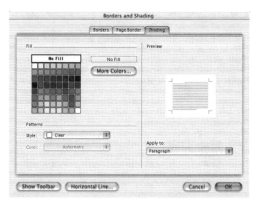

Figure 43 The Shading tab of the Borders and Shading dialog.

Figure 44 The Style pop-up menu in the Patterns area.

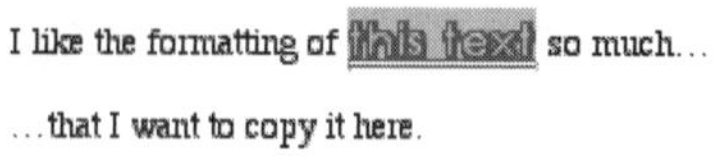

I like the formatting of **this text** so much...

...that I want to copy it here.

Figure 45 Select the text with the formatting you want to copy.

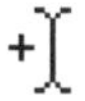

+I **Figure 46** When you click the Format Painter button, the mouse pointer turns into a Format Painter pointer.

I like the formatting of **this text** so much...

...that I want to copy it here.

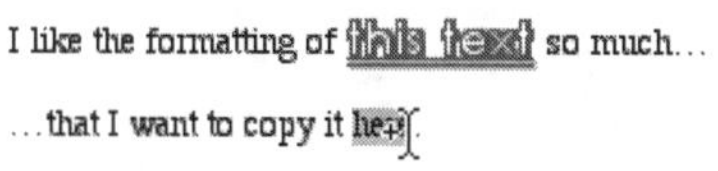

Figure 47 Use the Format Painter pointer to select the text you want to apply the formatting to.

I like the formatting of **this text** so much...

...that I want to copy it here.

Figure 48 When you release the mouse button, the formatting is applied.

The Format Painter

The Format Painter enables you to copy the font or paragraph formatting of selected text and apply it to other text. This can save time and effort when applying the same formatting in multiple places throughout a document.

✔ Tip

- Word offers two other methods to apply the same formatting in various places throughout a document:

  ▲ Select multiple blocks of text before applying formatting. I explain how to make multiple selections in **Chapter 2**.

  ▲ Define and apply paragraph or character styles. I begin my discussion of Word's styles feature on the next page.

To use the Format Painter

1. Select the text whose formatting you want to copy (**Figure 45**).

2. Click the Format Painter button 🖌 on the Standard toolbar. The Format Painter button becomes selected and the mouse pointer turns into an I-beam pointer with a plus sign beside it (**Figure 46**).

3. Use the mouse pointer to select the text to which you want to copy the formatting (**Figure 47**).

When you release the mouse button, the formatting is applied (**Figure 48**) and the mouse pointer returns to normal.

✔ Tips

- To copy paragraph formatting, be sure to select the entire paragraph in step 1, including the nonprinting Return character at the end of the paragraph. I tell you about nonprinting characters in **Chapter 2**.

- To copy the same formatting to more than one selection, double-click the Format Painter button. The mouse pointer remains a Format Painter pointer (**Figure 46**) until you press (Esc) or click the Format Painter button 🖌 again.

Styles

Word's styles feature enables you to define and apply sets of paragraph and/or font formatting to text throughout a document. This offers two main benefits over applying formatting using the basic techniques covered so far:

◆ **Consistency.** All text with a particular style applied will have the same formatting (**Figure 49**)—unless additional formatting has also been applied.

◆ **Flexibility.** Changing a style's definition is relatively easy. Once changed, the change automatically applies to all text formatted with that style (**Figure 50**).

There are two kinds of styles:

◆ **Character styles** affect the formatting of characters. The default character style is called *Default Paragraph Font* and is based on the font formatting of the currently applied paragraph style.

◆ **Paragraph styles** affect the formatting of entire paragraphs. The default paragraph style is called *Normal*.

✔ Tips

■ Like font or paragraph formatting, you can apply character or paragraph styles as you type or to text that has already been typed. Check **Chapter 3** for details.

■ Styles are sometimes known as *style sheets*.

■ Word includes a number of predefined styles that you can apply to text.

■ Word's outline feature automatically applies predefined Heading styles as you create an outline. You can learn more about outlines in **Chapter 8**.

■ Word automatically applies some styles as you type. For example, if you enter text at the top of a document, center it, and apply other formatting to it, Word redefines the Title style and applies it to the paragraph.

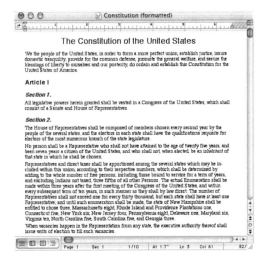

Figure 49 In this example, styles are applied to all text for consistent formatting.

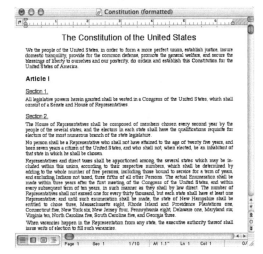

Figure 50 When two of the styles are modified, the formatting of text with those styles applied changes automatically. In this example, Normal style's paragraph formatting was changed from align left to justified and Heading 2 style's font formatting was changed from bold italic to regular with underline.

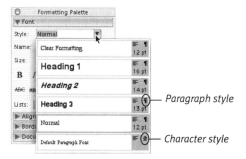

Figure 51 The Style pop-up menu on the Formatting Palette.

Figure 52 Click the style name to select it.

Figure 53 Type in the name of the style that you want to apply.

To apply a style with the Formatting Palette

Choose a style from the Style pop-up menu on the Formatting Palette (**Figure 51**).

or

1. Click the name of the style in the Style pop-up menu's text box to select it (**Figure 52**).

2. Type in the exact name of the style that you want to apply (**Figure 53**).

3. Press Return.

✔ Tips

- The Style pop-up menu displays only the styles that have been applied in the document, the first three Heading styles, and Default Paragraph Font (**Figure 51**).

- To include all built-in template styles on the Style pop-up menu, hold down Shift while clicking to display the menu.

- The Style pop-up menu displays each style name using the formatting of that style (**Figure 51**).

- You can distinguish between character styles and paragraph styles in the Style pop-up menu by the symbol to the right of the style name (**Figure 51**).

- If you enter the name of a style that does not yet exist in the document in step 2 above, Word creates a new style for you, based on the selected paragraph. The formatting of the paragraph does not change, but the new style name appears on the Style pop-up menu.

- The Clear Formatting option on the Formatting Palette's Style pop-up menu removes all manually applied formatting from a selection, returning its formatting to that of the style that is applied to the text. This is a brand new feature in Word X.

APPLYING STYLES WITH THE FORMATTING PALETTE

To apply a style with the Style dialog

1. Choose Format > Style (**Figure 5**) to display the Style dialog (**Figure 54**).

2. If necessary, use the List pop-up menu (**Figure 55**) to display a specific group of styles:

   ▲ **Styles in use** are the styles already applied within the document.

   ▲ **All styles** are the styles included within the template on which the document is based.

   ▲ **User-defined styles** are the styles that you add to the document.

3. Click on the name of the style that you want to apply to select it.

4. Click the Apply button.

✔ Tips

■ You can distinguish between character styles and paragraph styles in the Style dialog by the symbol to the left of the style name (**Figure 56**).

■ Triangle markers appear to the left of the currently applied character and paragraph styles (**Figure 56**).

■ The Description area of the Style dialog provides information about the formatting that the style includes (**Figure 54**).

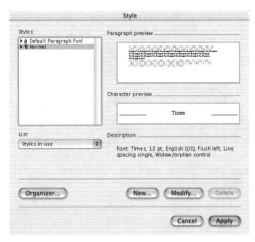

Figure 54 The Style dialog.

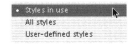

Figure 55 The List pop-up menu in the Style dialog.

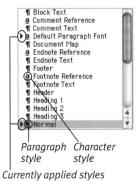

Figure 56 Another example of the Styles list in the Style dialog when Styles in use is chosen from the List pop-up menu.

Paragraph style   Character style

Currently applied styles

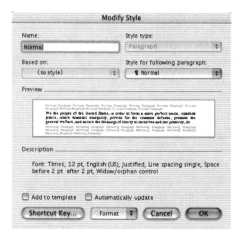

Figure 57 The Modify Style dialog.

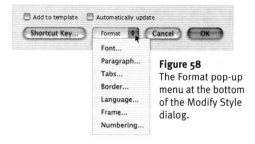

Figure 58
The Format pop-up menu at the bottom of the Modify Style dialog.

Figure 59 When you modify a style, the Cancel button at the bottom of the Style dialog turns into a Close button.

To modify a style

1. Choose Format > Style (**Figure 5**) to display the Style dialog (**Figure 54**).

2. If necessary, use the List pop-up menu (**Figure 55**) to display a specific group of styles.

3. Click the name of the style that you want to modify to select it.

4. Click the Modify button to display the Modify Style dialog (**Figure 57**).

5. To change the style's name, enter a new name in the Name text box.

6. To change the style's formatting, choose an option from the Format pop-up menu (**Figure 58**). Each option displays the appropriate formatting dialog.

7. Make changes as desired in the dialog that appears and click OK.

8. Repeat steps 6 and 7 as necessary to make all desired formatting changes.

9. To add the revised style to the template on which the document is based, turn on the Add to template check box.

10. To instruct Word to automatically update the style's definition whenever you apply manual formatting to text with the style applied, turn on the Automatically update check box. (This step only applies if you are modifying a paragraph style.)

11. Click OK to save changes in the Modify Style dialog.

12. Click the Close button (**Figure 59**) to dismiss the Style dialog without applying the style to the currently selected text.

    or

    Click the Apply button (**Figure 59**) to dismiss the Style dialog and apply the style to the currently selected text.

MODIFYING STYLES

To create a new style

1. Choose Format > Style (**Figure 5**) to display the Style dialog (**Figure 54**).

2. Click the New button to display the New Style dialog (**Figure 60**).

3. Enter a name for the style in the Name text box.

4. Choose the type of style that you want to create from the Style type pop-up menu (**Figure 61**).

5. To base the style on an existing style, choose the style from the Based on pop-up menu. This menu lists all styles of the type you selected in step 4 that are included in the template on which the document is based.

6. To specify the style's formatting, choose an option from the Format pop-up menu (**Figure 58**). Each option displays the appropriate formatting dialog.

7. Make changes as desired in the dialog that appears and click OK.

8. Repeat steps 6 and 7 as necessary to set all desired formatting options.

9. To add the new style to the template on which the document is based, turn on the Add to template check box.

10. To instruct Word to automatically update the style whenever you apply manual formatting to text with the style applied, turn on the Automatically update check box. (This step only applies if you are creating a paragraph style.)

11. Click OK to save changes in the New Style dialog.

12. At the bottom of the Style dialog (**Figure 59**), click the Apply button to apply the new style to selected text; otherwise click the Close button to dismiss the Style dialog.

Figure 60 The New Style dialog.

Figure 61 The Style type pop-up menu.

Figure 62 Word confirms that you want to delete a style.

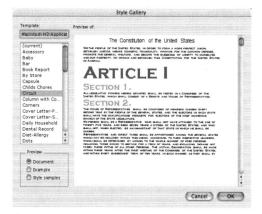

Figure 63 The Style Gallery showing a template's styles applied to the active document.

To delete a style

1. Choose Format > Style (**Figure 5**) to display the Style dialog (**Figure 54**).

2. If necessary, use the List pop-up menu (**Figure 55**) to display a specific group of styles.

3. Click to select the name of the style that you want to delete.

4. Click the Delete button.

5. A warning dialog (**Figure 62**) or Office Assistant balloon appears. Click Yes to delete the style.

✔ Tip

- When you delete a style, the default style (Normal for paragraph styles and Default Paragraph Font for character styles) is applied to any text to which the deleted style was applied.

To use the Style Gallery

1. Choose Format > Theme (**Figure 5**).

2. In the Themes dialog that appears, click the Style Gallery button to display the Style Gallery dialog.

3. Click the name of a template in the Template scrolling list to select it. An example of the document with the template's styles applied appears in the Preview area of the dialog (**Figure 63**).

4. To apply the styles of a selected template to the current document, click OK.

   or

   To close the Style Gallery dialog without changing styles, click Cancel.

✔ Tip

- I tell you about Word's themes feature in **Chapter 14**.

To attach a template to a document

1. Choose Tools > Templates and Add-Ins (**Figure 64**) to display the Templates and Add-ins dialog (**Figure 65**).

2. To update the current document's styles with styles from the template you are attaching, turn on the Automatically update document styles check box.

3. Click the Attach button.

4. Use the Choose a File dialog that appears (**Figure 66**) to locate, select, and open the template you want to attach to the document.

5. Back in the Templates and Add-ins dialog, click OK.

✔ Tips

- You can attach any Word template to a Word document—not just one of the templates that came with Microsoft Word.

- When you attach a template to a document, you make all the styles stored in the template available for use in the document.

- Attaching a template to a document is a good way to get an existing document to use standard formatting stored in a template file, even if the template was not available when the document was originally created.

Figure 64
Choose Templates and Add-Ins from the Tools menu.

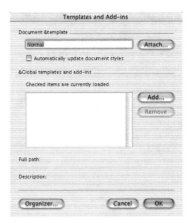

Figure 65 The Templates and Add-ins dialog.

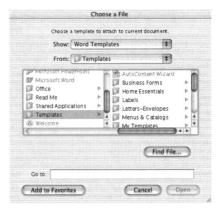

Figure 66 Use this dialog to locate, select, and open the template you want to attach.

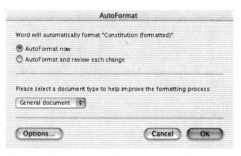

Figure 67 The AutoFormat dialog.

Figure 68 Use this pop-up menu to tell Word what kind of document it must format.

AutoFormat

Word's AutoFormat feature can automatically format a document either as you type or when the document is finished. Word formats documents by applying appropriate styles to text based on how the text is used in the document —for example, as titles, lists, headings, or body text. Word can also format Internet addresses as hyperlinks and replace typed symbols (such as --) with actual symbols (such as —).

✔ Tips

- AutoFormat As You Type is automatically turned on when you first use Word.

- I tell you more about Internet addresses and hyperlinks in **Chapter 14** and about symbols in **Chapter 7**.

To use AutoFormat on a completed document

1. Choose Format > AutoFormat (**Figure 5**) to display the AutoFormat dialog (**Figure 67**).

2. To use AutoFormat without reviewing changes, select the AutoFormat now radio button.

    or

    To review changes as you use AutoFormat, select the AutoFormat and review each change radio button.

3. Select the appropriate type of document from the pop-up menu (**Figure 68**).

4. Click OK to begin the AutoFormat process.

    ▲ If you selected the AutoFormat now radio button in Step 2, Word formats the document and displays the changes. The AutoFormat process is complete; the rest of the steps do not apply.

Continued on next page...

Continued from previous page.

▲ If you selected the AutoFormat and review each change radio button in step 2, Word formats the document. Continue with step 5.

5. A different AutoFormat dialog appears (**Figure 69**). Click one of its four buttons to proceed:

▲ **Accept All** accepts all changes to the document. The AutoFormat process is complete; the remaining steps do not apply.

▲ **Reject All** rejects all changes to the document. The AutoFormat process is reversed; the remaining steps do not apply.

▲ **Review Changes** enables you to review the changes one by one. The Review AutoFormat Changes dialog appears. Continue with step 6.

▲ **Style Gallery** displays the Style Gallery dialog so you can select a different template's styles. I tell you how to use the Style Gallery earlier in this chapter. When you are finished using the Style Gallery, you will return to this dialog; click one of the other buttons to continue.

6. In the Review AutoFormat Changes dialog, click the second Find button to begin reviewing changes throughout the document (**Figure 70**):

▲ To accept a change, click the Find button again.

▲ To reject a change and move to the next change, click the Reject button.

7. Repeat step 6 until you have reviewed every change.

8. Word displays a dialog when you reach the end of the document (**Figure 71**). Click Cancel to dismiss it.

Figure 69 This AutoFormat dialog appears when Word has finished the AutoFormat process and is waiting for you to review its changes.

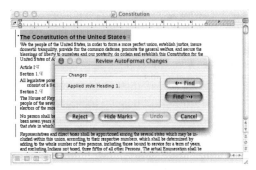

Figure 70 The Review AutoFormat Changes dialog lets you accept or reject each change as it is selected in the document window.

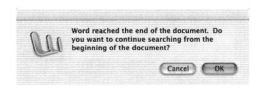

Figure 71 Word tells you when you reach the end of a document.

9. Click Cancel again to return to the Auto-Format Dialog (**Figure 69**).

10. Click Accept All to accept all changes that you did not reject.

USING AUTOFORMAT

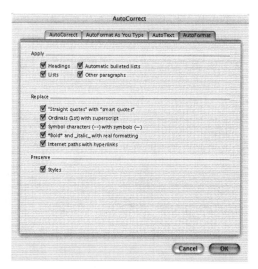

Figure 72 The AutoFormat tab of the AutoCorrect dialog.

To set AutoFormat options

1. Choose Format > AutoFormat (**Figure 5**) to display the AutoFormat dialog (**Figure 67**).

2. Click the Options button. The AutoFormat tab of the AutoCorrect dialog appears (**Figure 72**).

3. Set options as desired:

   ▲ **Headings** applies Heading styles to text that appears as a heading.

   ▲ **Lists** applies list and bullet styles to numbered, bulleted, and other lists.

   ▲ **Automatic bulleted lists** applies bulleted list formatting to paragraphs beginning with *, o, or - followed by a space or tab.

   ▲ **Other paragraphs** applies other styles such as Body Text, Inside Address, and Salutation.

   ▲ **"Straight quotes" with "smart quotes"** replaces plain quote characters with curly quote characters.

   ▲ **Ordinals (1st) with superscript** formats ordinals with superscript. For example, 1st becomes 1st.

   ▲ **Symbol characters (- -) with symbols (—)** replaces a single hyphen with an en dash (–) and a double hyphen with an em dash (—).

   ▲ ***Bold* and _italic_ with real formatting** formats text enclosed within asterisk characters (*) as bold and text enclosed within underscore characters as italic. For example, *hello* becomes **hello** and _goodbye_ becomes *goodbye*.

   ▲ **Internet paths with hyperlinks** formats e-mail addresses and URLs as clickable hyperlink fields.

   ▲ **Styles** prevents styles already applied in the document from being changed.

4. Click OK to save your settings.

✔ Tips

■ To convert other characters to corresponding symbols, such as (tm) to ™ or (c) to ©, use the AutoCorrect feature, which I explain in **Chapter 5**.

■ I tell you about hyperlinks and other Internet-related features in **Chapter 14**.

SETTING AUTOFORMAT OPTIONS

To set automatic formatting options

1. Choose Format > AutoFormat (**Figure 5**) to display the AutoFormat dialog (**Figure 67**).

2. Click the Options button. The AutoFormat tab of the AutoCorrect dialog appears (**Figure 72**).

3. Click the AutoFormat As You Type tab to display its options (**Figure 73**).

4. Set options as desired. Most of the options are the same as those in the AutoFormat tab, which I discuss on the previous page. Here are the others:

   ▲ **Borders** automatically applies paragraph border styles when you type three or more hyphens, underscores, or equal signs.

   ▲ **Tables** creates a table when you type a series of hyphens with plus signs to indicate column edges, such as +----------+-----+.

   ▲ **Automatic numbered lists** applies numbered list formatting to paragraphs beginning with a number or letter followed by a space or tab.

   ▲ **Format beginning of list item like the one before it** repeats character formatting that you apply to the beginning of a list item. For example, if the first word of the previous list item was formatted as bold, the first word of the next list item is automatically formatted as bold.

   ▲ **Define styles based on your formatting** automatically creates or modifies styles based on manual formatting that you apply in the document.

5. Click OK to save your settings.

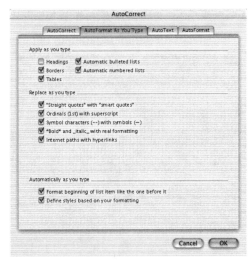

Figure 73 The AutoFormat As You Type tab of the AutoCorrect dialog.

✔ Tips

- I tell you about borders, list formatting, and styles earlier in this chapter and about tables in **Chapter 9**.

- Most AutoFormatting As You Type options are turned on by default. The only way to disable this feature is to turn off all options in the AutoFormat As You Type tab of the AutoCorrect dialog (**Figure 73**).

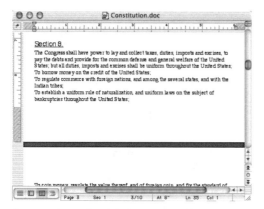

Figure 74 A page break in Page Layout view.

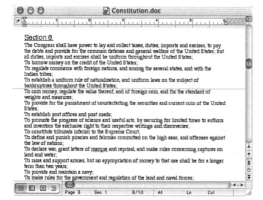

Figure 75 The same page break in Normal view.

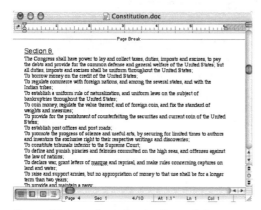

Figure 76 A manual page break adjusts all the subsequent automatic page breaks.

Page, Section, & Column Breaks

As you work with a document, Word automatically sets page breaks based on page size, margins, and contents. A *page break* marks the end of a page; anything after the page break will appear on the next page when the document is printed. This is easy to see in Page Layout view (**Figure 74**). In Normal view, automatic page breaks appear as dotted lines across the document (**Figure 75**).

Although you cannot change an automatic page break directly, you can change it indirectly by inserting a manual page break before it (**Figure 76**). This forces the page to end where you specify and, in most cases, forces subsequent automatic page breaks in the document to change.

In addition to page breaks, Word also enables you to insert section and column breaks. A *section break* marks the end of a document section. Sections are commonly used to divide a document into logical parts, each of which can have its own settings in the Document dialog. A *column break* marks the end of a column of text. Column breaks are usually used in conjunction with multi-column text.

✔ Tips

- Automatic page breaks do not appear in Online Layout, Outline, or Master Document view.

- As discussed in **Chapter 3**, section breaks may be automatically inserted by Word in a document when you change document formatting settings.

- I tell you more about columns and multi-column text a little later in this chapter.

To insert a break

1. Position the insertion point where you want the break to occur (**Figure 77**).

2. Choose an option from the Insert menu's Break submenu (**Figure 78**):

   ▲ **Page Break** inserts a page break. **Figure 76** shows an inserted page break.

   ▲ **Column Break** inserts a column break.

   ▲ **Section Break (Next Page)** inserts a section break that also acts as a page break.

   ▲ **Section Break (Continuous)** inserts a section break in the middle of a page.

   ▲ **Section Break (Odd Page)** inserts a section break that also acts as a page break. The following page will always be odd-numbered.

   ▲ **Section Break (Even Page)** inserts a section break that also acts as a page break. The following page will always be even-numbered.

   or

   Use one of the following shortcut keys:

   ▲ To insert a page break, press [Shift] [Enter].

   ▲ To insert a column break, press [⌃] [⌘] [Shift] [R].

   ▲ To insert a next page section break, press [⌃] [⌘] [Enter].

To remove a break

1. In Normal view, select the break by clicking in the selection bar to its left (**Figure 79**).

2. Press [Delete].

Insertion point

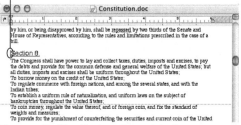

Figure 77 Position the insertion point where you want the break to occur.

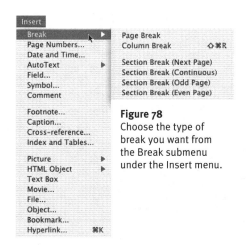

Figure 78 Choose the type of break you want from the Break submenu under the Insert menu.

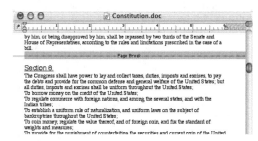

Figure 79 Click in the selection bar to the left of the break to select it.

Figure 80 Multi-column text in Page Layout view.

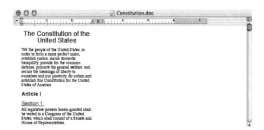

Figure 81 Multi-column text in Normal view.

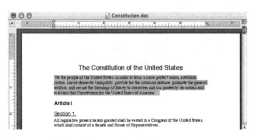

Figure 82 Select the text for which you want to set columns.

Figure 83
Choose the number of columns from the Columns button menu on the Standard toolbar.

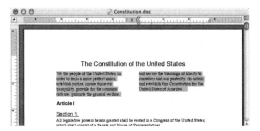

Figure 84 Word sets the columns for the selected text, inserting section breaks if necessary.

Columns

Word enables you to format text with multiple columns, like those in a newspaper.

✔ Tips

- Although you can edit multi-column text in any view, you must be in Page Layout view (**Figure 80**) to see the columns side by side. In Normal view, the text appears in the same narrow column (**Figure 81**).

- Column formatting applies to sections of text. You can insert section breaks as discussed on the previous page to set up various multi-column sections.

To set the number of columns

1. Select the text for which you want to set the number of columns (**Figure 82**).

2. Click the Columns button on the Standard toolbar to display a menu of columns and choose the number of columns (**Figure 83**).

If you are not in Page Layout view, Word switches to that view. The text is reformatted with the number of columns you specified (**Figure 84**).

✔ Tips

- To set the number of columns for an entire single-section document, in step 1 above, position the insertion point anywhere in the document.

- To set the number of columns for one section of a multi-section document, in step 1 above, position the insertion point anywhere in the section.

- If necessary, Word inserts section breaks to mark the beginning and end of multi-column text (**Figure 84**).

To set column options

1. Position the insertion point in the section for which you want to change column options.

   or

   Select the sections for which you want to change column options.

2. Choose Format > Columns (**Figure 5**) to display the Columns dialog (**Figure 85**).

3. To set the number of columns, click one of the icons in the Presets section or enter a value in the Number of columns text box.

4. To set different column widths for each column, make sure the Equal column width check box is turned off, then enter values in the Width text boxes for each column. You can also enter values in the Spacing text boxes to specify the amount of space between columns.

5. To put a vertical line between columns, turn on the Line between check box.

6. To specify the part of the document that you want the changes to apply to, choose an option from the Apply to pop-up menu (**Figure 86**).

   or

   To insert a column break at the insertion point, choose This point forward from the Apply to pop-up menu (**Figure 86**), then turn on the Start new column check box.

7. When you are finished setting options, click OK to save them.

✔ Tip

- You can see the effect of your changes in the Preview area as you change settings in the Columns dialog.

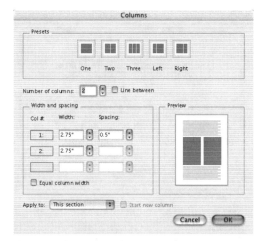

Figure 85 The Columns dialog, showing the settings for the two-column section in **Figure 84**.

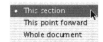

Figure 86 The Apply to pop-up menu in the Columns dialog when the insertion point is in a section of a multi-section document. The options on this menu vary depending on the document and what is selected.

Figure 87
Choose Header and Footer from the View menu.

Figure 88 The Header area of a document window.

Figure 89 The Footer area of a document window.

Headers & Footers

A header is a part of the document that appears at the top of every page. A footer is a part of the document that appears at the bottom of every page. Headers and footers are commonly used to place page numbers, revision dates, or other document information on document pages.

To display a header or footer

Choose View > Header and Footer (**Figure 87**).

If necessary, Word switches to Page Layout view and displays the Header area of the current document section and the Header and Footer toolbar (**Figure 88**).

◆ To view the footer for the current section, click the Switch Between Header and Footer button ▣ on the Header and Footer toolbar. The Footer area appears (**Figure 89**).

◆ To view the header or footer for the previous or next section of a multi-section document, click the Show Previous ▣ or Show Next ▣ button on the Header and Footer toolbar.

✔ Tip

■ If you are viewing a document in Page Layout view, you can view a header or footer by double-clicking in the header or footer area of a page.

To hide a header or footer

Click the Close button in the Header and Footer toolbar.

or

Double-click anywhere in the document window other than in the Header or Footer area.

The document returns to the view you were in before you viewed the header or footer and the Header and Footer toolbar disappears.

To create a header or footer

1. Display the header or footer area (**Figure 88** or **89**) for the header or footer that you want to create.

2. Enter the header (**Figure 90**) or footer (**Figure 91**) information.

3. When you're finished, hide the header or footer area to continue working on the document.

Header
The Constitution of the United States

Figure 90 A simple header.

Footer
Revised March 19, 1789

Figure 91 A simple footer.

✔ Tip

■ You can format the contents of a header or footer the same way that you format any other part of the document. You can find detailed formatting instructions in **Chapter 3** and earlier in this chapter.

To edit a header or footer

1. Display the header (**Figure 90**) or footer (**Figure 91**) area for the header or footer that you want to change.

2. Edit the header or footer information.

3. When you're finished, hide the header or footer area to continue working on the document.

CREATING & EDITING HEADERS & FOOTERS

Figure 92
The AutoText menu
on the Header and
Footer toolbar.

Figure 93 The Header and Footer toolbar.

Figure 94 This footer example uses the "Author, Page #, Date" AutoText entry to insert Word fields.

To insert AutoText entries or Word fields in a header or footer

1. Position the insertion point in the Header or Footer area where you want the Auto-Text entry or field to appear.

2. To insert an AutoText entry, click the AutoText button on the Header and Footer toolbar to display a menu of entries (**Figure 92**). Choose the one that you want to insert.

3. To insert a Word field, click the appropriate button on the Header and Footer toolbar (**Figure 93**) to insert the field.

✔ Tips

■ I tell you about AutoText entries and Word fields in **Chapter 7**.

■ To number pages, use the Insert Page Number button [#] on the Header and Footer toolbar or one of the first three options on the AutoText button menu (**Figure 92**) to insert a page number in the header or footer. **Figure 94** shows an example using the "Author, Page #, Date" AutoText Entry. This is the best way to number pages in a document. Using the Page Numbers command on the Insert menu inserts page numbers in frames that can be difficult to work with. The Page Numbers command is not covered in this book.

USING WORD FIELDS IN HEADERS & FOOTERS

To create a different first page or odd and even header and footer

1. Choose Format > Document (**Figure 5**) to display the Document dialog. If necessary, click the Layout tab.

   or

   Click the Document Layout button 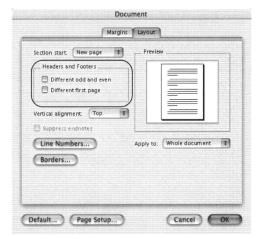 on the Header and Footer toolbar.

   The Layout tab of the Document dialog appears (**Figure 95**).

2. To create a different header and footer on odd- and even-numbered pages of the document, turn on the Different odd and even check box.

3. To create a different header and footer on the first page of the document or document section, turn on the Different first page check box.

4. Click OK.

5. Follow the instructions on the previous pages to create headers and footers as desired. Use the Show Previous ⬐ and Show Next ⬏ buttons on the Header and Footer toolbar to display and edit each header and footer.

To remove a header or footer

1. Display the Header or Footer area for the header or footer that you want to remove.

2. Select its contents and press (Delete). The header or footer is removed.

3. Hide the header or footer area to continue working on the document.

Figure 95 The Layout tab of the Document dialog.

WRITING TOOLS

Word's Writing Tools

Word includes a number of features to help you be a better writer. Some of these features can help you find and fix errors in your documents, while other features can help you fine tune your documents for publication.

Here are the writing tools covered in this chapter:

◆ The **spelling checker** compares words in your document to words in dictionary files to identify unknown words.

◆ The **grammar checker** checks sentences against a collection of grammar rules to identify questionable sentence construction.

◆ **AutoCorrect** automatically corrects common errors as you type.

◆ The **dictionary** helps you understand the meaning of words in a document.

◆ The **thesaurus** enables you to find synonyms or antonyms for words in your document.

◆ **Hyphenation** automatically hyphenates words based on hyphenation rules.

◆ **Word count** counts the words in a selection or the entire document.

✔ Tip

■ No proofing tool is a complete substitute for carefully rereading a document to manually check it for errors. Use Word's spelling and grammar checkers to help you find and fix errors, but don't depend on them to find all spelling or grammar errors in your documents.

The Spelling & Grammar Checkers

Word's spelling and grammar checkers help you to identify potential spelling and grammar problems in your documents. They can be set to check text automatically as you type or when you have finished typing.

The spelling checker compares the words in a document to the words in its main spelling dictionary, which includes many words and names. If it cannot find a match for a word, it then checks the active custom dictionaries—the dictionary files that you create. If Word still cannot find a match, it flags the word as unknown so you can act on it.

The grammar checker works in much the same way. It compares the structure of sentences in the document with predetermined rules for a specific writing style. When it finds a sentence or sentence fragment with a potential problem, it identifies it for you so you can act on it.

Both the spelling and grammar checkers are highly customizable so they work the way that you want them to.

✔ Tips

- The spelling checker cannot identify a misspelled word if it correctly spells another word. For example, if you type *from* when you meant to type *form*, the spelling checker would not find the error. The grammar checker, on the other hand, might find this particular error, depending on its usage.

- Do not add a word to a custom dictionary unless you *know* it is correctly spelled. Otherwise, the word will never be flagged as an error.

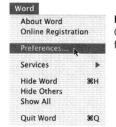

Figure 1
Choose Preferences
from the Word menu.

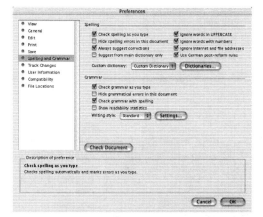

Figure 2 The default Spelling and Grammar settings in
the Preferences dialog.

To enable or disable automatic spelling and/or grammar checking

1. Choose Word > Preferences (**Figure 1**).

2. In the Preferences dialog that appears, click Spelling and Grammar in the list on the left to display Spelling and Grammar options (**Figure 2**).

3. To enable automatic spelling checking, turn on the Check spelling as you type check box.

   or

   To disable automatic spelling checking, turn off the Check spelling as you type check box.

4. To enable automatic grammar checking, turn on the Check grammar as you type check box.

   or

   To disable automatic grammar checking, turn off the Check grammar as you type check box.

5. Click OK.

✔ Tips

- By default, Word is set up to automatically check spelling and grammar, as you type.

- I explain how to set other spelling and grammar preferences in **Chapter 15**.

To check spelling as you type

1. Make sure that the automatic spelling checking feature has been enabled.

2. As you enter text into the document, a red wavy underline appears beneath each unknown word (**Figure 3**).

3. Hold down Control while clicking on a flagged word. The spelling shortcut menu appears (**Figure 4**).

4. Choose the appropriate option:

   ▲ Suggested spellings appear at the top of the shortcut menu. Choosing one of these spellings changes the word and removes the wavy underline.

   ▲ **Ignore All** tells Word to ignore all occurrences of the word in the document. Choosing this option removes the wavy underline from all occurrences of the word in the document.

   ▲ **Add** adds the word to the current custom dictionary. The wavy underline disappears and the word is never flagged again as unknown.

   ▲ **AutoCorrect** enables you to create an AutoCorrect entry for the word using one of the suggested spellings. Choose the appropriate word from the submenu (**Figure 5**). The word is replaced in the document and will be automatically replaced with the word you chose each time you type in the unknown word.

   ▲ **Spelling** opens the Spelling dialog (**Figure 6**), which offers additional options.

✔ Tips

■ As shown in **Figure 7**, Word's spelling checker also identifies repeated words and offers appropriate options.

■ I tell you more about AutoCorrect and the Spelling dialog later in this chapter.

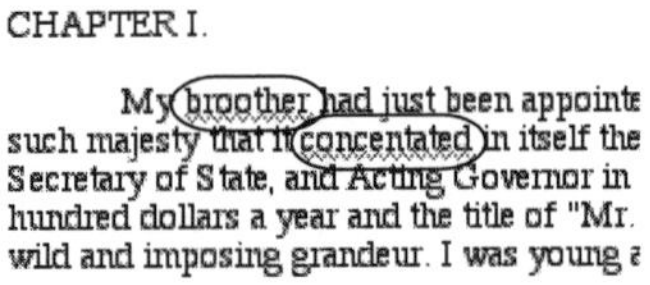

Figure 3 Two possible errors identified by the spelling checker.

Figure 4 A shortcut menu displays options to fix a possible spelling problem.

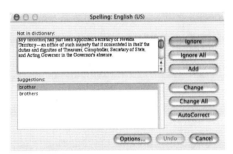

Figure 5 The AutoCorrect option displays a submenu with the suggested words. Choose one to create an AutoCorrect entry.

Figure 6 The Spelling dialog offers additional options for dealing with possible spelling errors. This dialog is very similar to the Spelling and Grammar dialog shown in **Figure 14**.

Figure 7 The shortcut menu offers different options for repeated words.

CHECKING SPELLING AS YOU TYPE

The Constitution of the United States

We the people of the United States, in order to form a more perfect union, establish justice, insure domestic tranquility, provide for the common defense, promote the general welfare, and secure the blessings of liberty to ourselves and our posterity, do ordain and establish this Constitution for the United States of America.

Article I

Section 1.

All legislative powers herein granted shall be vested in a Congress of the United States, which shall consist of a Senate and House of Representatives.

Figure 8 Two possible errors identified by the grammar checker.

Figures 9 & 10
Using the grammar shortcut menu to correct possible grammar problems. (I wonder what our founding fathers would have thought of this!)

Figure 11 The Office Assistant can explain grammar rules.

Figure 12 The Grammar dialog offers additional options for working with possible grammar problems. This dialog is very similar to the Spelling and Grammar dialog shown in **Figure 14**.

To check grammar as you type

1. Make sure that the automatic grammar checking feature has been enabled.

2. As you enter text into the document, a green wavy underline appears beneath each questionable word, phrase, or sentence (**Figure 8**).

3. Hold down Control while clicking on a flagged problem. The grammar shortcut menu appears (**Figures 9** and **10**).

4. Choose the appropriate option:

   ▲ Suggested corrections appear near the top of the shortcut menu (**Figures 9** and **10**). Choosing one of these corrections changes the text and removes the wavy underline.

   ▲ **Ignore** tells Word to ignore the problem. Choosing this option removes the wavy underline.

   ▲ **About this Sentence** provides information about the grammar rule that caused the sentence to be flagged (**Figure 11**). The Office Assistant must be enabled for this option to work.

   ▲ **Grammar** opens the Grammar dialog (**Figure 12**), which offers additional options.

✔ Tips

■ I tell you more about the Grammar dialog later in this chapter.

■ Word's grammar checker doesn't always have a suggestion to fix a problem.

■ Don't choose a suggestion without examining it carefully. The suggestion Word offers may not be correct.

■ I tell you about the Office Assistant in **Chapter 1**.

To check spelling and grammar all at once

1. Choose Tools > Spelling and Grammar (**Figure 13**) or press [Option] ⌃ ⌘ [L].

   Word begins checking spelling and grammar. When it finds a possible error, it displays the Spelling and Grammar dialog (**Figure 14**).

2. For a spelling or grammar problem:

   ▲ To ignore the problem, click Ignore.

   ▲ To ignore all occurrences of the problem in the document, click Ignore All.

   ▲ To use one of Word's suggested corrections, click to select the suggestion and then click Change.

   ▲ To change the problem without using a suggestion, edit it in the top part of the Spelling and Grammar dialog. Then click Change.

   For a spelling problem only:

   ▲ To add the word to the current custom dictionary, click Add.

   ▲ To change the word throughout the document to one of the suggested corrections, click to select it and then click Change All.

   ▲ To create an AutoCorrect entry for the word, select one of the suggestions and click AutoCorrect.

3. Word continues checking. It displays the Spelling and Grammar dialog for each possible error. Repeat step 2 until the entire document has been checked.

✔ Tips

■ The Spelling and Grammar dialog contains elements found in both the Spelling dialog (**Figure 6**) and the Grammar dialog (**Figure 12**).

■ If the Office Assistant is open, it explains each grammar problem Word finds (**Figure 11**).

Figure 13
Most of Word's writing tools can be accessed with commands on the Tools menu.

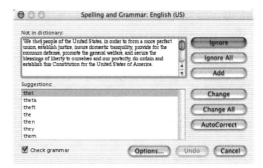

Figure 14 The Spelling and Grammar dialog displaying options for a spelling problem.

■ To disable grammar checking during a manual spelling check, turn off the Check grammar check box in the Spelling and Grammar dialog (**Figure 14**).

CHECKING SPELLING & GRAMMAR AT ONCE

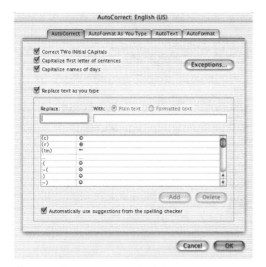

Figure 15 The AutoCorrect tab of the AutoCorrect dialog.

AutoCorrect

Word's AutoCorrect feature can correct common typographical errors as you make them. You set up AutoCorrect entries by entering the incorrect and correct text in the AutoCorrect dialog. Then, each time you make an error for which an AutoCorrect entry exists, Word automatically replaces the error with the correction.

✔ Tips

- Word comes preconfigured with hundreds of AutoCorrect entries based on abbreviations, online equivalents of special symbols, and common typographical errors and misspellings.

- AutoCorrect is enabled by default.

To set AutoCorrect options

1. Choose Tools > AutoCorrect (**Figure 13**).

2. The AutoCorrect dialog appears. If necessary, click the AutoCorrect tab to display its options (**Figure 15**).

3. Set options as desired:

   ▲ **Correct TWo INitial CApitals** changes the second letter in a pair of capital letters to lowercase.

   ▲ **Capitalize first letter of sentences** capitalizes the first letter following the end of a sentence.

   ▲ **Capitalize names of days** capitalizes the names of the days of the week.

   ▲ **Replace text as you type** enables the AutoCorrect feature for the AutoCorrect entries in the bottom of the dialog.

   ▲ **Automatically use suggestions from the spelling checker** tells Word to replace spelling errors with words from the dictionary as you type.

4. Click OK to save your settings.

✔ Tip

- To disable AutoCorrect, turn off all check boxes in the AutoCorrect tab of the Auto-Correct dialog.

To add an AutoCorrect entry

1. Choose Tools > AutoCorrect (**Figure 13**).
2. The AutoCorrect dialog appears. If necessary, click the AutoCorrect tab to display its options (**Figure 15**).
3. Type the text that you want to automatically replace in the Replace text box.
4. Type the text that you want to replace it with in the With text box (**Figure 16**).
5. Click the Add button.
6. Click OK.

✔ Tip

- To add a formatted text entry, enter and format the replacement text in your document. Then select that text and follow the steps above. Make sure the Formatted text radio button is selected before clicking the Add button in step 5.

To use AutoCorrect

In a document, type the text that appears on the Replace side of the AutoCorrect entries list (**Figure 17**). When you press Spacebar, Return, Shift Return, or some punctuation, the text you typed changes to the corresponding text on the With side of the AutoCorrect entries list (**Figure 18**).

To delete an AutoCorrect entry

1. Choose Tools > AutoCorrect (**Figure 13**).
2. The AutoCorrect dialog appears. If necessary, click the AutoCorrect tab to display its options (**Figure 15**).
3. Scroll through the list of AutoCorrect entries in the bottom half of the dialog to find the entry that you want to delete and click it once to select it.
4. Click the Delete button.
5. Click OK.

Replace:
With:
Plain text
Formatted text
mll
Maria L. Langer

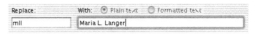

Figure 16 The two parts of an AutoCorrect entry.

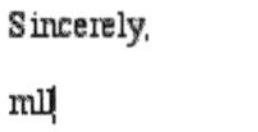

Sincerely,
mll

Figure 17 To use an AutoCorrect entry, type the text from the Replace part of the entry...

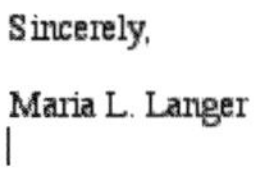

Sincerely,
Maria L. Langer

Figure 18 ...and the With part of the entry appears automatically as you continue typing.

Figure 19
Choose the Define option on the shortcut menu.

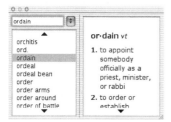

Figure 20 A word's definition and usage appears in a window like this one.

Figure 21 Word keeps track of all the words you've defined while working.

The Dictionary

Word includes a dictionary feature that enables you to look up word meanings and usage—right from within Word. You can use this feature to make sure the words you use in your documents are the right ones to get your message across. You can also use the dictionary to look up the meanings of words in Word documents written by others.

To view a definition

1. Hold down ⟨Control⟩ and click on the word for which you want a definition.

2. A shortcut menu appears (**Figure 19**). If the Define option is available, choose it.

or

1. Select the word for which you want a definition.

2. Choose Tools > Dictionary (**Figure 13**).

A definition window like the one in **Figure 20** appears. The word being defined is selected in the list on the left side of the window and its meanings and usage appear on the right side of the window.

✔ Tips

- You can define another word by either entering it in the text box or selecting it in the scrolling list of words in the definition window (**Figure 20**).

- A pop-up menu at the top of the definition window (**Figure 21**) keeps track of all the words you have defined during your Word session. Choose a word to see its definition again.

THE DICTIONARY

The Thesaurus

Word's thesaurus enables you to find synonyms or antonyms for words in your document—without leaving Word.

To find a synonym quickly

1. Hold down (Control) and click on the word for which you want to find a synonym.

2. A shortcut menu appears. If the Synonyms option is available, highlight it to display a submenu of synonyms for the word (**Figure 22**).

3. To replace the word with one of the synonyms, choose it from the submenu.

To use the Thesaurus dialog

1. Select the word for which you want to find a synonym or antonym.

2. Choose Tools > Thesaurus (**Figure 13**) or press (Option)(⌃ ⌘)(R) to display the Thesaurus dialog (**Figure 23**).

3. Click to select a meaning in the Can mean list. A list of synonyms (or antonyms) appears on the right side of the dialog.

4. To replace the selected word, click to select the synonym or antonym with which you want to replace it. Then click Replace. The dialog disappears.

    or

    To look up a synonym or antonym, click it to select it and then click Look Up. Then repeat step 3.

✔ Tips

■ The word pop-up menu (**Figure 24**) keeps track of all the words you looked up while using the Thesaurus dialog. Choose a word from the menu to look it up again.

■ To close the Thesaurus dialog without replacing a word, click its Cancel button.

Figure 22 The shortcut menu for a word may include synonyms.

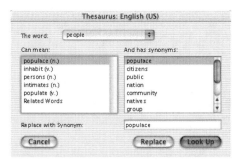

Figure 23 The Thesaurus dialog.

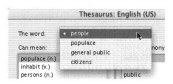

Figure 24 This pop-up menu keeps track of all the words you've looked up.

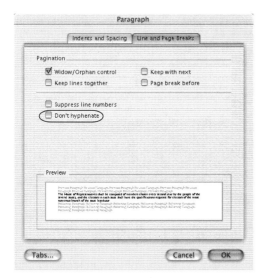

Figure 25 Use the Line and Page Breaks tab of the Paragraph dialog to prevent hyphenation in selected paragraphs.

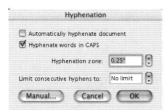

Figure 26 The default settings in the Hyphenation dialog.

✔ Tip

- To remove hyphenation inserted with the automatic hyphenation feature, turn off the Automatically hyphenate document check box in the Hyphenation dialog (**Figure 26**).

Hyphenation

Word's hyphenation feature can hyphenate words so they fit better on a line. Word can hyphenate the words in your documents automatically as you type or manually when you have finished typing.

✔ Tips

- Hyphenation helps prevent ragged right margins in left aligned text and large gaps between words in full justified text. I tell you about alignment in **Chapter 3**.

- To prevent text from being hyphenated, select it and then turn on the Don't hyphenate option in the Line and Page Breaks tab of the Paragraph dialog (**Figure 25**). I explain options in the Paragraph dialog in **Chapters 3** and **4**.

To set hyphenation options

1. Choose Tools > Hyphenation (**Figure 13**) to display the Hyphenation dialog (**Figure 26**).

2. Set options as desired:
   - ▲ **Automatically hyphenate document** enables automatic hyphenation as you type. (By default, this option is turned off.)
   - ▲ **Hyphenate words in CAPS** hyphenates words entered in all uppercase letters, such as acronyms.
   - ▲ **Hyphenation zone** is the distance from the right indent within which you want to hyphenate the document. The lower the value you enter, the more words are hyphenated.
   - ▲ **Limit consecutive hyphens to** is the maximum number of hyphens that can appear in a row.

3. Click OK.

To manually hyphenate a document

1. Follow steps 1 and 2 on the previous page to open the Hyphenation dialog (**Figure 26**) and set options. Be sure to leave the Automatically hyphenate document check box turned off.

2. Click the Manual button. Word begins searching for hyphenation candidates. When it finds one, it displays the Manual Hyphenation dialog (**Figure 27**).

3. Do one of the following:

   ▲ To hyphenate the word at the recommended break, click Yes.

   ▲ To hyphenate the word at a different break, click the hyphen at the desired break and then click Yes. (The hyphen that you click must be to the left of the margin line.)

   ▲ To continue without hyphenating the word, click No.

4. Word continues looking for hyphenation candidates. It displays the Manual Hyphenation dialog for each one. Repeat step 3 until the entire document has been hyphenated.

✔ Tips

■ To hyphenate only part of a document, select the part that you want to hyphenate before following the above steps.

■ You can also manually insert two types of special hyphens within words:

   ▲ Press ⌃ ⌘ – to insert an optional hyphen, which only breaks the word when necessary. Use this to manually hyphenate a word without using the Manual Hyphenation dialog.

   ▲ Press Shift ⌃ ⌘ – to insert a non-breaking hyphen, which displays a hyphen but never breaks the word.

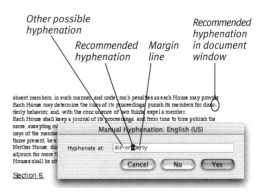

Other possible hyphenation   *Recommended hyphenation*   *Margin line*   *Recommended hyphenation in document window*

Figure 27 The Manual Hyphenation dialog.

Figure 28 The Live Word Count feature displays the current word number and total number of words in the status bar.

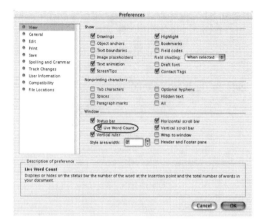

Figure 29 Turning on the Live Word Count check box enables the Live Word Count feature.

Word Count

The word count feature counts the pages, words, characters, paragraphs, and lines in a selection or the entire document.

Word also includes a Live Word Count feature. When enabled, it displays word count information in the status bar at the bottom of the document window (**Figure 28**):

◆ The first number is the number of the word at the insertion point or the number of words that are selected.

◆ The second number is the total number of words in the document.

✔ Tip

■ The word count feature is especially useful for writers who often have word count limitations or get paid by the word.

To enable/disable Live Word Count

1. Choose Word > Preferences (**Figure 1**) to display the Preferences dialog.

2. If necessary, click View in the list on the left side of the dialog (**Figure 29**).

3. To enable the Live Word Count feature, turn on the Live Word Count check box. (The Status bar check box must be turned on as well.)

   or

   To disable the Live Word Count feature, turn off the Live Word Count check box.

4. Click OK.

To count pages, words, characters, paragraphs, & lines

1. If necessary, select the text that you want to count.

2. Choose Tools > Word Count (**Figure 13**) to display the Word Count dialog (**Figure 30**).

   After a moment, complete count figures appear.

3. To include footnotes and endnotes in the count, turn on the Include footnotes and endnotes check box.

4. When you are finished working with the count figures, click OK to dismiss the dialog.

✔ Tip

- I explain how to insert footnotes and endnotes in **Chapter 7**.

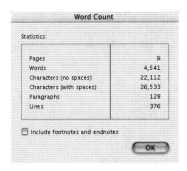

Figure 30 The Word Count dialog.

PRINTING DOCUMENTS

Printing Documents

In most cases, when you've finished writing, formatting, and proofreading a document, you'll want to print it. This chapter tells you about the three parts to the printing process:

- ◆ **Page Setup** enables you to specify information about the paper size, print orientation, and scale.

- ◆ **Print Preview** enables you to view the document on screen before you print it. You can also use this view to set page breaks and margins to fine-tune printed appearance.

- ◆ **Print** enables you to specify the page range, paper source, and other options for printing. It then sends the document to your printer.

✔ Tips

- ■ Although it's a good idea to go through all three of the above parts of the printing process, you don't have to. You can just print. But as I explain throughout this chapter, each part of the printing process has its own purpose that may benefit a print job.

- ■ When you save a document, Word saves many Page Setup and Print options with it.

- ■ I provide specific information for printing mailing labels, form letters, and envelopes in **Chapters 10** and **11**.

Print Center

Mac OS X introduced Print Center, a utility that enables you to identify printers and work with print jobs.

When you configure Mac OS X for printing, you add each of your printers to Print Center's Printer List (**Figure 1**). This list can include printers that are directly connected to your computer or those accessible via network. The printers on this list appear in pop-up menus in the Page Setup (**Figure 7**) and Print (**Figure 34**) dialogs.

Mac OS X includes *printer driver* software that enables your computer to communicate with printers. If you have a printer that is not recognized by Mac OS X, you will have to install the printer driver that came with the printer or that can be downloaded from the printer manufacturer's Web site.

Figure 1 Print Center's Printer List on my computer. The Printer List window on your computer will list your printers.

✔ Tips

- The options in the Print dialog will vary depending on the printer you choose. It is impossible to show all possibilities in this book. Instead, I provide specific information for two printers: a Hewlett-Packard LaserJet 2100TN PostScript laser printer (connected via Ethernet network) and an Epson Stylus Color 740 inkjet printer (directly connected via USB). The options supported by your printer will be similar to one of these.

- To learn more about Print Center and the printing options supported by your printer, consult the documentation that came with Mac OS or your printer. Or track down a copy of the Peachpit Press book, *Mac OS X: Visual QuickStart Guide.*

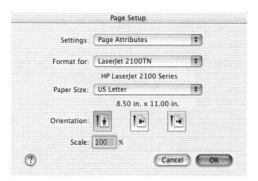

Figure 2 The Page Attributes settings of the Page Setup dialog.

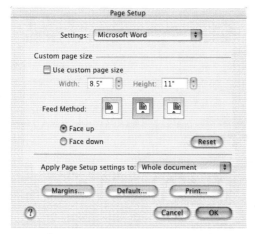

Figure 3 The Microsoft Word settings of the Page Setup dialog.

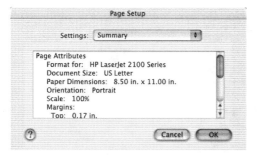

Figure 4 The Summary pane of the Page Setup dialog summarizes all of the Page Setup settings for the document.

Page Setup

The Page Setup dialog enables you to set a number of options for printing your document. It is broken down into two groups of settings:

◆ **Page Attributes** settings (**Figure 2**) include the printer, paper size, page orientation, and print scale.

◆ **Microsoft Word** settings (**Figure 3**) are those settings specific to Word, including custom page information, and paper feed method.

✔ Tips

■ Some Page Setup options—such as paper size and orientation—affect a page's margins. If you plan to use non-standard Page Setup options, consider setting them before you create and format your document.

■ I explain how to set up custom paper sizes later in this chapter.

■ You can review all Page Setup settings for a document in the Summary settings pane (**Figure 4**).

To open the Page Setup dialog

Choose File > Page Setup (**Figure 5**).

or

Click the Page Setup button at the bottom of the Document dialog (**Figure 12**).

To set Page Attributes options

1. Open the Page Setup dialog.

2. If necessary, choose Page Attributes from the Settings pop-up menu (**Figure 6**) to display Page Attributes options (**Figure 2**).

3. Choose a printer you want to print on from the Format for pop-up menu (**Figure 7**).

4. Choose the size of the paper you want to print on from the Paper Size pop-up menu (**Figures 8** and **9**).

5. Click to select an orientation icon. The first icon represents portrait orientation while the other two represent landscape orientation in two different directions.

6. To reduce or enlarge the print size, enter a value in the Scale text box.

7. Click OK to save your settings.

✔ Tip

■ As shown in **Figures 8** and **9**, the Paper Size pop-up menu may offer different options, depending on the printer you selected in step 3.

Figure 5
The File menu offers access to all three printing-related commands.

Figure 6 The Settings pop-up menu.

Figure 7 The Format for pop-up menu lists the printers in Print Center's Printer List.

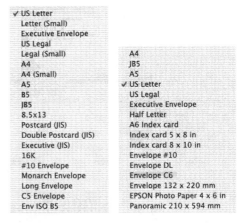

Figures 8 & 9 The Paper Size pop-up menu for a LaserJet 2100 TN printer (left) and Stylus Color 740 printer (right).

SETTING PAGE SETUP OPTIONS

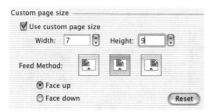

Figure 10 Use this part of the dialog to create and use a custom paper size.

Figure 11 Use this pop-up menu to specify which part of the document Page Setup options should apply to. The options that appear vary based on whether the document has multiple sections or text is selected.

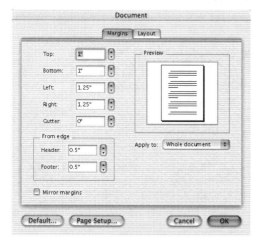

Figure 12 The Margins tab of the Document dialog.

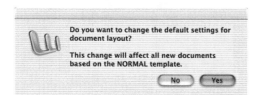

Figure 13 This dialog confirms that you want to save settings as Word document defaults.

To set Word-specific options

1. Open the Page Setup dialog.

2. Choose Microsoft Word from the Settings pop-up menu (**Figure 6**) to display Microsoft Word options (**Figure 3**).

3. To create a custom paper size, turn on the Use custom page size check box, enter dimensions for the paper, and select Feed Method options (**Figure 10**).

4. To apply Page Setup dialog settings to only a part of the document, choose an option from the Apply Page Setup settings pop-up menu (**Figure 11**).

5. Click OK to save your settings.

✔ Tips

- When the Use custom page size check box is turned on (**Figure 10**), the measurements in the dialog override the option chosen in the Page Attributes settings of the Page Setup dialog (**Figure 2**).

- Clicking the Reset button in the Custom page size area (**Figure 10**) resets Feed method options.

- Choosing an option other than Whole document from the Apply Page Setup Settings pop-up menu (**Figure 11**) may insert section breaks within your document. I tell you about section breaks in **Chapters 3** and **4**.

- Clicking the Margins button displays the Margins tab of the Document dialog (**Figure 12**) so you can change document margins settings. I explain how to use this dialog to change margins in **Chapter 3**.

- To save your settings as the defaults for Word documents, click the Default button. Then click OK in the confirmation dialog that appears (**Figure 13**).

- Clicking the Print button displays the Print dialog, which I discuss later in this chapter.

SETTING PAGE SETUP OPTIONS

Print Preview

Word's Print Preview (**Figure 14**) displays one or more pages of a document exactly as they will appear when printed. It also enables you to make last-minute changes to margins and document contents before printing.

✔ Tip

■ Print Preview can save a lot of time and paper—it's a lot quicker to look at a document on screen than wait for it to print, and it doesn't use a single sheet of paper!

To switch to Print Preview

Choose File > Print Preview (**Figure 5**).

or

Click the Print Preview button  on the Standard toolbar.

✔ Tip

■ The Print Preview toolbar (**Figure 15**) appears automatically at the top of the screen when you switch to Print Preview.

To zoom in or out

1. Select the Magnifier button 🔍 on the Print Preview toolbar (**Figure 15**).

2. Click on the page that you want to zoom in or out on. With each click, the view toggles between 100% and the current Zoom percentage on the Print Preview toolbar.

or

Choose an option from the Zoom pop-up menu on the Print Preview toolbar (**Figure 16**).

or

1. Click in the Zoom text box on the Print Preview toolbar.

2. Enter a value.

3. Press Return.

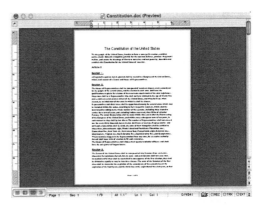

Figure 14 A single page of a document in Print Preview.

Figure 15 The Print Preview toolbar.

Figure 16
The Zoom pop-up menu on the Print Preview toolbar.

PREVIEWING PAGES

Figure 17
Use the Multiple Pages button's menu to choose a layout for displaying multiple document pages.

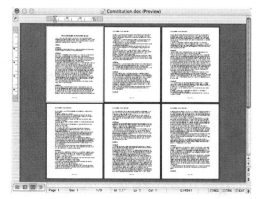

Figure 18 Six pages of a document displayed in Print Preview.

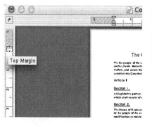

Figure 19
The mouse pointer changes when you position it on a margin on the ruler.

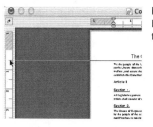

Figure 20
Drag to change the margin.

To view multiple pages

Click the Multiple Pages button 🔳 on the Print Preview toolbar to display a menu of page layouts and choose the one that you want (**Figure 17**).

The view and magnification change to display the pages as you specified (**Figure 18**).

✔ Tip

- To return to a single-page view, click the One Page button 🔳 on the Print Preview toolbar.

To change margins

1. If necessary, click the View Ruler button 🔳 on the Print Preview toolbar to display the ruler in the Print Preview window (**Figure 14**).

2. Position the mouse pointer on the ruler in the position corresponding to the margin you want to change. The mouse pointer turns into a box with arrows on either end and a yellow box appears, identifying the margin (**Figure 19**).

3. Press the mouse button down and drag to change the margin. As you drag, a dotted line indicates the position of the margin (**Figure 20**). When you release the mouse button, the margin changes.

✔ Tips

- A better way to change margins is with the Margins tab of the Document dialog (**Figure 12**), which I tell you about in **Chapter 3**.

- You can also use the ruler to change indentation for selected paragraphs. I explain how in **Chapter 3**.

To move from page to page

In Print Preview, click the Previous Page or Next Page button at the bottom of the vertical scroll bar (**Figure 21**).

To edit the document

1. If necessary, zoom in to get a better look at the text you want to edit.

2. Deselect the Magnifier button 🔍 on the Print Preview toolbar.

3. Click in the document window to position the insertion point.

4. Edit the document as desired.

To reduce the number of pages

Click the Shrink to Fit button 🗐 on the Print Preview toolbar.

Word squeezes the document onto one less page by making minor adjustments to font size and paragraph spacing. It then displays the revised document.

✔ Tips

- This feature is useful for squeezing a two-page letter onto one page when the second page only has a line or two.

- If you don't like the way Word has shrunk your document, you can choose Edit > Undo to restore it.

To switch to a full-screen view

Click the Full Screen button 🔲 on the Print Preview toolbar.

The screen redraws to remove the status bar (**Figure 22**). This enables you to get a slightly larger view of the document page(s).

✔ Tip

- To return to a regular Print Preview view, click the Close Full Screen button on the Full Screen toolbar.

Previous Page

Next Page

Figure 21 Use the Previous Page and Next Page buttons at the bottom of the vertical scroll bar to move from one page to another.

Full Screen toolbar

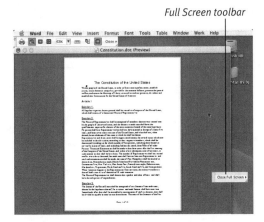

Figure 22 Full Screen view in Print Preview.

To leave Print Preview

Click the Close button on the Print Preview toolbar (**Figure 15**).

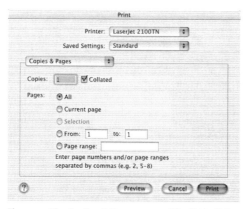

Figure 23 The Copies & Pages pane of the Print dialog.

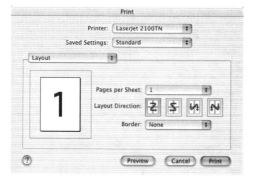

Figure 24 The Layout pane of the Print dialog.

Figure 25 The Output Options pane of the Print dialog.

Printing

The Print dialog enables you to set print options and send a document to the printer.

Print dialog options are broken down into a number of settings panes, which vary depending on the type of printer. For example, here are the panes available for my two printers:

◆ **Copies & Pages (Figure 23)** enables you to set the number of document copies and the range of document pages to print.

◆ **Layout (Figure 24)** enables you to specify the number of pages per sheet of paper, a layout direction, and border.

◆ **Output Options (Figure 25)** enables you to save a document as a PDF or PostScript file.

◆ **Paper Feed (Figure 26)** enables you to select paper feed methods or trays.

◆ **Error Handling (Figure 27)** enables you to specify how PostScript and other errors should be handled.

◆ **Printer Features (Figure 28)** enables you to set options for features specific to your printer.

Continued on next page...

Figure 26 The Paper Feed pane of the Print dialog. This pane is specific to a LaserJet 2100TN, which has several paper feed trays.

THE PRINT DIALOG

Continued from previous page.

- ◆ **Print Settings** (**Figure 29**) and **Advanced Settings** (**Figure 30**) enable you to set options for the type of paper, ink cartridge, print quality, and other print options.

- ◆ **Color Management** (**Figure 31**) enables you to set color options.

- ◆ **Microsoft Word** (**Figure 32**) enables you to specify what part of the Word document you want to print.

- ◆ **Summary** (**Figure 33**) summarizes all Print dialog settings.

After setting options, click the Print button to send the document to the selected printer.

✔ Tips

- ■ Remember, Print dialog panes and their options vary greatly depending on the selected printer.

- ■ This part of the chapter explains how to set options in the most commonly used Print dialog panes: Copies & Pages (**Figure 23**) and Microsoft Word (**Figure 32**). It also explains how to use the Output Options tab (**Figure 25**) to save a document as a PDF or PostScript file.

Figure 27 The Error Handling pane of the Print dialog. This pane appears for PostScript printers; the bottom half is specific to a LaserJet 2100TN.

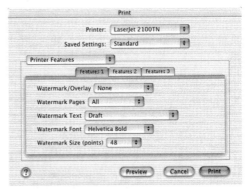

Figure 28 The Printer Features pane of the Print dialog. This tab only appears for some printers—in this example, the LaserJet 2100TN.

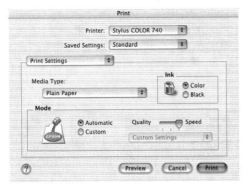

Figure 29 This Print Settings pane for a Stylus Color 740 offers some basic paper, ink, and mode options,...

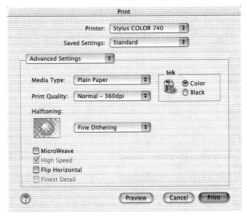

Figure 30 ...and this Advanced Settings pane for the same printer offers more advanced options.

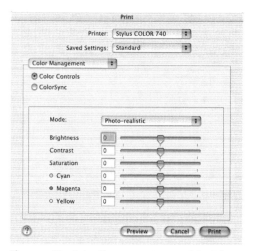

Figure 31 The Color Management pane of the Print dialog box offers color options for color printers.

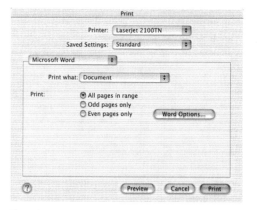

Figure 32 The Microsoft Word pane of the Print dialog.

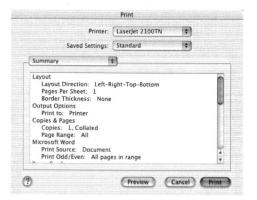

Figure 33 The Summary pane of the Print dialog summarizes all Print dialog settings.

To open the Print dialog

Choose File > Print (**Figure 5**) or press ⌃⌘P.

or

Click the Print button 🖨 on the Standard or Print Preview toolbar.

or

Click the Print button in the Page Setup dialog (**Figure 3**).

The Copies & Pages pane of the Print dialog appears (**Figure 23**).

To choose a destination printer

In the Print dialog (**Figure 23**), choose the printer you want to print on from the Printer pop-up menu (**Figure 34**).

✔ Tip

- Choosing Edit Printer List from the Printer pop-up menu (**Figure 34**) displays Print Center's Printer List (**Figure 1**) so you can add or remove printers.

✓ LaserJet 2100TN
Stylus COLOR 740

Edit Printer List...

Figure 34 The Printer pop-up menu lists all of the printers in Print Center's Printer List.

THE PRINT DIALOG

135

To specify the number of copies & pages to print

1. In the Print dialog, if necessary, choose Copies & Pages from the third pop-up menu (**Figure 35**) to display Copies & Pages options (**Figure 23**).

2. Enter the number of copies you want to print in the Copies text box.

3. If you want to print more than one copy and want the copies collated, turn on the Collated check box.

4. Select one of the Pages options:

   ▲ **All** sets the page range to all pages.

   ▲ **Current page** prints the page in which the insertion point is blinking.

   ▲ **Selection** prints selected text. This option is only available if text is selected in the document when you open the Print dialog.

   ▲ **From/to** enables you to enter the beginning and ending page numbers for a page range.

   ▲ **Page range** enables you to enter multiple individual pages and/or page ranges. Separate pages with commas and separate the beginning and ending page numbers in a range with a hyphen.

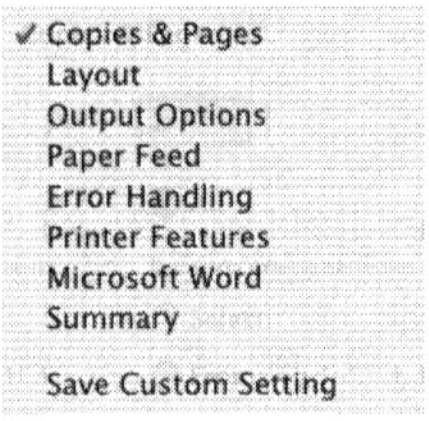

✓ Copies & Pages
Layout
Output Options
Paper Feed
Error Handling
Printer Features
Microsoft Word
Summary

Save Custom Setting

Figure 35
Use this pop-up menu to choose a category of Print dialog options.

✓ Document
Document properties
Comments
Styles
AutoText entries
Key assignments

Figure 36
The Print what pop-up menu enables you to print document information other than the document itself.

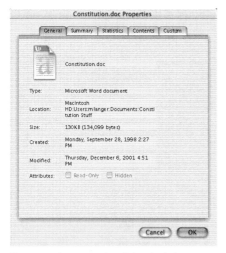

Figure 37 The Properties dialog includes additional information about a document.

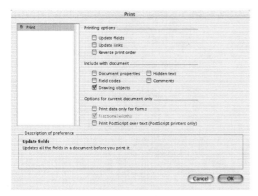

Figure 38 Use this dialog to set additional print options for the current document.

To set Word-specific options

1. In the Print dialog, choose Microsoft Word from the third pop-up menu (**Figure 35**) to display Microsoft Word options (**Figure 32**).

2. Choose an option from the Print what pop-up menu (**Figure 36**):

▲ **Document** prints the document.

▲ **Document properties** prints information in the Properties dialog (**Figure 37**) for the document.

▲ **Comments** prints comments stored in the document.

▲ **Styles** prints information about styles used in the document.

▲ **AutoText** entries prints a list of Auto-Text entries stored in the template on which the document is based.

▲ **Key assignments** prints shortcut keys stored in the document.

3. Select one of the Print options to print All pages, odd pages, or even pages in the range.

✔ Tips

■ I discuss Properties and Comments in **Chapter 12**, Styles in **Chapter 4**, AutoText in **Chapter 7**, and shortcut keys in **Chapter 1** and **Appendix A**.

■ Clicking the Word Options button displays Print options that appear in the Preferences dialog box (**Figure 38**). Use this dialog to set additional Word-specific print options for the document. I tell you more about Preferences in **Chapter 15**.

SETTING WORD-SPECIFIC OPTIONS

To set other Print dialog options

1. In the Print dialog, choose the category of option you want to set from the third pop-up menu (**Figure 35**). The pane for the option you selected appears (**Figures 23** through **33**).

2. Set options as desired.

3. Repeat steps 1 and 2 for each category of options you want to set.

✔ Tips

- These other options are specific to your printer, not to Microsoft Word.

- I tell you about Output Options on the next page.

To save Print options

In the Print dialog box, choose Save Custom Setting from the third pop-up menu (**Figure 35**).

After a moment, the settings are saved as Custom.

To use Custom Print options

In the Print dialog box, choose Custom from the Saved Settings pop-up menu (**Figure 39**).

All Print dialog settings are restored to the last settings you saved.

To print

Click the Print button in the Print dialog (**Figures 23** through **33**).

The document is sent to the printer.

✔ Tip

- To monitor a document's print status, open Print Center and double-click the name of the printer in the Printer List window (**Figure 1**).

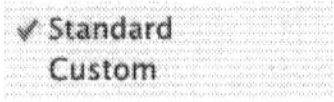

Figure 39 The Saved Settings pop-up menu after saving Print dialog settings.

Figure 40 When you turn on the Save as File check box, you can choose a file format and click a Save button to save the file.

Figure 41 The Format pop-up menu.

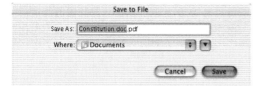

Figure 42 Use a standard Save As dialog to enter a name and specify a disk location for the file.

Saving a Document as a PDF or PostScript File

In Word X, you can use the Print dialog to save a document as a PDF or PostScript file. PDF (which stands for *Portable Document Format*) files can be opened and read with Preview on Mac OS X or Adobe Acrobat Reader on virtually any computer or operating system. PostScript files are often used to output documents to high-resolution printing devices such as imagesetters.

To save a document as a PDF or PostScript file

1. In the Print dialog, choose Output Options from the third pop-up menu (**Figure 35**) to display the Output Options pane (**Figure 25**).

2. Turn on the Save as File check box (**Figure 40**).

3. Choose an option from the Format pop-up menu (**Figure 41**).

4. Click Save.

5. Use the Save to File dialog that appears (**Figure 42**) to enter a name and specify a disk location for the file.

6. Click Save to save the file to disk.

✔ Tip

■ The PostScript option is only available on the Format pop-up menu (**Figure 41**) if a PostScript printer is chosen from the Printer pop-up menu (**Figure 34**).

INSERTING TEXT & MULTIMEDIA

Figure 1
The Insert menu.

✔ Tip

■ I discuss other Insert menu commands throughout this book:

  ▲ Break, in **Chapter 4**.

  ▲ Comment, in **Chapter 12**.

  ▲ Index and Tables, in **Chapter 8**.

  ▲ Hyperlink, in **Chapter 14**.

  ▲ Object, in **Chapter 13**.

Special Elements

Word's Insert menu (**Figure 1**) includes a number of commands that you can use to insert special text and multimedia elements into your documents:

◆ **AutoText** enables you to create and insert AutoText entries, which are commonly used text snippets, such as your name or the closing of a letter.

◆ **Field** enables you to insert Word fields, which are pieces of information that change as necessary, such as the date, file size, or page number.

◆ **Symbol** enables you to insert symbols and special characters such as bullets, smiley faces, and the registered trademark symbol (®).

◆ **Footnote** enables you to insert footnotes or endnotes, which are annotations that appear (and print) beneath text, at the bottom of the page, at the end of the section, or at the end of the document.

◆ **File** enables you to insert another file.

◆ **Picture** enables you to insert a variety of graphics, including clip art, AutoShapes, and WordArt.

◆ **Movie** enables you to insert a QuickTime movie, which can include video and/or sound.

AutoText & AutoComplete

Word's AutoText feature makes it quick and easy to insert text snippets that you use often in your documents. First, create the AutoText entry that you want to use. Then use one of two methods to insert it:

◆ Begin to type the entry or entry name. When an AutoComplete tip box appears (**Figure 7**), press Return to enter the rest of the entry. This feature is known as AutoComplete.

◆ Use options on the AutoText submenu under the Insert menu (**Figure 3**) to insert the entry.

✔ Tip

■ Word comes preconfigured with dozens of AutoText entries.

To create an AutoText entry

1. Select the text that you want to use as an AutoText entry (**Figure 2**).

2. Choose Insert > AutoText > New (**Figure 3**).

3. The Create AutoText dialog appears (**Figure 4**). It displays a default name for the entry. If desired, change the name.

4. Click OK.

or

1. Choose Insert > AutoText > AutoText (**Figure 3**) to display the AutoText tab of the AutoCorrect dialog (**Figure 5**).

2. Enter the text that you want to use as an AutoText entry in the Enter AutoText entries here text box.

3. Click Add. The entry appears in the scrolling list.

4. Repeat steps 2 and 3, if desired, to add additional entries.

5. When you are finished, click OK.

We the people of the United States, in order to insure domestic tranquility, provide for the com

Figure 2 Select the text that you want to use as an AutoText entry.

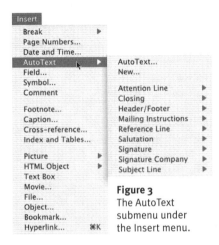

Figure 3
The AutoText submenu under the Insert menu.

Figure 4
The Create AutoText dialog.

Create AutoText

Word will create an AutoText entry from the current selection.

Please name your AutoText entry:

United States

Cancel   OK

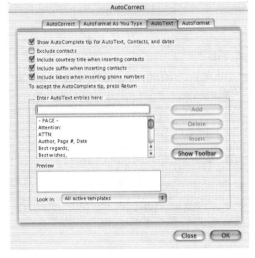

Figure 5 The AutoText tab of the AutoCorrect dialog.

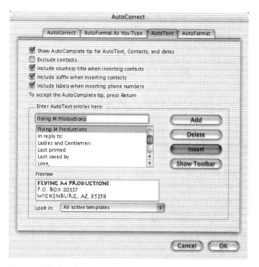

Figure 6 Selecting an AutoText entry.

To delete an AutoText entry

1. Choose Insert > AutoText > AutoText (**Figure 3**) to display the AutoText tab of the AutoCorrect dialog (**Figure 5**).

2. In the scrolling list of AutoText entries, click to select the entry that you want to delete (**Figure 6**). You can confirm that you have selected the correct entry by checking its contents in the Preview area.

3. Click Delete. The entry is removed from the scrolling list.

4. Repeat steps 2 and 3, if desired, to delete other entries.

5. When you are finished, click OK.

To configure AutoComplete

1. Choose Insert > AutoText > AutoText (**Figure 3**) to display the AutoText tab of the AutoCorrect dialog (**Figure 5**).

2. Toggle check boxes as desired at the top of the dialog:

   ▲ **Show AutoComplete tip for Auto-Text, Contacts, and dates** enables the AutoComplete feature.

   ▲ **Exclude contacts** does not display AutoComplete tips for Entourage contacts.

   ▲ **Include courtesy title when inserting contacts** includes the appropriate title (Mr., Ms., Dr., etc.) when inserting Entourage contacts.

   ▲ **Include suffix when inserting contacts** includes any name suffixes (Jr., Sr., III, etc.) when inserting Entourage contacts.

   ▲ **Include labels when inserting phone numbers** includes the identifying label (Home, Office, Cell, etc.) when inserting Entourage contact phone numbers.

3. Click OK.

✔ Tips

■ The AutoComplete feature is turned on by default.

■ Entourage is the personal information management software that's part of Microsoft Office. The AutoComplete feature can automatically use Entourage contact entries as you type.

To insert an AutoText entry with AutoComplete

1. Type text into your document.

2. When you type the first few characters of an AutoText entry, a yellow AutoComplete tip box appears (**Figure 7**).

3. To enter the text displayed in the Auto-Complete tip, press Return. The text you were typing is completed with the text from the AutoText entry (**Figure 8**).

   or

   To ignore the AutoComplete tip, keep typing.

To insert an AutoText entry with the AutoText submenu

1. Position the insertion point where you want the AutoText entry to appear.

2. Use your mouse to display the AutoText submenu under the Insert menu (**Figure 3**).

3. Select the submenu option that contains the entry that you want (**Figure 9**) and select the entry. It is inserted into the document.

Figure 7 When you begin to type text for which there is an AutoText entry, an AutoComplete tip box appears.

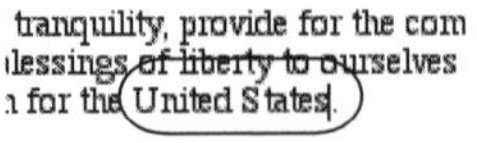

Figure 8 Press Return to complete the text you are typing with the AutoText entry.

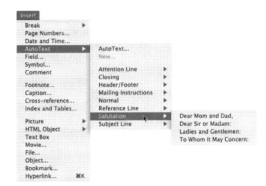

Figure 9 Each submenu on the AutoText submenu contains one or more AutoText entries.

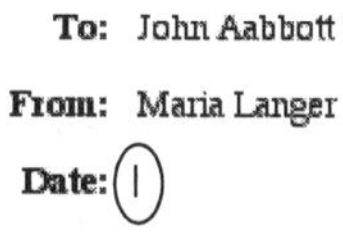

To: John Aabbott
From: Maria Langer
Date: (|)

Figure 10
Position the insertion point where you want the field to appear.

Figure 11
The Field dialog.

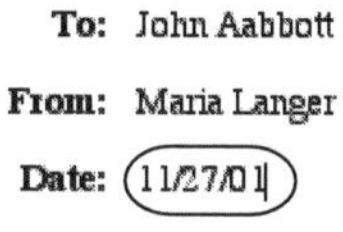

To: John Aabbott
From: Maria Langer
Date: (11/27/01|)

Figure 12
In this example, the Date field was inserted.

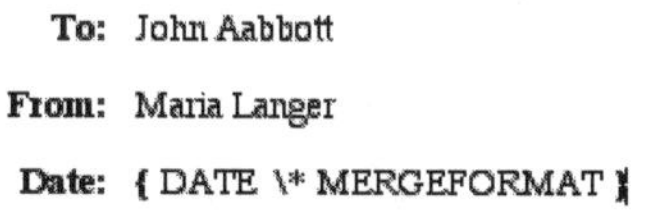

To: John Aabbott
From: Maria Langer
Date: { DATE * MERGEFORMAT }

Figure 13 Here's the same field with the field codes displayed rather than the field contents.

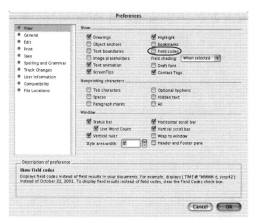

Figure 14 Make sure Field codes is turned off in the View pane of the Preferences dialog.

Word Fields

Word *fields* are special codes that, when inserted in a document, display specific information. But unlike typed text, Word fields can change when necessary so the information they display is always up-to-date.

For example, the PrintDate field displays the date the document was last printed. If you print it again on a later date, the contents of the PrintDate field will change to reflect the new date.

✔ Tip

- Word fields is a powerful feature of Word. A thorough discussion would go far beyond the scope of this book. Instead, the following pages will provide the basic information you need to get started using Word fields.

To insert a field

1. Position the insertion point where you want the field information to appear (**Figure 10**).

2. Choose Insert > Field (**Figure 1**) to display the Field dialog (**Figure 11**).

3. In the Categories scrolling list, click to select the category for the field you want to insert.

4. In the Field names scrolling list, click to select the name of the field you want to insert.

5. Click OK. The field is inserted in the document (**Figure 12**).

✔ Tip

- If field codes display instead of field contents (**Figure 13**), choose Word > Preferences, click View in the list on the left side of the Preferences dialog that appears, and turn off the Field codes check box (**Figure 14**).

WORD FIELDS

To select a field

1. In the document window, click the field once. It turns light gray and the insertion point appears within it (**Figure 15**).

2. Drag over the field. The field turns dark gray and is selected (**Figure 16**).

✔ Tip

■ Once you have selected a field, you can format it using formatting techniques discussed in **Chapter 3** or delete it by pressing (Delete).

To update a field

1. Use your mouse to point to the field.

2. Hold down (Control) while pressing the mouse button down to display the field's shortcut menu (**Figure 17**).

3. Choose Update Field. If necessary, the contents of the field changes.

✔ Tip

■ To ensure that all fields are automatically updated before the document is printed, choose Word > Preferences, click Print in the list on the left side of the Preferences dialog that appears, and turn on the Update fields check box (**Figure 18**).

Figures 15 & 16
When you click a field, it turns light gray and the insertion point appears within it (top). When you drag over the field, it turns dark gray and is selected (bottom).

Figure 17
A field's shortcut menu includes the Update Field command.

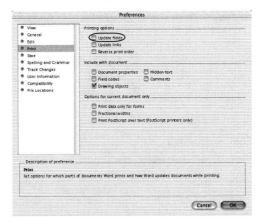

Figure 18 To ensure that all fields are updated before a document is printed, turn on the Update fields check box in the Print pane of the Preferences dialog.

WORD FIELDS

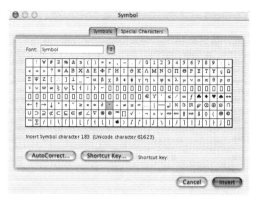

Figure 19 The Symbols tab of the Symbol window.

Figure 20 The Special Characters tab of the Symbol window.

Symbols & Special Characters

Symbols are special characters that don't appear on the keyboard. They include special characters within a font, such as ®, ©, ™, or é, and characters that appear only in special "dingbats" fonts, such as ■, ▲, →, and ♣.

Word offers the Symbol window (**Figures 19** and **20**), which makes it easy to insert all kinds of symbols and special characters in your documents.

✔ Tips

- You don't need to use the Symbol window to insert symbols or special characters in your documents. You just need to know the keystrokes and, if necessary, the font to apply. The Symbol window takes all the guesswork out of inserting these characters.

- Most special characters can be typed into a document by pressing Option or Shift Option in conjunction with another key.

- Symbols can be inserted with three types of fonts, as discussed on the next page:

  - ▲ Normal text, which is the current font.

  - ▲ Symbol, which is a font full of Greek characters and mathematical symbols.

  - ▲ Dingbats fonts, such as Hoefler Text Ornaments, Monotype Sorts, Webdings, Wingdings, or Zapf Dingbats.

- A *dingbats font* is a typeface that displays graphic characters rather than text characters. Monotype Sorts, Webdings, Wingdings, and Zapf Dingbats are four examples.

- In the Special Characters tab of the Symbol window (**Figure 20**), special characters appear in the current font.

To insert a symbol or special character

1. Position the insertion point where you want the character to appear (**Figure 21**).

2. Choose Insert > Symbol (**Figure 1**).

3. If necessary, click the Symbols tab in the Symbol window that appears to display its options (**Figure 19**).

4. Choose the font that you want to use to display the character from the Font pop-up menu (**Figure 22**). The characters displayed in the Symbol window change accordingly.

5. Click the character that you want to insert to select it (**Figure 23**).

6. Click Insert. The character that you clicked appears at the insertion point (**Figure 24**).

7. Repeat steps 4 through 6, if desired, to insert additional characters.

8. When you are finished inserting characters, click the close button to dismiss the Symbol window.

✔ Tips

- When inserting a symbol or special character in the normal font, you may prefer to use the Special Characters tab of the Symbol window (**Figure 20**). The list of special characters includes the shortcut key you can use to type the character without using the Symbol window.

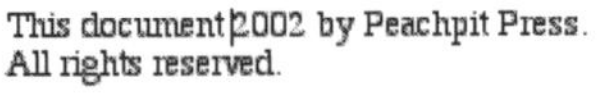

This document 2002 by Peachpit Press.
All rights reserved.

Figure 21 Position the insertion point where you want the symbol or special character to appear.

Figure 22 The Font pop-up menu in the Symbol window.

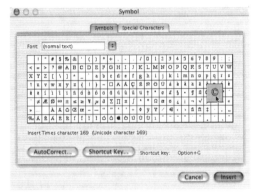

Figure 23 An example of the Symbols tab of the Symbol window being used to insert a special character in the normal font.

This document ©2002 by Peachpit Press.
All rights reserved.

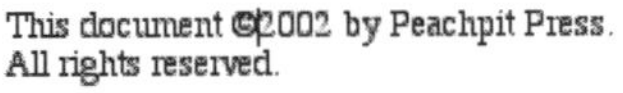

Figure 24 The character you selected appears at the insertion point.

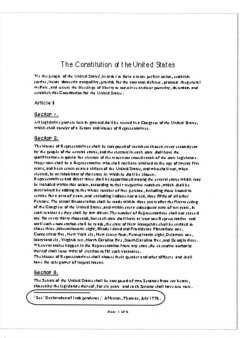

The Constitution of the United States

Figure 25 A page with a footnote. Word automatically inserts the footnote separator line, too.

Footnotes & Endnotes

Footnotes and endnotes are annotations for specific document text. You insert a marker—usually a number or symbol—right after the text, tell Word where you want the note to go, and enter the note. When you view the document in Page Layout view or print the document, the note appears where you specified.

The difference between a footnote and an endnote is its position in the document:

◆ **Footnotes** appear either after the last line of text on the page on which the annotated text appears or at the bottom of the page on which the annotated text appears (**Figure 25**).

◆ **Endnotes** appear either at the end of the section in which the annotated text appears or at the end of the document.

✔ Tips

■ Footnotes and endnotes are commonly used to show the source of a piece of information or provide additional information that may not be of interest to every reader.

■ I tell you about multiple-section documents in **Chapter 4**.

■ Word automatically renumbers footnotes or endnotes when necessary when you insert or delete a note.

■ If you're old enough to remember preparing high school or college term papers on a typewriter, you'll recognize this feature as another example of how easy kids have it today. (Sheesh! I sound like my grandmother!)

FOOTNOTES & ENDNOTES

To insert a footnote or endnote

1. Position the insertion point immediately after the text that you want to annotate (**Figure 26**).

2. Choose Insert > Footnote (**Figure 1**) to display the Footnote and Endnote dialog (**Figure 27**).

3. In the Insert part of the dialog, select the radio button for the type of note you want to insert.

4. In the Numbering part of the dialog, select the type of mark you want to insert.

5. If you select the Custom mark radio button in step 4, enter the character for the mark in the text box beside it.

6. Click OK. Word inserts a marker at the insertion point, then one of two things happens:

   ▲ If you are in Normal or Online Layout view, the window splits to display a footnote or endnote pane with the insertion point blinking beside the marker (**Figure 28**).

   ▲ If you are in Page Layout view, the view shifts to the location of the footnote or endnote where a separator line is inserted. The insertion point blinks beside the marker (**Figure 29**).

7. Enter the footnote or endnote text (**Figure 30**).

✔ Tips

■ In step 5, You can click the Symbol button to display the Symbol window (**Figure 19**), click a symbol to select it, and click OK to insert it in the text box.

■ In Normal view, to close the footnote pane, click the Close button at the top of the pane.

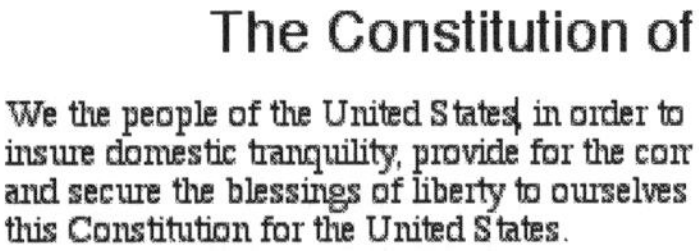

The Constitution of

We the people of the United States, in order to insure domestic tranquility, provide for the comm and secure the blessings of liberty to ourselves this Constitution for the United States.

Figure 26 Position the insertion point immediately after the text that you want to annotate.

Figure 27
The Footnote and Endnote dialog.

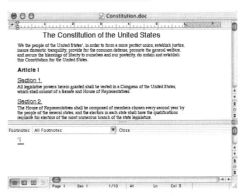

Figure 28 Entering a footnote in Normal view.

Figure 29 Entering a footnote in Page Layout view.

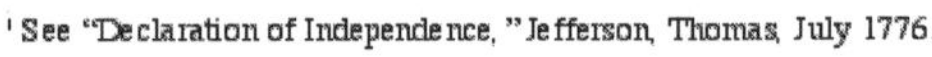

¹ See "Declaration of Independence," Jefferson, Thomas, July 1776|

Figure 30 Enter footnote text right after the marker.

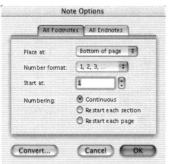

Figure 31
The All Footnotes tab of the Note Options dialog.

Figure 32
The All Endnotes tab of the Note Options dialog.

Figures 33 & 34 The Place at pop-up menu for footnotes (left) and endnotes (right).

Figure 35
The Number format pop-up menu.

Figure 36 When you make changes in the Note Options dialog, the Cancel button in the Footnote and Endnote dialog turns into a Close button so you can close it without inserting a note.

To set options for footnotes or endnotes

1. Choose Insert > Footnote (**Figure 1**).

2. Click the Options button in the Footnote and Endnote dialog (**Figure 27**).

3. In the Note Options dialog that appears, click the All Footnotes tab to display footnote options (**Figure 31**) or the All Endnotes tab to display endnote options (**Figure 32**).

4. Set options as desired:
   - ▲ Use the Place at pop-up menu (**Figures 33** and **34**) to set the note position.
   - ▲ Use the Number format pop-up menu (**Figure 35**) to specify the note numbering scheme.
   - ▲ Enter a value in the Start at text box to specify the start number.
   - ▲ Select one of the Numbering radio buttons to specify whether numbering should be continuous throughout the document, restarted in each section, or, in the case of footnotes, restarted on each page.

5. Click OK to save your settings and dismiss the Note Options dialog.

6. To insert a new footnote or endnote at the insertion point, follow steps 3 through 7 on the previous page.

   or

   To save your settings without inserting a new footnote or endnote, click the Close button in the Footnote and Endnote dialog (**Figure 36**).

✔ Tip

- ■ The last three options in the Note Options dialog apply only if you selected Auto-Number in the Footnote and Endnote dialog (**Figure 27**).

To convert notes

1. Choose Insert > Footnote (**Figure 1**) to display the Footnote and Endnote dialog (**Figure 27**).

2. Click Options to display the Note Options dialog (**Figures 31** and **32**).

3. Click the Convert button to display the Convert Notes dialog (**Figure 37**).

4. Select the radio button for the type of conversion that you want to do.

5. Click OK to dismiss the Convert Notes dialog.

6. Click OK to dismiss the Note Options dialog.

7. Click Close to dismiss the Footnote and Endnote dialog.

✔ Tip

■ The options available in the Convert Notes dialog (**Figure 37**) vary depending on the type(s) of notes in the document.

To delete a note

1. In the document window (not the note area or pane), select the note marker (**Figure 38**).

2. Press (Delete). The note marker and corresponding note are removed from the document. If the note was numbered using the AutoNumber option, all notes after it are properly renumbered.

✔ Tip

■ If you have trouble selecting the tiny note marker in the document, use the Zoom pop-up menu on the Standard toolbar (**Figure 39**) to increase the window's magnification so you can see it better. I tell you more about zooming a window's view in **Chapter 1**.

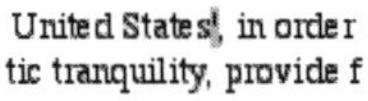

Figure 37 The Convert Notes dialog for a document that contains both footnotes and endnotes.

United States, in order tic tranquility, provide f

Figure 38 To delete a footnote or endnote, begin by selecting the note marker.

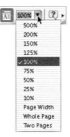

Figure 39 You can use the Zoom pop-up menu on the Standard toolbar to increase the window's magnification so you can see tiny note markers.

Figure 40 Position the insertion point where you want to insert the file.

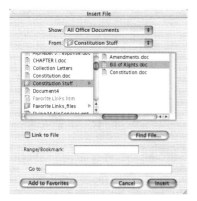

Figure 41 The Insert File dialog.

Figure 42 An inserted file.

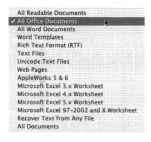

Figure 43
The Show
pop-up menu.

Files

You can use the File command under the Insert menu to insert one file (the source file) within another file (the destination file). The source file then becomes part of the destination file.

✔ Tips

- The source file can be in any format that Word recognizes.

- Copy and paste and drag and drop are two other methods for inserting the contents of one file into another. I explain these techniques in **Chapter 2**.

- A file can be inserted with or without a link. If the source file is linked, when you update the link, the destination file is updated with fresh information from the source. This means that changes in the source file are reflected in the destination file.

To insert a file

1. Position the insertion point where you want the source file to be inserted (**Figure 40**).

2. Choose Insert > File (**Figure 1**).

3. Use the Insert File dialog that appears (**Figure 41**) to locate and select the file that you want to insert.

4. Click the Insert button.

   The file is inserted (**Figure 42**).

✔ Tip

- You can use the Show pop-up menu (**Figure 43**) to view only specific types of files in the Insert File dialog (**Figure 41**).

To insert a file as a link

Follow all of the steps on the previous page to insert a file. In step 3, be sure to turn on the Link to File check box (**Figure 41**).

✔ Tips

- When you click the contents of a linked file, it turns gray (**Figure 44**).

- Any changes you make in the destination file to the contents of a linked file are lost when the link is updated.

- A linked file is inserted as a field. I tell you about fields earlier in this chapter.

To update a link

1. Position the mouse pointer over the linked file.

2. Hold down Control and click to display the link's shortcut menu (**Figure 45**).

3. Choose Update Field.

The link's contents are updated to reflect the current contents of the source file.

✔ Tip

- If Word cannot find the source file when you attempt to update a link, it replaces the contents of the source file with an error message (**Figure 46**). There are three ways to fix this problem:
  - ▲ Undo the update.
  - ▲ Remove the link and reinsert it.
  - ▲ Choose Edit > Links to fix the link with the Links dialog.

To remove an inserted file

1. Select the contents of the inserted file.

2. Press Delete.

Figure 44 When you click the contents of a linked file, it turns gray.

Figure 45 The shortcut menu for a linked file.

Figure 46 Word displays an error message when you attempt to update a link and it can't find the source file.

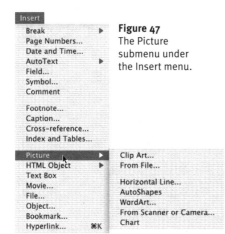

Figure 47
The Picture submenu under the Insert menu.

Pictures

Pictures are graphic objects. Word's Picture submenu (**Figure 47**) enables you to insert a variety of picture types:

◆ **Clip Art** inserts clip art, pictures, sounds, and videos from the Clip Gallery.

◆ **From File** inserts an existing picture file.

◆ **Horizontal Line** inserts a picture file as a horizontal divider.

◆ **AutoShapes** displays the AutoShapes and Drawing toolbars, which you can use to draw shapes and lines.

◆ **WordArt** inserts stylized text.

◆ **From Scanner or Camera** enables you to import images directly from a scanner or digital camera into a Word document.

◆ **Chart** inserts a Microsoft Graph chart.

This section covers all of these options.

✔ Tip

■ When a graphic object is inserted into a Word document, it appears on either the drawing layer or the document layer.

▲ AutoShapes, WordArt, charts, and movies appear on the *drawing layer*. This layer is separate from the text in your Word documents.

▲ ClipArt and pictures, including scans and photos, are inserted in the *document layer* as *inline images*—images that appear on text baselines like any other text.

PICTURES

To insert clip art

1. Position the insertion point where you want the clip art to appear.

2. Choose Insert > Picture > Clip Art (**Figure 47**) to display the Clip Gallery window (**Figure 48**).

3. Click a category name in the list on the left side of the window to display the clips within that category.

4. Click to select the clip that you want to insert.

5. Click the Insert button.

   The clip is inserted as an inline image at the insertion point (**Figure 49**).

✔ Tips

■ You can add your own clips to the Clip Gallery. Click the Import button and use the Import dialog that appears to locate, select, and import a picture file on disk.

■ More clip art is available online. If you have an Internet connection, you can click the Online button to launch your Web browser and visit the Microsoft Web site where you can download additional clips.

Figure 48 The Clip Gallery window.

Figure 49 Clip art inserted into a document.

INSERTING CLIP ART

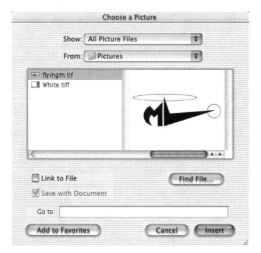

Figure 50 Use the Choose a Picture dialog to insert a picture from a file on disk.

Figure 51 When you insert a picture from a file on disk, it appears at the insertion point.

To insert a picture from a file

1. Position the insertion point where you want the picture to appear.

2. Choose Insert > Picture > From File (**Figure 47**) to display the Choose a Picture dialog (**Figure 50**).

3. Locate and select the file that you want to insert.

4. Click the Insert button.

   The file is inserted as an inline image at the insertion point (**Figure 51**).

✔ Tips

- By default, the Choose a Picture dialog displays the contents of the Clipart folder inside the Microsoft Office X folder. This enables you to insert clip art that comes with Word without using the Clip Gallery.

- To create a link between the file on disk and the Word document, turn on the Link to File check box in step 3. I tell you more about links earlier in this chapter.

INSERTING PICTURES FROM FILES

To insert a horizontal line

1. Position the insertion point where you want the horizontal line to appear.

2. Choose Insert > Picture > Horizontal Line (**Figure 47**) to display the Choose a Picture dialog (**Figure 52**).

3. Locate and select the line that you want to insert.

4. Click the Insert button.

   The line is inserted as an inline image at the insertion point (**Figure 53**).

✔ Tips

■ As shown in **Figure 52**, the dialog automatically displays the contents of the Lines folder within the Clipart folder in the Microsoft Office X folder.

■ To create a link between the file on disk and the Word document, turn on the Link to File check box in step 3. I tell you more about links earlier in this chapter.

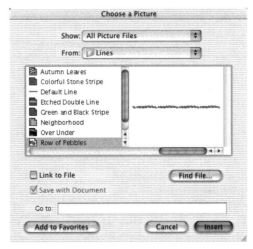

Figure 52 The Choose a Picture dialog automatically looks in the Lines folder for horizontal lines.

Figure 53 The line appears at the insertion point.

Drawing   AutoShapes
toolbar   toolbar

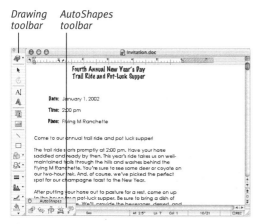

Figure 54 The AutoShapes and Drawing toolbars appear when you choose the AutoShapes command.

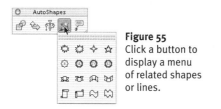

Figure 55
Click a button to display a menu of related shapes or lines.

Figure 56 Position the crosshairs pointer where you want to begin the shape.

Figure 57 Press the mouse button down and drag; the shape begins to emerge.

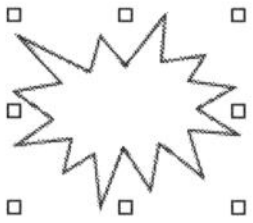

Figure 58 When you release the mouse button, the shape appears as a selected picture in the document.

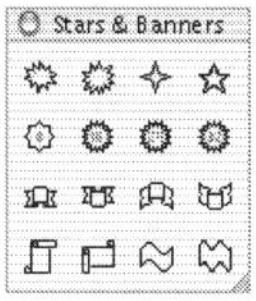

Figure 59
AutoShapes toolbar pop-up menus can be torn off to form their own toolbars.

To display the AutoShapes & Drawing toolbars

Choose Insert > Picture > AutoShapes (**Figure 47**). The AutoShapes and Drawing toolbars appear (**Figure 54**).

✔ Tips

- To display either of these toolbars individually, choose its name from the Toolbars submenu under the View menu. I tell you more about displaying and hiding toolbars in **Chapter 1**.

- The Drawing toolbar has many options you can use to draw lines and shapes or format selected objects—far too many options to cover in this book. Experiment with the toolbar on your own to see how you can use it to enhance drawn objects in your Word documents.

To draw a shape or line

1. Display the AutoShapes toolbar.

2. Click a button to display a pop-up menu of shapes (**Figure 55**) or lines and choose the shape or line that you want to draw.

3. Move the mouse pointer, which becomes a crosshairs pointer (**Figure 56**), into the document window where you want to begin to draw the shape or line.

4. Press the mouse button down and drag. As you drag, the shape (**Figure 57**) or line appears.

5. Release the mouse button to complete the shape (**Figure 58**) or line as an object on the drawing layer.

✔ Tip

- The shape or line pop-up menu that appears when you click an AutoShapes toolbar button (**Figure 55**) can be dragged off the toolbar to create its own toolbar (**Figure 59**).

DRAWING SHAPES & LINES

To insert WordArt

1. Display the Word document in which you want the WordArt image to appear.

2. Choose Insert > Picture > WordArt (**Figure 47**).

3. In the WordArt Gallery dialog that appears (**Figure 60**), click to select a WordArt style.

4. Click OK.

5. In the Edit WordArt Text dialog that appears next (**Figure 61**), change the sample text to the text that you want to display. You can also select a different font and font size and turn on bold and/or italic formatting.

6. Click OK. The WordArt image is inserted in your document's drawing layer and the WordArt toolbar appears (**Figure 62**).

✔ Tips

■ Once you have created a WordArt image, you can use buttons on the WordArt toolbar to modify it. The toolbar only appears when the WordArt image is selected.

■ In many instances, the WordArt image will appear right over document text. To move a WordArt image, simply drag it with your mouse pointer.

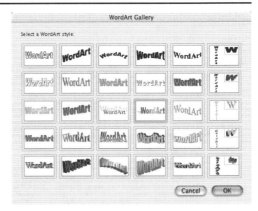

Figure 60 The WordArt Gallery dialog.

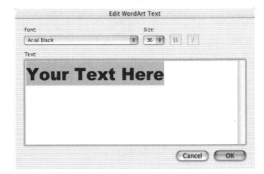

Figure 61 The default text in the Edit WordArt Text dialog.

Figure 62 A WordArt image and the WordArt toolbar.

Figure 63 Use this dialog to select the scanner or camera you want to access.

Figure 64 Word launches your scanner or camera software. In this example, it has launched the software for my new HP ScanJet 4470c. (My old ScanJet IIcx finally died after eight years of service.)

Figure 65 The picture appears at the insertion point in your Word document.

To insert a picture from a scanner or a digital camera

1. Make sure the scanner software is properly installed and that the scanner is connected to your computer and turned on. Then place the image you wish to scan on the scanning surface.

   or

   Make sure the digital camera software is properly installed and that the camera is connected to your computer and turned on.

2. In the Word document, position the insertion point where you want the picture to appear.

3. Choose Insert > Picture > From Scanner or Camera (**Figure 47**).

4. The Insert Picture from Scanner or Camera dialog appears (**Figure 63**). If necessary, use the menu to choose the device you wish to access, then click Acquire.

5. Word launches the software for your device to access the picture(s) (**Figure 64**). Use that software to either scan or select the image you want to use.

   When you are finished, the image appears in the Word document as an inline image (**Figure 65**).

✏ Important Note

- The instructions on this page are based on the steps to complete the task in Word 2001. Although I could not obtain a compatible scanner or digital camera to test and illustrate these steps, I am confident that the steps are virtually identical for Word X.

✔ Tip

- If the Insert Picture from Scanner or Camera dialog (**Figure 63**) does not appear after step 3, your scanner or camera is either not installed or connected correctly or is incompatible with Mac OS X.

To insert a chart

1. Activate the Word document in which you want the chart to appear.

2. Choose Insert > Picture > Chart (**Figure 47**). Word launches Microsoft Graph and displays its windows atop the Word document window (**Figure 66**).

3. Edit the contents of the Datasheet window to reflect the data that you want to chart; the Chart window is updated automatically.

4. Use commands on Microsoft Graph's menus to format the chart as desired.

5. When you are finished, choose Graph > Quit and Return. The chart is inserted in the document as an object on the drawing layer (**Figure 67**).

✔ Tips

- To move a chart, simply drag it with your mouse pointer.

- You can edit a chart by double-clicking it to re-launch the Microsoft Graph application.

- Microsoft Graph is a highly simplified version of the charting feature within Microsoft Excel. I explain how you can use Excel objects within Microsoft Word documents in **Chapter 13**.

Word document window *Datasheet window* *Chart window*

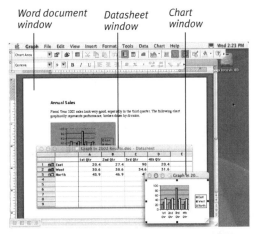

Figure 66 The Microsoft Graph windows appear atop the Word document window.

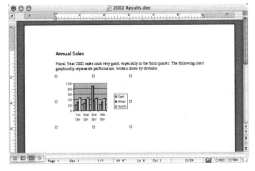

Figure 67 The completed chart appears in the document window on the drawing layer.

INSERTING CHARTS

Figure 68 Use this dialog to insert a QuickTime movie into a Word document.

Figure 69 An inserted QuickTime movie and the Movie toolbar.

Figure 70 An inserted movie with its controller displayed. (In case you're wondering, that's me with Three-Niner-Lima at Henderson Airport in Nevada; Las Vegas is in the background.)

Movies

The Insert menu's Movie command (**Figure 1**) enables you to insert a QuickTime movie into a Word document.

✔ Tip

- QuickTime must be properly installed on your computer to use this feature. You can obtain QuickTime for free from Apple's Web site, http://www.apple.com/quicktime/.

To insert a movie

1. Position the insertion point where you want the movie to appear.

2. Choose Insert > Movie (**Figure 1**) to display the Insert Movie dialog.

3. Locate and select the movie file that you want to insert (**Figure 68**).

4. Click the Choose button. The movie is inserted in the document's drawing layer and the Movie toolbar appears (**Figure 69**).

✔ Tips

- You can use the Movie toolbar (**Figure 69**) to play and set options for a selected movie.

- Click the icon within the movie frame (**Figure 69**) to display the movie's controller (**Figure 70**).

Working with Graphic Objects

Word includes many powerful image-editing tools that you can use to work with the graphic objects in your Word documents. Although a complete discussion of all of these tools is far beyond the scope of this book, here are some instructions for performing some common image manipulation tasks.

To move a graphic object

Drag it with the mouse pointer.

◆ A graphic object in the drawing layer can be moved anywhere in the document window.

◆ A graphic object in the document layer can be moved like a text character.

To resize a graphic object

1. Click the object to select it. White or black "handles" appear around it (**Figures 58**, **62**, **67**, **69**, and **71**).

2. Position the mouse pointer on a handle, press the mouse button down, and drag as follows:

   ▲ Drag away from the object to make it larger.

   ▲ Drag toward the center of the object to make it smaller (**Figure 72**).

   When you release the mouse button, the object resizes (**Figure 73**).

✔ Tip

■ To resize the object proportionally, hold down ⟨Shift⟩ while dragging a corner handle.

Figure 71 When you click a graphic object in the document layer, a black selection box and handles surround it and the Picture toolbar appears.

Figure 72 Drag the selection handle toward the center of the picture to make the picture smaller.

Figure 73 When you release the mouse button, the picture resizes.

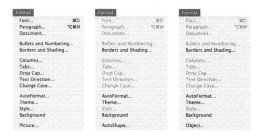

Figures 74a, 74b, and 74c The last command on the Format menu changes depending on what kind of object is selected in the document window.

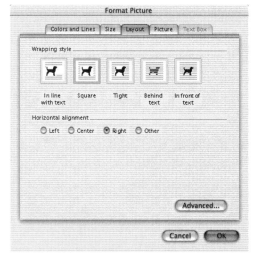

Figure 75 The Layout tab of the Format dialog enables you to set Word wrap options for a selected graphic object.

To wrap text around a graphic object

1. Click the object to select it.

2. Choose the last command under the Format menu. As shown in **Figures 74a, 74b**, and **74c**, this command's name changes depending on what is selected.

3. In the Format dialog that appears, click the Layout tab to display its options (**Figure 75**).

4. Select one of the Wrapping style options:

   ▲ **In line with text** places the object in the document layer as an inline image.

   ▲ **Square** wraps text around all sides of the object with some space to spare.

   ▲ **Tight** wraps text tightly around all sides of the object.

   ▲ **Behind text** places the object behind the document layer. There is no word wrap.

   ▲ **In front of text** places the object in front of the document layer. There is no word wrap.

5. Choose one of the Horizontal alignment options to determine how the object will be aligned in the document window.

6. Click OK.

✔ Tip

■ The Other option in step 5 enables you to drag the object anywhere you like within the document window.

To remove a graphic object

1. Click the object once to select it. White or black handles appear around it (**Figures 58, 62, 67, 69**, and **71**).

2. Press (Delete). The object disappears.

OUTLINES

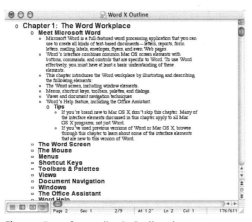

Figure 1 Part of an outline in Outline view.

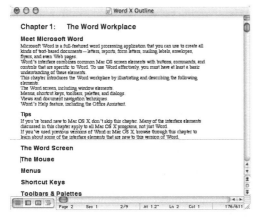

Figure 2 The outline in **Figure 1** in Normal view.

Outlines

An outline is a great tool for organizing ideas. By grouping topics and subtopics under main headings, you can set up the logical flow of a lengthy or complex document. A well-prepared outline is like a document "skeleton"—a solid framework on which the document can be built.

An outline has two components (**Figure 1**):

◆ Headings are topic names. Various levels of headings (1 through 9) are arranged in a hierarchy to organize and develop relationships among them.

◆ Body text provides information about each heading.

Word's Outline view makes it easy to build and refine outlines. You start by adding headings that you can set to any level of importance. Then add body text. You can use drag-and-drop editing to rearrange headings and body text. You can also switch to Normal view (**Figure 2**) or another view to continue working with your document.

✔ Tips

■ Word's Outline feature automatically applies the Heading and Normal styles as you work. You can redefine these styles to meet your needs; I tell you how in **Chapter 4**.

■ You can distinguish headings from body text in Outline view by the symbols that appear before them. Hollow dashes or plus signs appear to the left of headings while small hollow boxes appear to the left of body text (**Figure 1**).

Building an Outline

Building an outline is easy. Just create a new document, switch to Outline view, and start adding headings and body text.

✔ Tip

■ You can turn an existing document into an outline by simply switching to Outline view and adding headings.

To create an outline

1. Create a new blank document.

2. Choose View > Outline (**Figure 3**).

   or

   Click the Outline View button at the bottom of the document window (**Figure 4**).

   The document switches to Outline view and the Outlining toolbar appears (**Figure 5**).

✔ Tip

■ The Outlining toolbar (**Figure 6**) appears automatically any time you switch to Outline view. If it does not appear, you can display it by choosing View > Toolbars > Outline. I tell you more about displaying and hiding toolbars in **Chapter 1**.

Figure 3
One way to switch to Outline view is to choose Outline from the View menu.

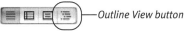

Figure 4 The View buttons at the bottom of the document window.

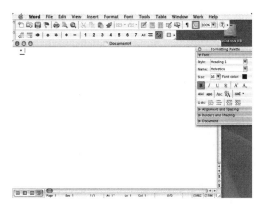

Figure 5 The document window in Outline view. The Outlining toolbar is right above the window.

Figure 6 The Outlining toolbar.

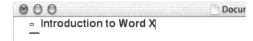

Figure 7 Enter the text that you want to use as a heading.

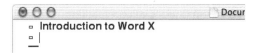

Figure 8 When you press Return, Word creates a new paragraph with the same heading level.

Figure 9 To create a new heading on the same level, simply type it in.

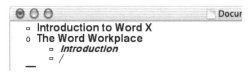

Figure 10 To create a heading at a lower level, click the Demote button before typing it in. When you press Return, Word creates a new paragraph with the same (lower) heading level.

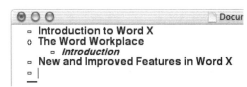

Figure 11 To create a heading at a higher level, click the Promote button while the insertion point is in the heading. When you press Return, Word creates a new paragraph with the same (higher) heading level.

To add headings

1. Type the text that you want to use as a heading (**Figure 7**).

2. Press Return. A new paragraph at the same heading level appears (**Figure 8**).

3. To add a heading at the same level, repeat steps 1 and 2 (**Figure 9**).

   or

   To add a heading at the next lower level, press Tab or click the Demote button on the Outlining toolbar. Then repeat steps 1 and 2 (**Figure 10**).

   or

   To add a heading at the next higher level, press Shift Tab or click the Promote button on the Outlining toolbar. Then repeat steps 1 and 2 (**Figure 11**).

✔ Tips

- By default, the first heading you create is Heading 1—the top level. You can see the heading level in the Style box on the Formatting Palette when the insertion point is in the heading paragraph.

- When you create a lower level heading beneath a heading, the marker to the left of the heading changes to a hollow plus sign to indicate that the heading has subheadings (**Figure 10**).

- Don't worry about entering a heading at the wrong level. You can promote or demote a heading at any time—I tell you how next.

To promote or demote a heading

1. Click anywhere in the heading to position the insertion point within it (**Figure 12**).

2. To promote the heading, press [Shift][Tab] or click the Promote button on the Outlining toolbar. The heading shifts to the left and changes into the next higher level heading (**Figure 13**).

   or

   To demote the heading, press [Tab] or click the Demote button on the Outlining toolbar. The heading shifts to the right and changes into the next lower level heading.

✔ Tips

- You cannot promote a Heading 1 level heading. Heading 1 is the highest level.

- You cannot demote a Heading 9 level heading. Heading 9 is the lowest level.

- To promote or demote multiple headings at the same time, select the headings, then follow step 2 above.

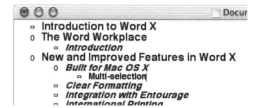

Figure 12 Position the insertion point in the heading that you want to promote or demote.

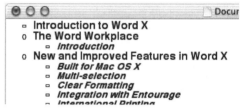

Figure 13 Clicking the Promote button shifts the heading to the left and changes it to the next higher heading level.

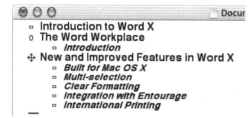

Figure 14 Position the mouse pointer over a heading marker; it turns into a four-headed arrow.

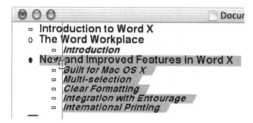

Figure 15 When you drag the heading marker, a line indicates the heading's level when you release the mouse button.

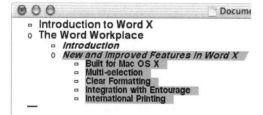

Figure 16 Release the mouse button to change the level of the heading and its subheadings.

To promote or demote a heading with its subheadings

1. Position the mouse pointer over the hollow plus sign to the left of the heading. The mouse pointer turns into a four-headed arrow (**Figure 14**).

2. To promote the headings, press the mouse button down and drag to the left.

   or

   To demote the headings, press the mouse button down and drag to the right (**Figure 15**).

   The heading and its subheadings are selected. As you drag, a line indicates the level to which the heading will be moved when you release the mouse button. You can see all this in **Figure 15**.

3. Release the mouse button to change the level of the heading and its subheadings (**Figure 16**).

✔ Tips

- You can also use this method to promote or demote a heading with no subheadings. Simply drag the hollow dash as instructed in step 2 to change its level.

- Another way to promote or demote a heading with its subheadings is with the Promote or Demote button on the Outlining toolbar. Just click the hollow plus sign marker (**Figure 14**) to select the heading and its subheadings. Then click the Promote or Demote button to change the selected headings' levels.

To add body text

1. Position the insertion point at the end of the heading after which you want to add body text (**Figure 17**).

2. Press [Return] to create a new line with the same heading level (**Figure 18**).

3. Click the Demote to Body Text button [➡] on the Outlining toolbar. The marker to the left of the insertion point changes into a small hollow square to indicate that the paragraph is body text (**Figure 19**).

4. Type the text that you want to use as body text (**Figure 20**).

✔ Tips

- Word automatically applies the Normal style to body text. You can modify the style to meet your needs; I tell you how in **Chapter 4**.

- Each time you press [Return] while typing body text, Word creates a new paragraph of body text.

- You can convert body text to a heading by clicking the the Promote [🔼] or Demote [🔽] button on the Outlining toolbar.

To remove outline components

1. To remove a single heading or paragraph of body text, click the hollow dash or small square marker to the left of the heading or body text. This selects the entire paragraph of the heading or body text.

   or

   To remove a heading with its subheadings and body text, click the hollow plus sign marker to the left of the heading. This selects the heading and all of its subheadings and body text (**Figure 21**).

2. Press [Delete]. The selection is removed.

ADDING BODY TEXT, REMOVING COMPONENTS

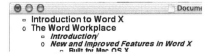

Figure 17 Position the insertion point.

Figure 18 Press [Return].

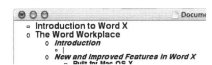

Figure 19 When you click the Demote to Body Text button, the level changes to body text.

Figure 20 Type the text that you want to appear as body text.

Figure 21 When you click the marker to the left of a heading, Word selects the heading and all of its subheadings and body text.

✔ Tip

- You can edit an outline in any of Word's views. Just use commands under the View menu to switch to your favorite view and edit the outline as desired.

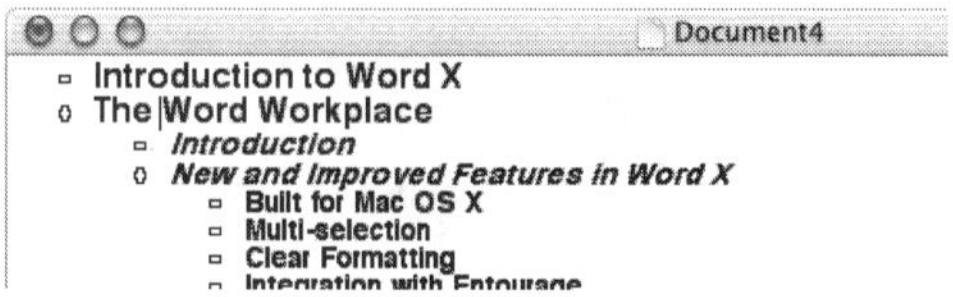

Figure 22 Click to position the insertion point.

Figure 23 When you click the Move Down button, the heading moves down.

Rearranging Outline Components

Word's Outline feature offers two methods to rearrange outline components:

◆ You can click the Move Up [⬆] or Move Down [⬇] button to move selected outline components up or down.

◆ You can drag heading or body text markers to move selected outline components up or down.

✔ Tips

■ Rearranging outline components using these methods changes the order in which they appear but not their level of importance.

■ Either of these methods can be used to move a single heading or paragraph of body text, multiple headings, or a heading with all of its subheadings and body text.

To move headings and/or body text with toolbar buttons

1. To move a single heading or paragraph of body text, click to position the insertion point within it (**Figure 22**).

    or

    To move a heading with its subheadings and body text, click the hollow plus sign marker to the left of the heading to select the heading, its subheadings, and its body text (**Figure 21**).

2. To move the heading up, click the Move Up button [⬆] on the Outlining toolbar. The heading moves one paragraph up.

    or

    To move the heading down, click the Move Down button [⬇] on the Outlining toolbar. The heading moves one paragraph down (**Figure 23**).

To move headings and/or body text by dragging

1. To move a single heading or paragraph of body text, position the mouse pointer over the hollow dash or small square marker to its left.

   or

   To move a heading with its subheadings and body text, position the mouse pointer on the plus sign marker to its left (**Figure 24**).

   The mouse pointer turns into a four-headed arrow (**Figure 24**).

2. To move the component(s) up, press the mouse button down and drag up (**Figure 25**).

   or

   To move the component(s) down, press the mouse button down and drag down.

   The components are selected. As you drag, a line indicates the location to which they will be moved when you release the mouse button. You can see this in **Figure 25**.

3. Release the mouse button to move the component(s) (**Figure 26**).

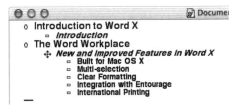

Figure 24 Position the mouse pointer over the heading marker.

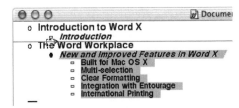

Figure 25 As you drag, a line indicates the new position when you release the mouse button.

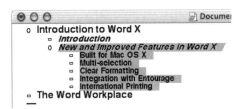

Figure 26 When you release the mouse button, the headings move.

REARRANGING OUTLINE COMPONENTS

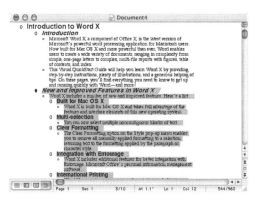

Figure 27 Click a heading's marker to select its contents.

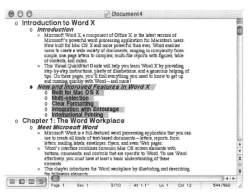

Figure 28 When you click the Collapse button, the lowest displayed level—in this example, the body text—is hidden.

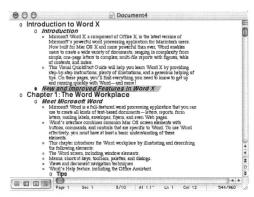

Figure 29 You can click the Collapse button repeatedly to hide multiple levels.

Viewing Outlines

Buttons on the Outlining toolbar (**Figure 6**) enable you to change your view of an outline:

◆ Collapse headings to hide subheadings and body text

◆ Expand headings to show subheadings and body text

◆ Show only specific heading levels

◆ Show all heading levels

◆ Show only the first line of text in each paragraph

◆ Show all lines of text in each paragraph

◆ Show or hide formatting

✔ Tip

■ These viewing options do not change the document's content—just your view of it.

To collapse a heading

1. Click the marker to the left of the heading that you want to collapse to select the heading, its subheadings, and its body text (**Figure 27**).

2. Click the Collapse button [−] on the Outlining toolbar. The heading collapses to hide the lowest displayed level (**Figure 28**).

3. Repeat step 2 until only the levels you want to see are displayed (**Figure 29**).

or

Double-click the marker to the left of the heading that you want to collapse. The heading collapses to its level (**Figure 29**).

✔ Tip

■ When you collapse a heading with sub-headings or body text, a gray line appears beneath it to indicate hidden items (**Figures 28** and **29**).

To expand a heading

1. Click the marker to the left of the heading that you want to expand to select the heading and all of its subheadings and body text.

2. Click the Expand button ![+] on the Outlining toolbar. The heading expands to display the highest hidden level.

3. Repeat step 2 as desired to display all of the levels you want to see.

or

Double-click the marker to the left of the heading that you want to expand. The heading expands to show all levels.

To view only certain heading levels

Click the numbered button on the Outlining toolbar (**Figure 6**) that corresponds to the lowest level of heading that you want to display.

The outline collapses or expands to show just that level (**Figures 30** and **31**).

To view all heading levels

Click the Show All Headings button ![All] on the Outlining toolbar.

The outline expands to show all headings and body text (**Figure 32**).

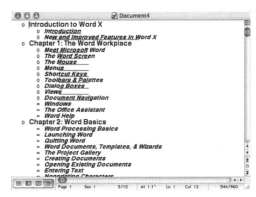

Figure 30 In this example, the Show Heading 2 button was clicked to display heading levels 1 and 2.

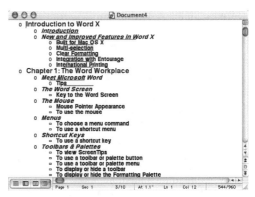

Figure 31 In this example, the Show Heading 3 button was clicked to display heading levels 1, 2, and 3.

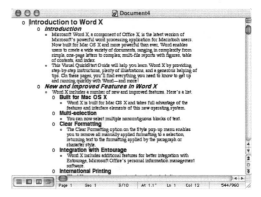

Figure 32 Clicking the Show All Headings button displays all levels of headings and the body text.

VIEWING HEADING LEVELS

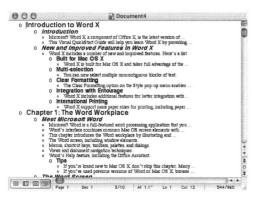

Figure 33 Turning on the Show First Line Only button displays only the first line of each heading or paragraph of body text.

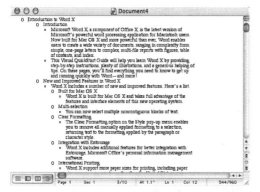

Figure 34 Turning off the Show Formatting button displays all text in the default paragraph font for the Normal style—in this case, 12-point Times.

To display only the first line of every paragraph

Click the Show First Line Only button ☰ on the Outlining toolbar.

The Outline view changes to display only the first line of each heading and paragraph of body text (**Figure 33**).

✔ Tip

- The Show First Line Only button works like a toggle switch. When turned on, only the first line of every paragraph is displayed. When turned off, all lines of every paragraph are displayed. This button is turned off by default.

To hide formatting

Click the Show Formatting button ⅍ on the Outlining toolbar.

The Outline view changes to display all headings and body text in the default paragraph font for the Normal style (**Figure 34**).

✔ Tip

- The Show Formatting button works like a toggle switch. When turned on, paragraph formatting is displayed. When turned off, all text appears in the default paragraph font for the Normal style. This button is turned on by default.

Working with an Outline in Another View

You can switch to Normal (**Figure 35**), Page Layout (**Figure 36**), or Online Layout (**Figure 37**) view while working with an outline. There's nothing special about an outline except the additional outlining features available in Outline view. It's the same document when you switch to another view.

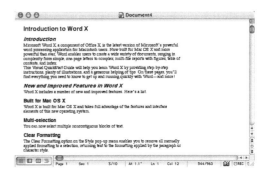

Figure 35 An outline in Normal view,...

✔ Tips

- You can switch between any of Word's views at any time.

- I explain how to switch from one view to another in **Chapter 1**.

- Once the structure of a lengthy or complex document has been established in Outline view, you may find it easier to complete the document in Normal or Page Layout view.

- In Normal, Page Layout, and Online Layout views, you can apply the Heading and Normal styles using the Style menu on the Formatting toolbar. I tell you more about styles in **Chapter 4**.

- The Document Map lists all of the outline's headings (**Figure 37**). Double-click a heading to move quickly to that part of the document. You can show the Document Map in Normal or Online Layout view. I tell you more about the Document Map in **Chapter 1**.

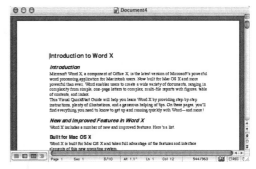

Figure 36 ...Page Layout view,...

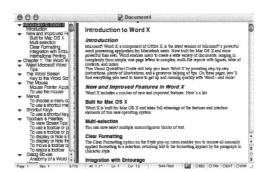

Figure 37 ...and Online Layout view with the Document Map showing.

Insert

Figure 38
Choose Index and Tables from the Insert menu.

Creating a Table of Contents

One of the benefits of using Word's Outline feature is that headings are easily gathered together to create a table of contents.

✔ Tip

- Although there are other ways to generate a table of contents in Word, basing a table of contents on an outline is the easiest way.

To create a table of contents based on an outline

1. Position the insertion point where you want the table of contents to appear.
2. Choose Insert > Index and Tables (**Figure 38**).
3. In the Index and Tables dialog that appears, click the Table of Contents tab to display its options (**Figure 39**).
4. Click to select one of the formats in the Formats list. Each time you click, a sample appears in the Preview area.
5. Set options in the bottom of the dialog:
   ▲ **Show levels** enables you to specify the number of heading levels that should be included in the table of contents.
   ▲ **Show page numbers** tells Word to include page references for each table of contents entry.
   ▲ **Right align page numbers** aligns page numbers along the right side of the page.
   ▲ **Tab leader** enables you to select the characters that should appear between the table of contents entry and its page number.
6. Click OK.

Word generates the table of contents and inserts it as a field at the insertion point (**Figure 40**).

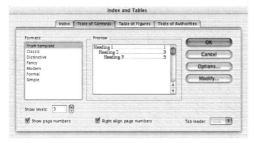

Figure 39 The Table of Contents tab of the Index and Tables dialog.

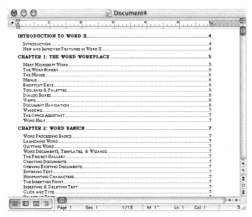

Figure 40 A table of contents for two heading levels, generated using the Formal format.

TABLES

Tour Name	Description	Approx Length	Price per Person
Basic Wickenburg Tour	Circle downtown Wickenburg.	10-15 minutes	$30
Grand Tour of Wickenburg	Our most popular tour offers a complete look at Wickenburg and the surrounding areas, including Vulture Peak, Big Spar Mine, Rancho de los Caballeros, Cemetery Wash, downtown Wickenburg, the Hassayampa River, Box Canyon and the narrow slot canyon beyond, and many of the town's ranches and homes.	20-30 minutes	$75
Ghost Towns and Mines of the Wickenburg Area	Tour the area's hard-to-reach ghost towns and mines. This tour includes sites from Wickenburg to Congress and features Vulture Peak, Vulture City, Big Spar Mine, Mammoth Mine, Dragon Mine, Monte Cristo Mine, Constellation, Gold Bar Mine, Octave, Stanton, and Senate Mine.	50-70 minutes	$150

Figure 1 A four-column, four-row table with borders and some formatting. Each box is an individual cell.

Tables

Microsoft Word's table feature enables you to create tables of information.

A table consists of table cells arranged in columns and rows (**Figure 1**). You enter information into each cell, which is like a tiny document of its own. You can put multiple paragraphs of text into a cell and format characters or paragraphs as discussed in **Chapters 3** and **4**.

Table structure and format are extremely flexible and can be modified to meet your needs. A cell can expand vertically to accommodate long blocks of text or graphics; you can also resize it manually as desired. You can format cells, merge cells, split cells, and put a table within a table cell. These capabilities make the table feature a good choice for organizing and presenting all kinds of data.

✔ Tip

- You can also use tab stops and tab characters to create simple tables without cells. I explain how to do this in **Chapter 3**. This method, however, is not nearly as flexible as using cell tables.

Creating a Table

Word offers three ways to create a table:

◆ Use the **Insert Table** command or toolbar button to create a table at the insertion point.

◆ Use the **Draw Table** command to draw a table anywhere on a page.

◆ Use the **Convert Text to Table** command to convert existing text to a table.

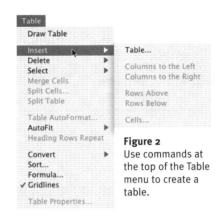

Figure 2
Use commands at the top of the Table menu to create a table.

To insert a table with the Insert Table dialog

1. Position the insertion point where you want the table to appear.

2. Choose Table > Insert > Table (**Figure 2**) to display the Insert Table dialog (**Figure 3**).

3. Enter the number of columns and rows for the table in the Number of columns and Number of rows text boxes.

4. Choose an AutoFit behavior option:

   ▲ **Initial column width** sets the width of each column regardless of its contents or the window width. If you select this option, enter Auto in the text box to set the table as wide as the print area and divide the table into columns of equal width or enter a value in the text box to specify the width of each column.

   ▲ **AutoFit to contents** sets each column to fit the contents of the widest cell in the column and makes the table as wide as all of the columns combined.

   ▲ **AutoFit to window** sets the table's width based on the width of the window and divides the table into columns of equal width.

5. Click OK.

   The table appears, with the insertion point in the top-left cell (**Figure 5**).

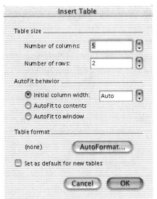

Figure 3
The Insert Table dialog.

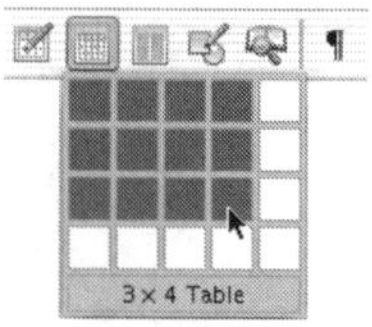

Figure 4
The Insert Table button's menu of columns and rows.

Here are some of the tours we offer:

Figure 5 An empty four-column, three-row table inserted after some text.

✔ Tips

- You can click the AutoFormat button in the Insert Table dialog (**Figure 3**) to format the table as you create it. I tell you about AutoFormatting tables later in this chapter.

- To set the options in the Insert Table dialog (**Figure 3**) as the default options for all new tables you create, turn on the Set as default for new tables check box.

- You can use this technique to insert a table into a table cell. Just make sure the insertion point is within a table cell before you choose Table > Insert > Table (**Figure 2**).

To insert a table with the Insert Table button

1. Position the insertion point where you want the table to appear.

2. Click the Insert Table button 🖽 on the Standard toolbar to display a menu of columns and rows.

3. Select the number of columns and rows you want in the table (**Figure 4**).

   The table appears, with the insertion point in the top-left cell (**Figure 5**).

✔ Tips

- This is probably the fastest way to insert an empty table into a document.

- You can use this technique to insert a table into a table cell. Just make sure the insertion point is within a table cell before you use the Insert Table button's menu.

To draw a table

1. Choose Table > Draw Table (**Figure 2**).

2. If you are not in Page Layout view, Word switches to that view. The Tables and Borders toolbar appears (**Figure 6**). If necessary, click the Draw Table button to select it.

3. Position the Draw Table tool where you want the upper-left corner of the table.

4. Press the mouse button down and drag diagonally to draw a box the size and shape of the table you want (**Figure 7**). When you release the mouse button, the outside border of the table appears (**Figure 8**).

5. Drag the Draw Table tool from the top border of the table to the bottom to draw each column boundary (**Figure 9**).

6. Drag the Draw Table tool from the left border of the table to the right to draw each row boundary (**Figure 10**).

   When you're finished, the table might look something like the one in **Figure 11**.

✔ Tips

- The first time you draw a table, if the Office Assistant is enabled, it appears and provides instructions (**Figure 6**). I explain how to enable and disable the Office Assistant in **Chapter 1**.

- Don't worry if you can't draw column and row boundaries exactly where you want them. I tell you how to change column widths and row heights later in this chapter.

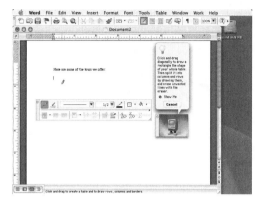

Figure 6 The Tables and Borders toolbar appears when you draw a table.

Figure 7 Drag diagonally to draw a box the size and shape of the table you want.

Figure 8 The outside border for a single-cell table appears.

Figure 9 Draw vertical lines for column boundaries...

Figure 10 ...and horizontal lines for row boundaries.

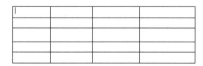

Figure 11 A drawn table.

Figure 12 Tab-separated text selected for conversion to a table.

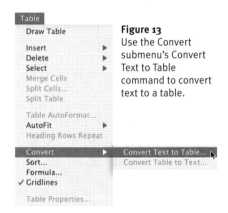

Figure 13
Use the Convert submenu's Convert Text to Table command to convert text to a table.

Figure 14
The Convert Text to Table dialog.

To convert text to a table

1. Select the text that you want to convert to a table (**Figure 12**).

2. Choose Table > Convert > Convert Text to Table (**Figure 13**).

3. In the Convert Text to Table dialog that appears (**Figure 14**), confirm that the correct separator has been selected and the correct values appear in the text boxes. Make any required changes.

4. Click OK.

   The text turns into a table (**Figure 15**).

✔ Tips

- This method works best with tab- or comma-separated text.

- The AutoFit behavior options in the Convert Text to Table dialog (**Figure 14**) are the same as in the Insert Table dialog. I explain them earlier in this chapter.

- In most instances, Word will correctly "guess" the settings for the Convert Text to Table dialog (**Figure 14**) and no changes will be required in step 3 above.

Substance	Date Tested	Tested By	Results
MSG	5/18/98	Maria Langer	452.6589
Magnesium	6/4/98	John Aabbott	51.84
Sulfur	6/15/98	Mary Johannesburg	14596.25489
Aspirin	10/17/98	Tim Jones	1.1

Figure 15 The text in Figure 12 converted to a table.

Anatomy of a Table

A table includes a variety of different elements (**Figure 16**):

◆ **Column boundaries** appear on either side of a column.

◆ **Row boundaries** appear on the top and bottom of a row.

◆ **Cell boundaries** are the portions of column and row boundaries that appear around an individual cell.

◆ **End-of-cell markers** appear within each table cell. They indicate the end of the cell's contents—just like the end-of document marker marks the end of a Word document.

◆ **Borders** are lines that can appear on any column, row, or cell boundary. These lines print when the table is printed.

◆ **Gridlines** (**Figure 17**) are lines that appear on any column, row, or cell boundary. Unlike borders, however, gridlines don't print.

✔ Tips

■ To see the end-of-cell marker, display nonprinting characters by turning on the Show/Hide ¶ button ¶ on the Standard toolbar. I tell you more about nonprinting characters and the Show/Hide ¶ button in **Chapter 1**.

■ By default, Word creates tables with borders on all column and row boundaries. You can change or remove them using techniques discussed in **Chapter 4**.

■ You can only see gridlines on boundaries that do not have borders (**Figure 17**). In addition, the Gridlines option on the Table menu (**Figure 18**) must be turned on for gridlines to appear.

End-of-cell marker

Figure 16 Table elements include column, row, and cell boundaries, end-of-cell markers, and, in this example, borders.

Figure 17 When a table has no borders, gridlines can identify the boundaries.

Figure 18
The Table menu.

ANATOMY OF A TABLE

Figure 19 Position the mouse pointer in the cell's selection bar.

Figure 20 Click to select the cell.

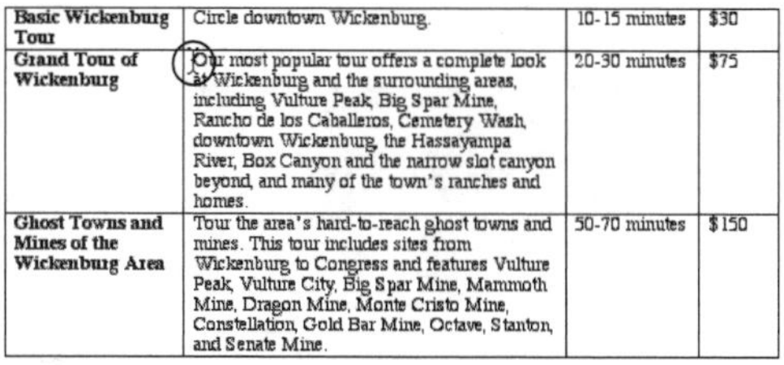

Basic Wickenburg Tour	Circle downtown Wickenburg.	10-15 minutes	$30
Grand Tour of Wickenburg	Our most popular tour offers a complete look at Wickenburg and the surrounding areas, including Vulture Peak, Big Spar Mine, Rancho de los Caballeros, Cemetery Wash, downtown Wickenburg, the Hassayampa River, Box Canyon and the narrow slot canyon beyond, and many of the town's ranches and homes.	20-30 minutes	$75
Ghost Towns and Mines of the Wickenburg Area	Tour the area's hard-to-reach ghost towns and mines. This tour includes sites from Wickenburg to Congress and features Vulture Peak, Vulture City, Big Spar Mine, Mammoth Mine, Dragon Mine, Monte Cristo Mine, Constellation, Gold Bar Mine, Octave, Stanton and Senate Mine.	50-70 minutes	$150

Figure 21 Position the I-beam pointer at the beginning of the cell's contents.

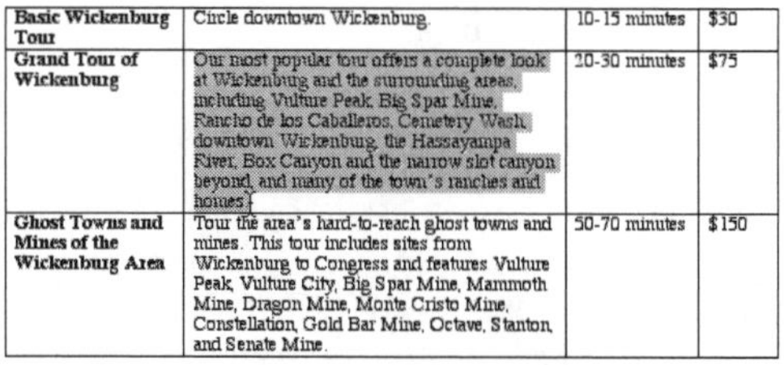

Basic Wickenburg Tour	Circle downtown Wickenburg.	10-15 minutes	$30
Grand Tour of Wickenburg	Our most popular tour offers a complete look at Wickenburg and the surrounding areas, including Vulture Peak, Big Spar Mine, Rancho de los Caballeros, Cemetery Wash, downtown Wickenburg, the Hassayampa River, Box Canyon and the narrow slot canyon beyond, and many of the town's ranches and homes.	20-30 minutes	$75
Ghost Towns and Mines of the Wickenburg Area	Tour the area's hard-to-reach ghost towns and mines. This tour includes sites from Wickenburg to Congress and features Vulture Peak, Vulture City, Big Spar Mine, Mammoth Mine, Dragon Mine, Monte Cristo Mine, Constellation, Gold Bar Mine, Octave, Stanton and Senate Mine.	50-70 minutes	$150

Figure 22 Drag through the cell's contents to select it.

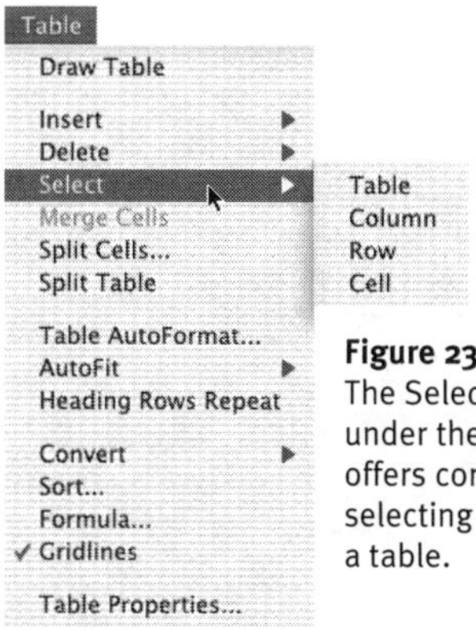

Selecting Table Cells

In many cases, to format the contents of table cells or restructure a table, you must begin by selecting the cells you want to change. Selecting table cells is very similar to selecting other document text, but there are some tricks to make it easier.

To select a cell

1. Position the mouse pointer in the far-left side of the cell so it points to the right (**Figure 19**). This is the cell's selection bar.

2. Click once. The cell becomes selected (**Figure 20**).

or

1. Position the mouse pointer at the beginning of a cell's contents. The mouse pointer must look like an I-beam pointer (**Figure 21**).

2. Press the mouse button down and drag through the contents of the cell. When you release the mouse button, the cell is selected (**Figure 22**).

or

1. Position the insertion point anywhere within the cell you want to select.

2. Choose Table > Select > Cell (**Figure 23**).

Figure 23
The Select submenu under the Table menu offers commands for selecting all or part of a table.

Figure 24 Double-click in a cell's selection bar to select the entire row.

To select a row

1. Position the mouse pointer in the selection bar of any cell in the row (**Figure 19**).

2. Double-click. The entire row becomes selected (**Figure 24**).

or

1. Click to position the blinking insertion point in any cell in the row (**Figure 25**) or select any cell in the row (**Figure 22**).

2. Choose Table > Select > Row (**Figure 23**). The entire row is selected (**Figure 26**).

Basic Wickenburg Tour	Circle downtown Wickenburg	10-15 minutes	$30
Grand Tour of Wickenburg	Our most popular tour offers a complete look at Wickenburg and the surrounding areas, including Vulture Peak, Big Spar Mine, Rancho de los Caballeros, Cemetery Wash, downtown Wickenburg, the Hassayampa River, Box Canyon and the narrow slot canyon beyond, and many of the town's ranches and homes.	20-30 minutes	$75
Ghost Towns and Mines of the Wickenburg Area	Tour the area's hard-to-reach ghost towns and mines. This tour includes sites from Wickenburg to Congress and features Vulture Peak, Vulture City, Big Spar Mine, Mammoth Mine, Dragon Mine, Monte Cristo Mine, Constellation, Gold Bar Mine, Octave, Stanton and Senate Mine.	50-70 minutes	$150

Figure 25 Position the insertion point in any cell in the row.

Basic Wickenburg Tour	Circle downtown Wickenburg	10-15 minutes	$30
Grand Tour of Wickenburg	Our most popular tour offers a complete look at Wickenburg and the surrounding areas, including Vulture Peak, Big Spar Mine, Rancho de los Caballeros, Cemetery Wash, downtown Wickenburg, the Hassayampa River, Box Canyon and the narrow slot canyon beyond, and many of the town's ranches and homes.	20-30 minutes	$75
Ghost Towns and Mines of the Wickenburg Area	Tour the area's hard-to-reach ghost towns and mines. This tour includes sites from Wickenburg to Congress and features Vulture Peak, Vulture City, Big Spar Mine, Mammoth Mine, Dragon Mine, Monte Cristo Mine, Constellation, Gold Bar Mine, Octave, Stanton and Senate Mine.	50-70 minutes	$150

Figure 26 The entire row is selected.

To select a column

1. Position the mouse pointer over the top boundary of the column that you want to select. It turns into an arrow pointing down (**Figure 27**).

2. Click once. The column is selected (**Figure 28**).

or

Hold down (Option) while clicking anywhere in the column that you want to select.

or

1. Click to position the blinking insertion point in any cell in the column (**Figure 25**) or select any cell in the column (**Figure 22**).

2. Choose Table > Select > Column (**Figure 23**). The entire column is selected (**Figure 29**).

Figure 27 Position the insertion point on the top boundary of the column.

Figure 28 Click once to select the column.

Basic Wickenburg Tour	Circle downtown Wickenburg	10-15 minutes	$30
Grand Tour of Wickenburg	Our most popular tour offers a complete look at Wickenburg and the surrounding areas, including Vulture Peak, Big Spar Mine, Rancho de los Caballeros, Cemetery Wash, downtown Wickenburg, the Hassayampa River, Box Canyon and the narrow slot canyon beyond, and many of the town's ranches and homes.	20-30 minutes	$75
Ghost Towns and Mines of the Wickenburg Area	Tour the area's hard-to-reach ghost towns and mines. This tour includes sites from Wickenburg to Congress and features Vulture Peak, Vulture City, Big Spar Mine, Mammoth Mine, Dragon Mine, Monte Cristo Mine, Constellation, Gold Bar Mine, Octave, Stanton and Senate Mine.	50-70 minutes	$150

Figure 29 The entire column is selected.

To select the entire table

Hold down (Option) while double-clicking anywhere in the table. The table is selected (**Figure 30**).

or

1. Click to position the blinking insertion point in any cell in the table (**Figure 25**) or select any cell in the table (**Figure 22**).

2. Choose Table > Select > Table (**Figure 23**). The entire table is selected (**Figure 31**).

Figure 30 A selected table.

Basic Wickenburg Tour	Circle downtown Wickenburg	10-15 minutes	$30
Grand Tour of Wickenburg	Our most popular tour offers a complete look at Wickenburg and the surrounding areas, including Vulture Peak, Big Spar Mine, Rancho de los Caballeros, Cemetery Wash, downtown Wickenburg, the Hassayampa River, Box Canyon and the narrow slot canyon beyond, and many of the town's ranches and homes.	20-30 minutes	$75
Ghost Towns and Mines of the Wickenburg Area	Tour the area's hard-to-reach ghost towns and mines. This tour includes sites from Wickenburg to Congress and features Vulture Peak, Vulture City, Big Spar Mine, Mammoth Mine, Dragon Mine, Monte Cristo Mine, Constellation, Gold Bar Mine, Octave, Stanton and Senate Mine.	50-70 minutes	$150

Figure 31 Another selected table.

Figure 32 Position the insertion point in the cell in which you want to enter text.

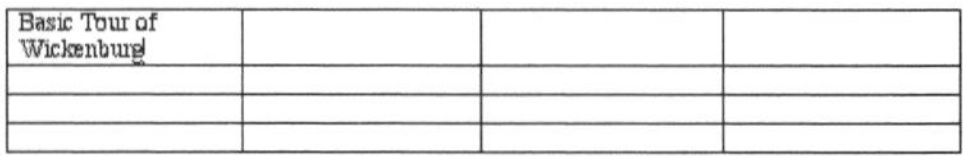

Basic Tour of Wickenburg			

Figure 33 Type to enter the text.

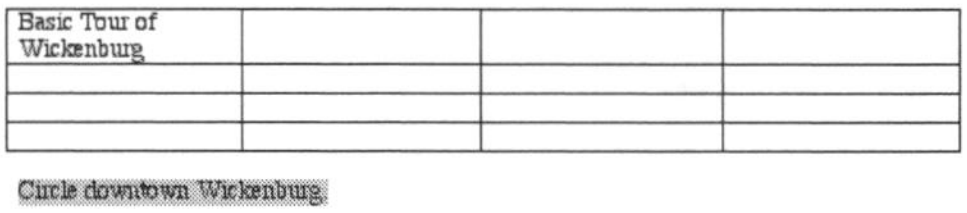

Basic Tour of Wickenburg			

Circle downtown Wickenburg.

Figure 34 Select the text that you want to move into a cell.

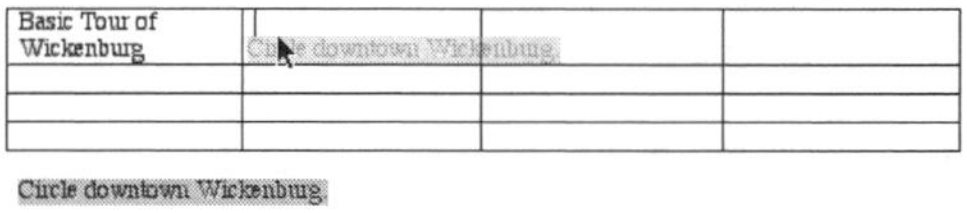

Basic Tour of Wickenburg	Circle downtown Wickenburg.		

Circle downtown Wickenburg.

Figure 35 Drag the selection into the cell.

Basic Tour of Wickenburg	Circle downtown Wickenburg.		

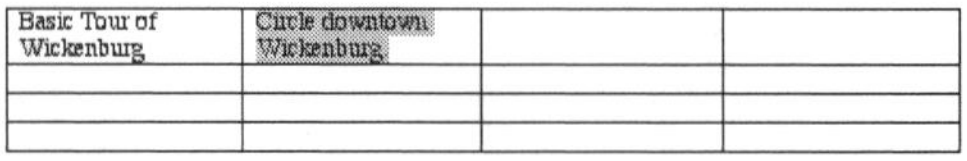

Figure 36 When you release the mouse button, the selection moves into the cell.

Entering & Formatting Table Information

You enter text and other information into a table the same way you enter it into any document: type, paste, or drag it in. Then format it as desired using techniques in **Chapters** 3 and 4.

✔ Tips

- ■ Think of each cell as a tiny document window. The cell boundaries are like document margins. You can enter as much information as you like and apply any kind of formatting.

- ■ As you enter information into a cell, the cell expands vertically as necessary to accommodate the text.

- ■ I tell you about copying and moving text with the Cut, Copy, and Paste commands and drag-and-drop text editing in **Chapter 2**.

To enter text into a cell

1. Position the insertion point in the cell (**Figure 32**).

2. Type the text that you want to appear in the cell (**Figure 33**).

   or

   Use the Paste command to paste the Clipboard contents (a previously copied or cut selection) into the cell.

or

1. Select text in another part of the document (**Figure 34**) or another document.

2. Drag the selected text into the cell in which you want it to appear (**Figure 35**). When you release the mouse button, the text appears in the cell (**Figure 36**).

✔ Tip

- ■ To enter a tab character in a cell, press Control Tab.

ENTERING TEXT INTO TABLE CELLS

To enter special text or objects into a cell

1. Position the insertion point in the cell.

2. Choose the appropriate command from the Insert menu (**Figure 37**) to insert special text or objects.

   or

   Use the Paste command to paste the Clipboard contents (a previously copied or cut selection) into the cell.

or

1. Select special text or objects in another part of the document (**Figure 38**) or another document.

2. Drag the selection into the cell in which you want it to appear. When you release the mouse button (**Figure 39**), it appears in the cell (**Figure 40**).

✔ Tip

- I tell you about options under the Insert menu in **Chapter 7**.

To advance from one cell to another

To advance to the next cell in the table, press Tab.

or

To advance to the previous cell in the table, press Shift Tab.

✔ Tip

- If you use either of these techniques to advance to a cell that is not empty, the cell's contents become selected. Otherwise, the insertion point appears in the cell.

Figure 37
You can use the Insert menu to insert special text or objects into a table.

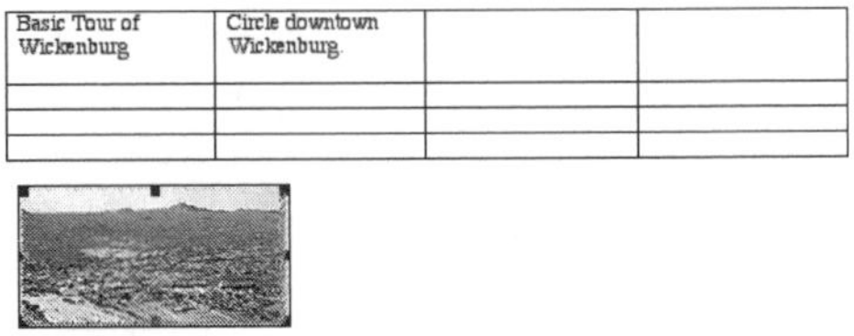

Figure 38 Select the object that you want to move into a cell.

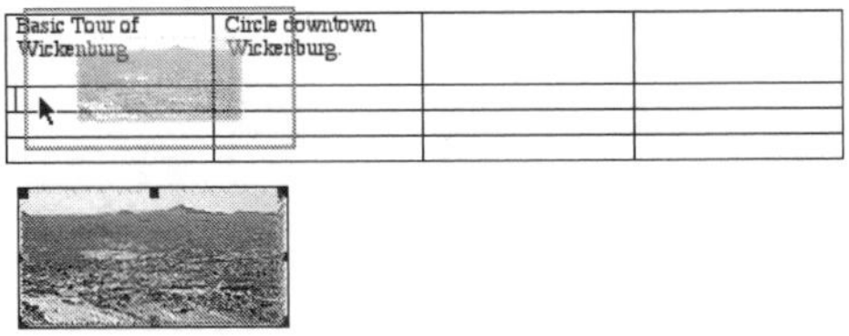

Figure 39 Drag the object into the cell.

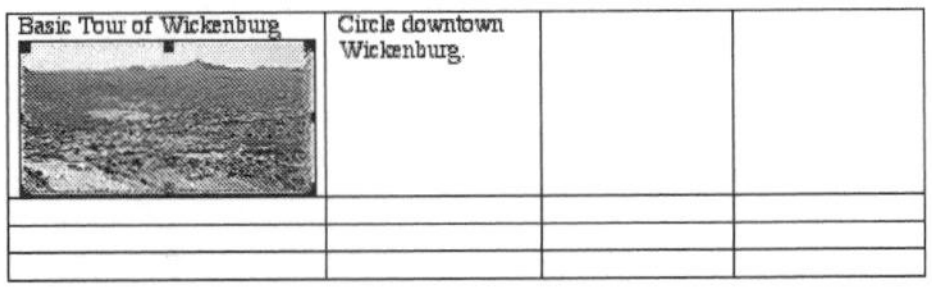

Figure 40 When you release the mouse button, the object moves.

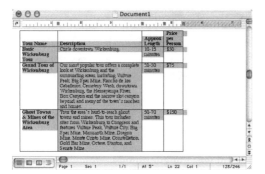

Figure 41 Select the table that you want to align.

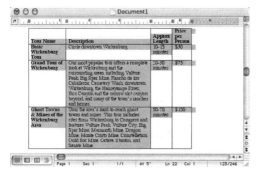

Figure 42 When you click the Center button on the Formatting toolbar, the table centers between the left and right document margins.

To format characters or paragraphs in a cell

1. Select the characters that you want to format.

2. Apply font formatting (such as font, font size, and font style) and/or paragraph formatting (such as alignment, indentation, and line spacing) as discussed in **Chapters 3** and **4**.

✔ Tips

- Almost every kind of font or paragraph formatting can be applied to the contents of individual cells.

- I tell you more about formatting tables when I discuss the Table AutoFormat feature later in this chapter.

To align a table

1. Select the entire table (**Figure 41**).

2. Click one of the alignment buttons on the Formatting Palette:

   ▲ **Align Left** 📄 shifts the table against the left margin. This is the default setting.

   ▲ **Align Center** 📄 shifts the table to center it between the left and right margins (**Figure 42**).

   ▲ **Align Right** 📄 shifts the table against the right margin.

✔ Tips

- The Justify button 📄 does not move the table. Instead it applies full justification to all paragraphs within the table.

- You will only notice a change in a table's alignment if the table is narrower than the printable area between the document's left and right margins.

Inserting & Deleting Cells

You can insert or remove columns, rows, or individual cells at any time to change the structure of a table.

Substance	Date Tested	Tested By	Results
MSG	5/18/98	Maria Langer	452.6589
Magnesium	6/4/98	John Aabbott	51.84
Sulfur	6/15/98	Mary Johannesburg	14596.25489
Aspirin	10/17/98	Tim Jones	1.1

Figure 43 Select the column adjacent to where you want to insert a column.

To insert a column

1. Select a column adjacent to where you want to insert a column (**Figure 43**).

2. To insert a column to the left of the selected column, choose Table > Insert > Columns to the Left (**Figure 44**) or click the Insert Columns button ⊞ on the Standard toolbar.

   or

   To insert a column to the right of the selected column, choose Table > Insert > Columns to the Right (**Figure 44**).

   An empty column is inserted (**Figure 45**).

✔ Tip

- To insert multiple columns, select the same number of columns that you want to insert (if possible) in step 1 or repeat step 2 until the number of columns that you want to insert have been inserted.

To insert a row

1. Select a row adjacent to where you want to insert a row (**Figure 46**).

2. To insert a row above the selected row, choose Table > Insert > Rows Above (**Figure 44**) or click the Insert Rows button ⊡ on the Standard toolbar.

   or

   To insert a row below the selected row, choose Table > Insert > Rows Below (**Figure 44**).

   An empty row is inserted (**Figure 47**).

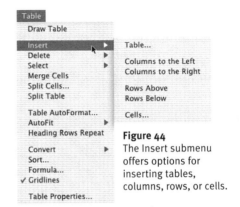

Figure 44
The Insert submenu offers options for inserting tables, columns, rows, or cells.

Substance		Date Tested	Tested By	Results
MSG		5/18/98	Maria Langer	452.6589
Magnesium		6/4/98	John Aabbott	51.84
Sulfur		6/15/98	Mary Johannesburg	14596.25489
Aspirin		10/17/98	Tim Jones	1.1

Figure 45 When you choose Columns to the Left from the Insert submenu, a column is inserted to the left of the selected column.

Substance	Date Tested	Tested By	Results
MSG	5/18/98	Maria Langer	452.6589
Magnesium	6/4/98	John Aabbott	51.84
Sulfur	6/15/98	Mary Johannesburg	14596.25489
Aspirin	10/17/98	Tim Jones	1.1

Figure 46 Select a row adjacent to where you want to insert the row.

Substance	Date Tested	Tested By	Results
MSG	5/18/98	Maria Langer	452.6589
Magnesium	6/4/98	John Aabbott	51.84
Sulfur	6/15/98	Mary Johannesburg	14596.25489
Aspirin	10/17/98	Tim Jones	1.1

Figure 47 When you choose Rows Above from the Insert submenu, a row is inserted above the selected row.

INSERTING COLUMNS & ROWS

Substance	Date Tested	Tested By	Results
MSG	5/18/98	Maria Langer	452.6589
Magnesium	6/4/98	John Aabbott	51.84
Sulfur	6/15/98	Mary Johannesburg	14596.25489
Aspirin	10/17/98	Tim Jones	1.1

Figure 48 Pressing ⟨Tab⟩ while the insertion point is in the last cell of the table adds a row at the bottom of the table.

Substance	Date Tested	Tested By	Results
MSG	5/18/98	Maria Langer	452.6589
Magnesium	6/4/98	John Aabbott	51.84
Sulfur	6/15/98	Mary Johannesburg	14596.25489
Aspirin	10/17/98	Tim Jones	1.1

Figure 49 Select the cell where you want to insert a cell.

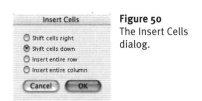

Figure 50
The Insert Cells dialog.

Substance	Date Tested	Tested By	Results	
MSG	5/18/98	Maria Langer		452.6589
Magnesium	6/4/98	John Aabbott	51.84	
Sulfur	6/15/98	Mary Johannesburg	14596.25489	
Aspirin	10/17/98	Tim Jones	1.1	

Substance	Date Tested	Tested By	Results
MSG	5/18/98	Maria Langer	
Magnesium	6/4/98	John Aabbott	452.6589
Sulfur	6/15/98	Mary Johannesburg	51.84
Aspirin	10/17/98	Tim Jones	14596.25489
			1.1

Figures 51a & 51b You can shift cells to the right (top) or down (bottom) when you insert a cell.

✔ Tips

■ Another way to insert a row at the bottom of the table is to position the insertion point in the last cell of the table and press ⟨Tab⟩. An empty row is inserted (**Figure 48**).

■ To insert multiple rows, select the same number of rows that you want to insert (if possible) in step 1 or repeat step 2 until the number of rows that you want to insert have been inserted.

To insert a cell

1. Select the cell at the location where you want to insert a cell (**Figure 49**).

2. Choose Table > Insert > Cells (**Figure 44**) or click the Insert Cells button on the Standard toolbar.

3. In the Insert Cells dialog that appears (**Figure 50**), select an option:

   ▲ **Shift cells right** inserts a cell in the same row and moves the cells to its right to the right (**Figure 51a**).

   ▲ **Shift cells down** inserts a cell in the same column and moves the cells below it down (**Figure 51b**).

   ▲ **Insert entire row** inserts a row above the selected cell.

   ▲ **Insert entire column** inserts a column to the left of the selected cell.

4. Click OK.

✔ Tip

■ To insert multiple cells, select the same number of cells that you want to insert (if possible) in step 1 or repeat steps 2 and 3 until the number of cells that you want to insert have been inserted.

INSERTING CELLS

To delete a column, row, or cell

1. Select the column (**Figure 52**), row (**Figure 55**), or cell (**Figure 57**) that you want to remove.

2. Choose the appropriate command from the Table menu's Delete submenu (**Figure 53**) to delete the selected column, row, or cell.

or

Press Delete.

3. If you delete a column, it disappears and the columns to its right shift to the left (**Figure 54**).

or

If you delete a row, it disappears and the rows below it shift up (**Figure 56**).

or

If you delete a cell, choose an option in the Delete Cells dialog that appears (**Figure 58**):

▲ **Shift cells left** deletes the cell and moves the cells to its right to the left (**Figure 59a**).

▲ **Shift cells up** deletes the cell and moves the cells below it up (**Figure 59b**).

▲ **Delete entire row** deletes the row.

▲ **Delete entire column** deletes the column.

Then click OK.

✔ Tips

■ The contents of a column, row, or cell are deleted with it.

■ You can select multiple contiguous columns, rows, or cells in step 1 above to delete them all at once.

Substance	Date Tested	Tested By	Results
MSG	5/18/98	Maria Langer	452.6589
Magnesium	6/4/98	John Aabbott	51.84
Sulfur	6/15/98	Mary Johannesburg	14596.25489
Aspirin	10/17/98	Tim Jones	1.1

Figure 52 Select the column that you want to delete.

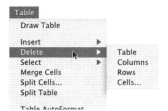

Figure 53 Use commands on the Delete submenu to delete a selected table, column, row, or cell.

Substance	Date Tested	Results
MSG	5/18/98	452.6589
Magnesium	6/4/98	51.84
Sulfur	6/15/98	14596.25489
Aspirin	10/17/98	1.1

Figure 54 The column is deleted.

Substance	Date Tested	Tested By	Results
MSG	5/18/98	Maria Langer	452.6589
Magnesium	6/4/98	John Aabbott	51.84
Sulfur	6/15/98	Mary Johannesburg	14596.25489
Aspirin	10/17/98	Tim Jones	1.1

Figure 55 Select the row that you want to delete.

Substance	Date Tested	Tested By	Results
Magnesium	6/4/98	John Aabbott	51.84
Sulfur	6/15/98	Mary Johannesburg	14596.25489
Aspirin	10/17/98	Tim Jones	1.1

Figure 56 The Rows command deletes it.

Substance	Date Tested	Tested By	Results
MSG	5/18/98	Maria Langer	452.6589
Magnesium	6/4/98	John Aabbott	51.84
Sulfur	6/15/98	Mary Johannesburg	14596.25489
Aspirin	10/17/98	Tim Jones	1.1

Figure 57 Select the cell that you want to delete.

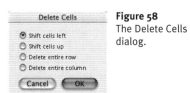

Figure 58
The Delete Cells dialog.

Substance	Date Tested	Tested By	Results
MSG	5/18/98	Maria Langer	
Magnesium	6/4/98	John Aabbott	51.84
Sulfur	6/15/98	Mary Johannesburg	14596.25489
Aspirin	10/17/98	Tim Jones	1.1

Substance	Date Tested	Tested By	Results
MSG	5/18/98	Maria Langer	51.84
Magnesium	6/4/98	John Aabbott	14596.25489
Sulfur	6/15/98	Mary Johannesburg	1.1
Aspirin	10/17/98	Tim Jones	

Figures 59a & 59b You can shift cells to the left (left) or up (right) when you delete a cell.

DELETING COLUMNS, ROWS, & CELLS

Tour Name	Description	Approx Length	Price per Person
Basic Wickenburg Tour	Circle downtown Wickenburg	10-15 minutes	$30
Grand Tour of Wickenburg	Our most popular tour offers a complete look at Wickenburg and the surrounding areas, including Vulture Peak, Big Spar Mine, Rancho de los Caballeros, Cemetery Wash, downtown Wickenburg, the Hassayampa River, Box Canyon and the narrow slot canyon beyond, and many of the town's ranches and homes.	20-30 minutes	$75

Figure 60 Select the cells that you want to merge.

Tour Name	Description	Approx Length	Price per Person
Basic Wickenburg Tour Circle downtown Wickenburg		10-15 minutes	$30
Grand Tour of Wickenburg	Our most popular tour offers a complete look at Wickenburg and the surrounding areas, including Vulture Peak, Big Spar Mine, Rancho de los Caballeros, Cemetery Wash, downtown Wickenburg, the Hassayampa River, Box Canyon and the narrow slot canyon beyond, and many of the town's ranches and homes.	20-30 minutes	$75

Figure 61 The cells are merged into one cell.

Tour Name	Description	Approx Length	Price per Person
Basic Wickenburg Tour	Circle downtown Wickenburg	10-15 minutes	$30
Grand Tour of Wickenburg	Our most popular tour offers a complete look at Wickenburg and the surrounding areas, including Vulture Peak, Big Spar Mine, Rancho de los Caballeros, Cemetery Wash, downtown Wickenburg, the Hassayampa River, Box Canyon and the narrow slot canyon beyond, and many of the town's ranches and homes.	20-30 minutes	$75

Figure 62 Select the cell that you want to split.

Figure 63 The Split Cells dialog.

Tour Name	Description	Approx Length	Price per Person
Basic Wickenburg Tour	Circle downtown Wickenburg	10-15 minutes	$30
Grand Tour of Wickenburg	Our most popular tour offers a complete look at Wickenburg and the surrounding areas, including Vulture Peak, Big Spar Mine, Rancho de los Caballeros, Cemetery Wash, downtown Wickenburg, the Hassayampa River, Box Canyon and the narrow slot canyon beyond, and many of the town's ranches and homes.	20-30 minutes	$75

Figure 64 A cell split into one column and two rows.

Merging & Splitting Cells & Tables

You can modify the structure of a table by merging and splitting cells or splitting the table:

◆ Merging cells turns multiple cells into one cell that spans multiple columns or rows.

◆ Splitting a cell turns a single cell into multiple cells in the same column or row.

◆ Splitting a table turns a single table into two separate tables.

To merge cells

1. Select the cells that you want to merge (**Figure 60**).

2. Choose Table > Merge Cells (**Figure 18**). The cells become a single cell (**Figure 61**).

✔ Tip

■ When you merge cells containing text, each cell's contents appear in a separate paragraph of the merged cell (**Figure 61**).

To split cells

1. Select the cell(s) that you want to split (**Figure 62**).

2. Choose Table > Split Cells (**Figure 18**) to display the Split Cells dialog (**Figure 63**).

3. Enter the number of columns and rows for the cell split in the Number of columns and Number of rows text boxes.

4. Click OK. The cell splits as specified (**Figure 64**).

Continued on next page...

MERGING & SPLITTING CELLS

Continued from previous page.

Figure 65 The cells selected in **Figure 60** after merging and splitting them into one column and three rows.

✔ Tips

- To split a cell in the middle of its contents, in step 1 above position the insertion point where you want the split to occur.

- To merge and split multiple cells at the same time, in step 1, select all the cells (**Figure 60**). Then, in step 3, make sure the Merge cells before split check box is turned on (**Figure 63**). When you click OK, the cells are merged and split (**Figure 65**).

To split a table

1. Position the insertion point anywhere in the row below where you want the split to occur (**Figure 66**).

2. Choose Table > Split Table (**Figure 18**).

   The table splits above the row you indicated (**Figure 67**).

Figure 66 Position the insertion point in the row below where you want the split to occur.

Figure 67 The table splits above the insertion point.

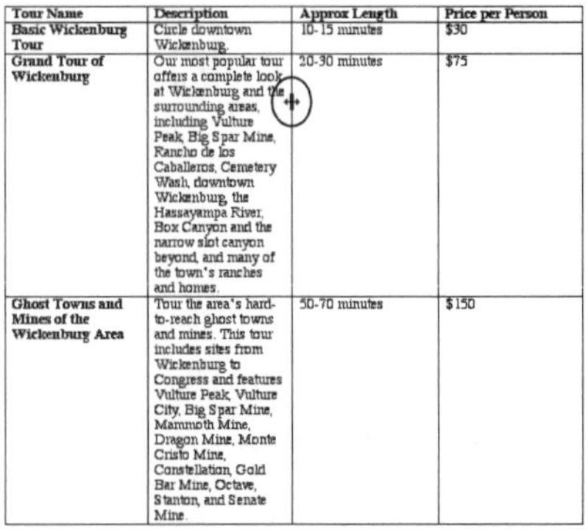

Figure 68 Position the mouse pointer on the column's right boundary.

Figure 69 Drag the column boundary.

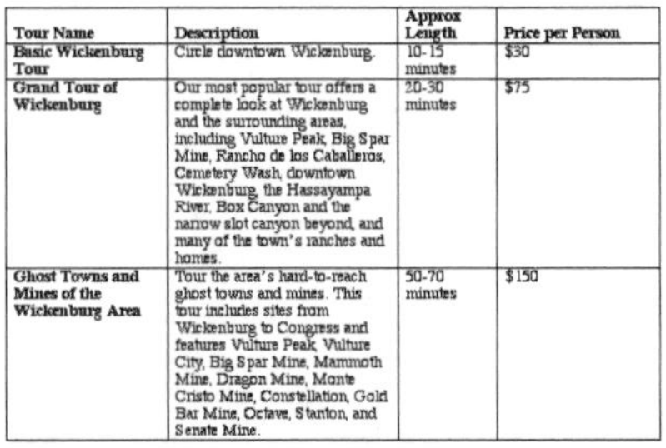

Figure 70 When you release the mouse button, the column and the column to its right resize.

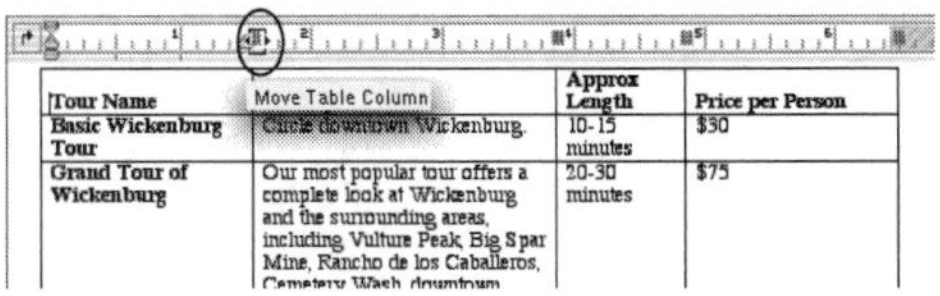

Figure 71 You can also resize a column by dragging the Move Table Column area for the column's right boundary.

Resizing Columns & Rows

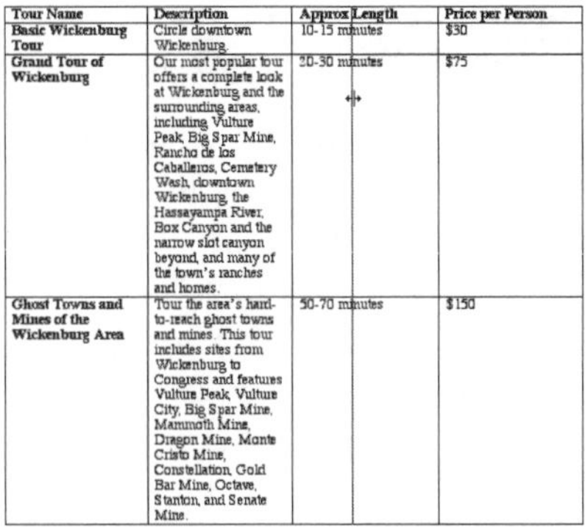

Word offers two ways to manually change the width of columns or height of rows:

◆ Drag to change column widths and row heights.

◆ Use the Table Properties dialog to change column widths and row heights.

To change a column's width by dragging

1. Position the mouse pointer on the boundary between the column that you want to change and the one to its right. The mouse pointer turns into a double-line with arrows (**Figure 68**).

2. Press the mouse button down and drag:

   ▲ Drag to the right to make the column wider.

   ▲ Drag to the left to make the column narrower.

   As you drag, a dotted line indicating the new boundary moves with the mouse pointer (**Figure 69**).

3. Release the mouse button. The column boundary moves to the new position, resizing both columns (**Figure 70**).

✔ Tips

■ To resize a column without changing the width of other columns, in step 1, position the mouse pointer on the Move Table Column area for the column's right boundary (**Figure 71**). Because this method changes only one column's width, it also changes the width of the table.

■ If a cell is selected when you drag to resize a column, only the selected cell's width changes.

CHANGING COLUMN WIDTH BY DRAGGING

To change a row's height by dragging

1. If necessary, switch to Page Layout view.

2. Position the mouse pointer on the boundary between the row that you want to change and the one below it. The mouse pointer turns into a double-line with arrows (**Figure 72**).

3. Press the mouse button down and drag:

   ▲ Drag up to make the row shorter.

   ▲ Drag down to make the row taller.

   As you drag, a dotted line indicating the new boundary moves with the mouse pointer (**Figure 73**).

4. Release the mouse button. The row boundary moves to the new position. The rows beneath it shift accordingly (**Figure 74**).

✔ Tips

■ Another way to resize a row by dragging is to position the mouse pointer on the Adjust Table Row area of the row's bottom boundary (**Figure 75**). Then follow steps 3 and 4 above.

■ Changing a row's height changes the total height of the table.

■ You can't make a row's height shorter than the height of the text within the row.

Substance	Date Tested	Tested By	Results
MSG	5/18/98	Maria Langer	452.6589
Magnesium	6/4/98	John Aabbott	51.84
Sulfur	6/15/98	Mary Johannesburg	14596.25489
Aspirin	10/17/98	Tim Jones	1.1

Figure 72 Position the mouse pointer on the bottom boundary.

Substance	Date Tested	Tested By	Results
MSG	5/18/98	Maria Langer	452.6589
Magnesium	6/4/98	John Aabbott	51.84
Sulfur	6/15/98	Mary Johannesburg	14596.25489
Aspirin	10/17/98	Tim Jones	1.1

Figure 73 Drag the row boundary.

Substance	Date Tested	Tested By	Results
MSG	5/18/98	Maria Langer	452.6589
Magnesium	6/4/98	John Aabbott	51.84
Sulfur	6/15/98	Mary Johannesburg	14596.25489
Aspirin	10/17/98	Tim Jones	1.1

Figure 74 When you release the mouse button, the boundary moves, changing the row's height.

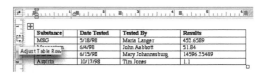

Figure 75 You can also resize a row by dragging the Adjust Table Row area for the row's bottom boundary.

CHANGING ROW HEIGHT BY DRAGGING

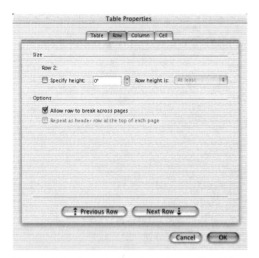

Figure 76 The Row tab of the Table Properties dialog.

Figure 77 Use this pop-up menu to specify how the row height measurement you enter should be used.

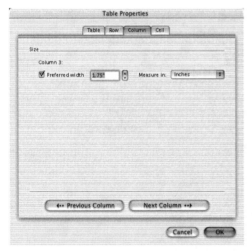

Figure 78 The Column tab of the Table Properties dialog.

Figure 79 Use this pop-up menu to specify how the column width measurement you enter should be used.

To set row height or column width

1. Select a cell in the row or column for which you want to set height or width.

2. Choose Table > Table Properties (**Figure 18**) to display the Table Properties dialog.

3. To set row height, click the Row tab to display its options (**Figure 76**). Turn on the Specify height check box, enter a value in the text box beside it, and choose an option from the Row height is pop-up menu (**Figure 77**).

   or

   To set column width, click the Column tab to display its options (**Figure 78**). Turn on the Preferred width check box, enter a value in the text box beside it, and choose an option from the Measure in pop-up menu (**Figure 79**).

4. Click OK.

✔ Tips

- To set column width and row height at the same time, in step 1, select a cell that is in both the column and row that you want to change. Then follow the remaining steps, including both parts of step 3.

- You can click the Previous Row and Next Row buttons in the Row tab (**Figure 76**) and the Previous Column and Next Column buttons in the Column tab (**Figure 78**) of the Table Properties dialog to cycle through and set values for all the rows and columns in the table.

- The Table Properties dialog offers a number of advanced features for formatting tables, rows, columns, and cells that are beyond the scope of this book.

SETTING ROW HEIGHT & COLUMN WIDTH

Using AutoFit

Table AutoFit options (**Figure 81**) instruct Word to automatically set the column width or row height depending on the table or window width or cell contents. The options are:

◆ **AutoFit to Contents** automatically sizes a column's width based on its contents.

◆ **AutoFit to Window** automatically sizes a table's width to fill the space between the margins.

◆ **Fixed Column Width** locks a column's width so it does not automatically change.

◆ **Distribute Rows Evenly** equalizes the height of rows.

◆ **Distribute Columns Evenly** equalizes the width of columns.

To adjust columns to best fit contents

1. To adjust all table columns, click anywhere in the table (**Figure 80**).

   or

   To adjust just one or more columns, select the column(s).

2. Choose Table > AutoFit > AutoFit to Contents (**Figure 81**).

   The column(s) adjust to minimize word wrap (**Figure 82**).

To adjust a table's width to fill the window

1. Click anywhere in the table (**Figure 80**).

2. Choose Table > AutoFit > AutoFit to Window (**Figure 81**).

   The table's width adjusts to fill the space between the margins (**Figure 83**). Columns are resized proportionally.

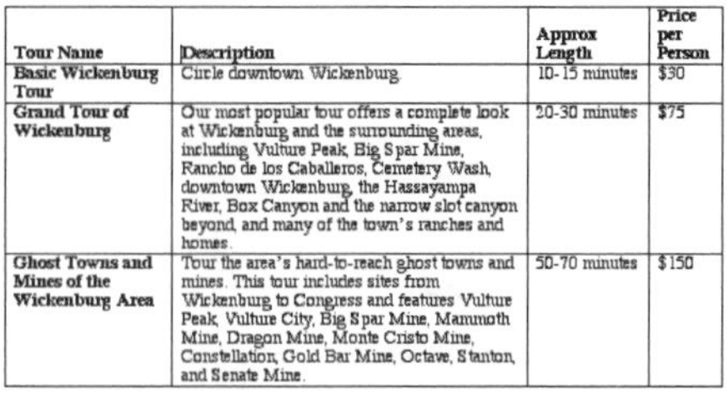

Figure 80 Position the insertion point anywhere in the table.

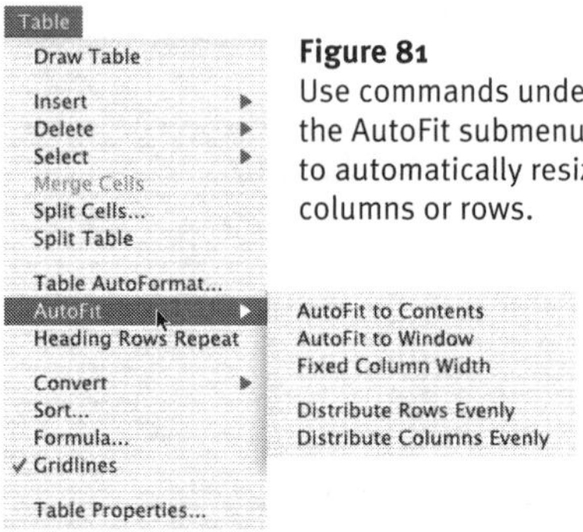

Figure 81
Use commands under the AutoFit submenu to automatically resize columns or rows.

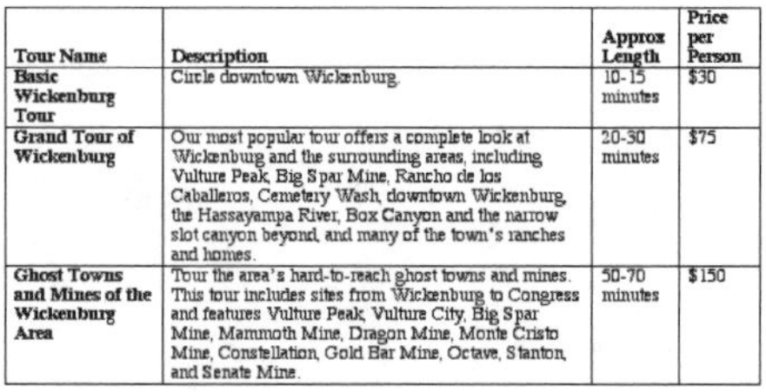

Figure 82 The AutoFit to Contents command minimizes word wrap within cells.

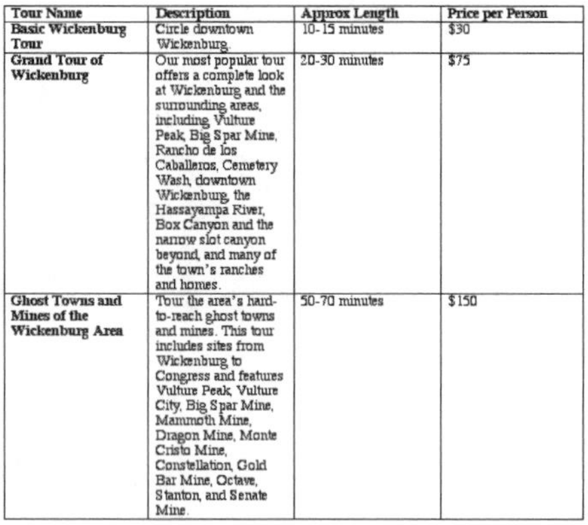

Figure 83 The AutoFit to Window command resizes columns proportionally so the table fits in the space between the margins.

Figure 84 Select the columns for which you want to equalize width.

Figure 85 The space used by the columns is distributed evenly between them.

Figure 86 Select the rows for which you want to equalize height.

Figure 87 The row heights change as necessary so each selected row is the same height.

To equalize the width of columns

1. Select the columns for which you want to equalize width (**Figure 84**).

2. Choose Table > AutoFit > Distribute Columns Evenly (**Figure 81**). The column widths change to evenly distribute space within the same area (**Figure 85**).

To equalize the height of rows

1. Select the rows for which you want to equalize height (**Figure 86**).

2. Choose Table > AutoFit > Distribute Rows Evenly (**Figure 81**). The row heights change so that all selected rows are the same height (**Figure 87**).

✔ Tip

■ Using the Distribute Rows Evenly command usually increases the height of the table, since all selected rows become the same height as the tallest row.

EQUALIZING COLUMN WIDTH & ROW HEIGHT

Table Headings

A table heading consists of one or more rows that appear at the top of the table. If page breaks occur within a table, the table heading appears at the top of each page of the table (**Figure 88**).

✔ Tip

- Setting a row as a table heading does not change its appearance. You must manually apply formatting or use the Table AutoFormat command to make headings look different from other data in the table. I tell you about formatting text in **Chapters 3** and **4** and about the Table AutoFormat command on the next page.

To set a table heading

1. Select the row(s) that you want to use as a table heading (**Figure 89**).

2. Choose Table > Heading Rows Repeat (**Figure 18**).

   The selected rows are set as headings.

To remove a table heading

1. Select the row(s) that comprise the heading (**Figure 89**).

2. Choose Table > Heading Rows Repeat (**Figure 90**).

   The headings setting is removed from the selected rows.

✔ Tip

- Removing the heading feature from selected row(s) does not delete the row(s) from the table.

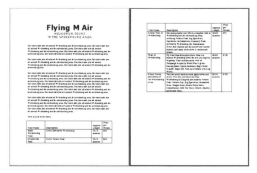

Figure 88 If a page break splits a table into multiple pages, the headings appear at the top of each page of the table.

Tour Name	Description	Approx Length	Price per Person
Basic Wickenburg Tour	Circle downtown Wickenburg.	10-15 minutes	$30
Around the Peak	Circle Vulture Peak.	10-15 minutes	$30
Grand Tour of Wickenburg	Our most popular tour offers a complete look at Wickenburg and the surrounding areas, including Vulture Peak, Big Spar Mine, Rancho de los Caballeros, Cemetery Wash, downtown Wickenburg, the Hassayampa River, Box Canyon and the narrow slot canyon beyond, and many of the town's ranches and homes.	20-30 minutes	$75
West of Wickenburg	Fly west from the airport to see what lies beyond Wickenburg down the old Los Angeles Highway. Tour includes aerial view of Forepaugh Airport (a World War II glider training base), Aguila farmland, Eagle Roost Airpark, Eagle Eye Peak, and Robson's Mining World.	40-50 minutes	$130
Ghost Towns and Mines of the Wickenburg Area	Tour the area's hard-to-reach ghost towns and mines. This tour includes sites from Wickenburg to Congress and features Vulture Peak, Vulture City, Big Spar Mine, Mammoth Mine, Dragon Mine, Monte Cristo Mine, Constellation, Gold Bar Mine, Octave, Stanton, and Senate Mine.	50-70 minutes	$150

Figure 89 Select the row(s) that you want to use as a heading.

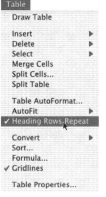

Figure 90
Choose Heading Rows Repeat from the Table menu a second time to remove the heading feature from selected row(s).

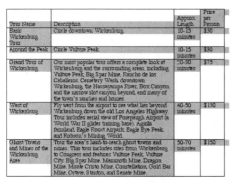

Figure 91 Select the table that you want to format.

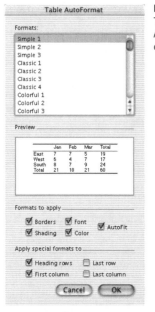

Figure 92
The Table
AutoFormat
dialog.

Table AutoFormat

Word's Table AutoFormat feature offers a quick and easy way to combine many formatting options for an entire table.

To use Table AutoFormat

1. Select the table that you want to format (**Figure 91**).

2. Choose Table > Table AutoFormat (**Figure 18**) to display the Table AutoFormat dialog (**Figure 92**).

3. Click to select one of the formats in the scrolling list.

4. Toggle check boxes in the Formats to apply area to specify which part(s) of the Auto-Format should be applied to the selection.

5. Toggle check boxes in the Apply special formats to area to specify which part(s) of the table should get the special formatting.

6. When you're finished setting options, click OK. The formatting for the AutoFormat is applied to the table (**Figure 93**).

✔ Tips

■ Each time you make a change in the Table AutoFormat dialog (**Figure 92**), the Pre-view area changes to show the effect of your changes.

■ If you don't like the formatting applied by the Table AutoFormat feature, use the Undo command to reverse it. Then try again or format the table manually.

To remove AutoFormatting

Follow steps 1 and 2 above, but select (none) in the scrolling list in step 3, and then click OK.

Figure 93 The table from Figure 91 with the Colorful 2 format applied.

TABLE AUTOFORMAT

Removing a Table

You can remove a table two ways:

♦ Delete the table, thus removing it and its contents from the document.

♦ Convert the table to text, thus removing the structure of the table from the document but not the table's contents.

To delete a table

1. Select the table that you want to delete.

2. Choose Table > Delete > Table (**Figure 53**).

   or

   Press Delete.

   The table and all of its data are removed from the document.

To convert a table to text

1. Select the table that you want to convert to text.

2. Choose Table > Convert > Convert Table to Text (**Figure 94**).

3. In the Convert Table to Text dialog that appears (**Figure 95**), select the radio button for the type of delimiter that you want to use to separate the contents of table cells when the cell boundaries are removed.

4. Click OK.

   The table is converted to text.

Figure 94
Use the Convert Table to Text command to remove a table without removing its contents.

Figure 95
The Convert Table to Text dialog.

ENVELOPES & LABELS

Envelopes & Labels

Microsoft Word's Envelopes and Labels feature can create and print addressed envelopes and mailing labels based on document contents or other information you provide. This feature makes it easy to print professional-looking envelopes and labels for all of your mailing needs.

✔ Tips

- Word supports a wide variety of standard envelope and label sizes and formats. Settings can also be changed for printing on nonstandard envelopes or labels.

- You can use the Data Merge Manager feature to create envelopes and labels based on database information. I tell you how in **Chapter 11**.

Creating an Envelope

In Word, you create an envelope with the Envelope dialog (**Figure 1**). This dialog enables you to provide several pieces of information:

◆ **Delivery address** is the address the envelope will be mailed to. You can also indicate that you want barcode information included on the envelope.

◆ **Return address** is the address that appears in the upper-left corner of the envelope. You can use your own address, specify another address, or omit the address entirely.

◆ **Printing Options** include options related to the envelope size and feed method. Word can get these settings from your printer or you can set them manually.

✔ Tip

■ You can also specify the font and position of the delivery and return addresses.

To open the Envelope dialog

Choose Tools > Envelopes (**Figure 2**).

✔ Tip

■ You cannot choose the Envelopes command from the Tools menu unless a document window is open.

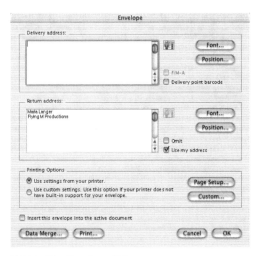

Figure 1 The Envelope dialog.

Figure 2 The Tools menu offers commands for creating both envelopes and labels from within Word.

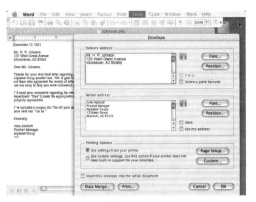

Figure 3 When you create an envelope for a letter, Word is usually "smart" enough to fill in the Delivery address for you.

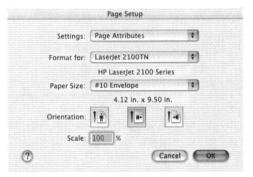

Figure 4 The Page Setup dialog. Note the option chosen from the Paper Size pop-up menu.

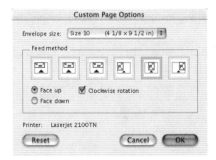

Figure 5 You can set envelope and feed options for your printer in the Custom Page Options dialog.

To set envelope options

1. Open the Envelope dialog (**Figure 1** or **3**).

2. Enter the name and address of the person to whom the envelope should be addressed in the Delivery address box.

3. If desired, enter a return address in the Return address box.

   or

   To create an envelope without a return address, turn on the Omit check box. This omits the return address from the envelope, even if one appears in the Return address box.

4. Select one of the radio buttons in the Printing Options area:

   ▲ **Use settings from your printer** tells Word to use your printer's settings for the envelope. If you select this option, you can click the Page Setup button and use the Page Setup dialog that appears (**Figure 4**) to select the correct envelope options.

   ▲ **Use custom settings** tells Word that you will provide envelope settings. If you select this option, click the Custom button to display the Custom Page Options dialog (**Figure 5**). Select envelope size and feed method options that will work with your printer, and click OK.

✔ Tips

■ If you are creating an envelope for a letter in the active document window, the Delivery address may already be filled in based on the inside address of the letter (**Figure 3**). You can "help" Word enter the correct address in this box by selecting the recipient's address before opening the Envelope dialog.

Continued on next page...

SETTING ENVELOPE OPTIONS

Continued from previous page.

- To include a postal barcode on the envelope, turn on the Delivery point barcode check box in the Delivery address area (**Figure 1**). You can then also turn on the FIM-A check box if desired to add additional postal coding to the face of the envelope.

- If you entered your address in the User Information pane of the Preferences dialog (**Figure 6**) or in Entourage (software that's part of Microsoft Office), you can automatically enter your return address by turning on the Use my address check box in the Envelope dialog (**Figure 1**). I discuss User Information preferences in **Chapter 15** and Entourage in **Chapter 13**.

- To set the font options for either address, click the Font button in its area. Then use the Font dialog that appears (**Figure 7**) to set formatting options. I tell you more about font formatting in **Chapters 3** and **4**.

- To override Word's automatic positioning of addresses, click either Position button. Then use the Address Position dialog that appears (**Figure 8**) to enter measurements for address positioning.

To print an envelope

1. Click the Print button in the Envelope dialog (**Figure 1**).

2. Word creates a new document for the envelope (**Figure 9**) and displays the Print dialog (**Figure 10**).

3. Change options if necessary for the envelope and click Print to print it.

   Word prints the envelope. When it is finished, the document window containing the envelope is the active window.

✔ Tip

- I tell you more about printing in **Chapter 6**.

Figure 6 The User Information pane of the Preferences dialog.

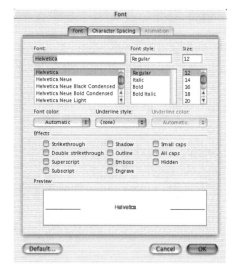

Figure 7 You can format the characters of either address with the Font dialog.

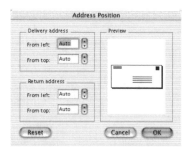

Figure 8 You can override Word's automatic address positioning by entering measurements in the Address Position dialog.

SETTING OPTIONS, PRINTING ENVELOPES

Figure 9 Word creates a new document for the envelope.

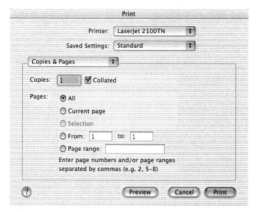

Figure 10 The Print dialog.

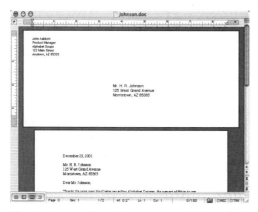

Figure 11 An envelope added as a separate document section when viewed in Page Layout view.

To save the envelope

1. Print the envelope as instructed on the previous page.

   or

   Click OK in the Envelope dialog (**Figure 1**).

   The envelope appears in the active document window (**Figure 9**).

2. Choose File > Save to display the Save As dialog and save the document on disk.

To save the envelope as part of the active document

1. In the Envelope dialog (**Figure 1**), turn on the Insert this envelope into the active document check box.

2. Click Print to print the envelope as instructed on the previous page.

   or

   Click OK to create the envelope without printing it.

   Word adds a new section to the document with the proper settings to print that section as an envelope (**Figure 11**).

✔ Tips

- When you use the Print command to print a document that includes an envelope, Word displays a separate Print dialog for the envelope and the rest of the document.

- I tell you about document sections in **Chapter 4**.

Creating Labels

In Word, you create labels with the Labels dialog (**Figure 12**). This dialog enables you to provide several pieces of information:

◆ **Address** is the address that should appear on the label. You can also indicate that you want barcode information included on the label.

◆ **Label** options include printer information and the size of the label. Word supports most standard label products—including Avery labels—and enables you to set a custom label size if necessary.

◆ **Number of Labels** is the number of labels you want to print. If you're printing less than a full sheet, you can specify the location of the label you want to print.

◆ **Printing Options** enable you to specify the feed method and sheet size for non-standard labels.

To open the Labels dialog

Choose Tools > Labels (**Figure 2**).

✔ Tip

■ You cannot choose the Labels command from the Tools menu unless a document window is open.

Figure 12 The Labels dialog.

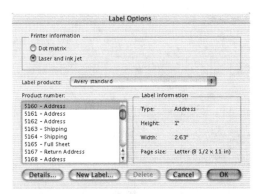

Figure 13 Use the Label Options dialog to indicate the type of printer you will use and to choose a label product.

Figure 14 Word supports label products from a wide variety of label makers.

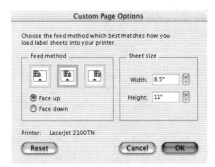

Figure 15 Use this dialog to provide additional printing information for non-standard label sizes and feed methods.

To set label options

1. Open the Labels dialog (**Figure 12**).

2. Enter the name and address of the person to whom the label should be addressed in the Address box.

3. To select the type of label you want to print on, click the Options button in the Label area to display the Label Options dialog (**Figure 13**). Select the appropriate Printer information radio button, then choose an option from the Label products pop-up menu (**Figure 14**) and select the product number for the label you want to use. Then click OK.

4. Back in the Labels dialog (**Figure 12**), select an option in the Number of Labels area:

   ▲ **Full page of the same label** prints the entire page of labels with the name and address that appears in the Address box.

   ▲ **Single label** prints only one label. If you select this option, be sure to enter the row and column number (if applicable) for the label you want to print.

5. If the label uses non-standard paper size, click the Customize button in the Printing Options area. Then use the Custom Page Options dialog that appears (**Figure 15**) to set options for the feed method and sheet size. Click OK.

✔ Tips

■ If you are creating a label for a letter in the active document window, the Address may already be filled in based on the inside address of the letter. You can "help" Word enter the correct address in this box by selecting the recipient's address before opening the Labels dialog.

Continued on next page...

SETTING LABEL OPTIONS

Continued from previous page.

- To include a postal barcode on the label, turn on the Delivery point barcode check box in the Address area (**Figure 12**).

- If you entered your address in the User Information pane of the Preferences dialog (**Figure 6**) or in Entourage (software that's part of Microsoft Office), you can automatically enter your own address by turning on the Use my address check box in the Labels dialog (**Figure 12**). This is a handy way to create a sheet of return address labels. I discuss User Information preferences in **Chapter 15** and Entourage in **Chapter 13**.

- If you're not sure which Product number to select in step 3, consult the information on the box of labels.

- You can create your own custom label settings. In step 3, click the New Label button to display the New Custom dialog (**Figure 16**). Enter a name and measurements for the label, and click OK. The name of your new labels will appear in the Product number area of the Label Options dialog (**Figure 13**) when Other is selected from the Label products pop-up menu (**Figure 14**).

- In step 3, you can customize the selected label by clicking the Details button. The dialog that appears looks and works very much like the one in **Figure 16**. Make changes as desired and click OK.

- When printing single labels on a laser or inkjet printer, print on the labels at the bottom of the sheet first. This helps prevent printer jamming when labels at the top of the sheet have been removed.

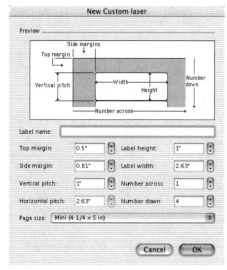

Figure 16 Use a dialog like this one to create your own custom label sizes.

SETTING LABEL OPTIONS

Figure 17 In this example, only one label was created. It was set up to print in the 1st column and 5th row of the sheet of labels.

To print labels

1. Click the Print button in the Labels dialog (**Figure 12**).

2. Word creates a new document for the envelope and displays the Print dialog (**Figure 10**).

3. Change options if necessary for the labels, and click Print to print them.

   Word prints the labels. When it is finished, the document window containing the labels is the active window (**Figure 17**).

✔ Tip

- I tell you more about printing in **Chapter 6**.

To save the labels

1. Print the labels as instructed above.

   or

   Click OK in the Labels dialog (**Figure 12**).

   The labels appear in the active document window (**Figure 17**).

2. Choose File > Save to display the Save As dialog and save the document on disk.

DATA MERGE

Data Merge

Microsoft Word's data merge feature enables you to create mailing labels, form letters, and other documents based on database information. This feature merges fields or categories of information with static text to produce merged documents.

The data merge process uses two special kinds of documents:

◆ A **main document** contains the information that remains the same for each version of the merged document. In a form letter, for example, the main document would consist of the letter text that appears in every letter.

◆ A **data source** contains the information that changes for each version of a merged document. In a form letter, the data source would consist of the names and addresses of the individuals who will receive the letter.

The results of a data merge can be sent directly to the printer or saved as a file on disk.

✔ Tips

■ You can use a single main document with any number of data sources. Similarly, you can use a data source with any number of main documents.

■ You can create a data source with Word as I explain in this chapter or with another application such as Microsoft Excel or FileMaker Pro.

■ Word's data merge feature also includes powerful query and conditional functions. These are advanced features that are beyond the scope of this book.

■ This feature was referred to as Mail Merge in some previous versions of Word.

The Data Merge Manager

Word's Data Merge Manager (**Figure 1**) is a floating palette that helps you create or identify the main document and data source for a merge and merge the files.

To open the Data Merge Manager

Choose Tools > Data Merge Manager (**Figure 2**).

✔ Tips

- The Data Merge Manager appears automatically when you open a main or data source document.

- The Data Merge Manager is a reworked version of the Mail Merge Helper that was in previous versions of Word.

To use the Data Merge Manager: an overview

1. Open the Data Merge Manager (**Figure 1**).

2. Choose an option from the Create pop-up menu in the Main Document area (**Figure 3**).

3. If desired, edit the main document's static text.

4. Choose an option from the Get Data pop-up menu in the Data Source area (**Figure 4**).

5. If desired, edit the data source's contents.

6. If necessary, edit the main document to include fields from the data source.

7. Click a Merge button to perform the merge.

✔ Tips

- I provide details for all of these steps throughout this chapter.

- To use the Data Merge Manager for an existing main document, open the main document first, then follow these steps.

Figure 1
The Data Merge Manager.

Figure 2
Choose Data Merge Manager from the Tools menu.

Figure 3
The Create pop-up menu.

Figure 4
The Get Data pop-up menu.

Figure 5 An example of a main document for a form letter.

Creating a Main Document

A main document (**Figure 5**) has two components:

◆ **Static text** that does not change. In a form letter, for example, static text would be the information that remains the same for each individual who will get the letter.

◆ **Data merge fields** that indicate what data source information should be merged into the document and where it should go. In a form letter, the static text *Dear* might be followed by the field *«FirstName»*. When merged, the contents of the FirstName field are merged into the document after the word *Dear* to result in *Dear Joe*, *Dear Sally*, etc.

Normally, a main document can be created with one or two steps:

◆ Enter the static text first, then insert the fields when the data source is complete. This method is useful when you use an existing document as a main document.

◆ Enter the static text and insert the fields at the same time when the data source document is complete. This method may save time and prevent confusion when creating a main document from scratch.

✔ Tips

■ You cannot insert fields into a main document until after the data source has been created and associated with the main document.

■ You enter and edit static text in a main document the same way you do in any other Word document.

To create a main document

1. Open a document on which you want to base the main document (**Figure 6**).

   or

   Create a new document.

2. Open the Data Merge Manager (**Figure 1**).

3. Choose an option from the Create pop-up menu (**Figure 3**):

   ▲ **Form Letters** are letters customized for multiple recipients.

   ▲ **Labels** are labels addressed to multiple recipients. If you choose this option, the Label Options dialog appears (**Figure 7**). Use it to specify the type of printer, choose a label product, and select a product number. Then click OK.

   ▲ **Envelopes** are envelopes addressed to multiple recipients. If you choose this option, the Envelope dialog appears (**Figure 8**). Use it to specify return address and printing options for the envelope. Then click OK.

   ▲ **Catalog** is a collection of information about multiple items.

   The name and type of the main document appears in the Data Merge Manager (**Figure 9**).

4. Add or edit static text as desired.

5. Save the document.

✔ Tips

■ Do not add any static text at this point for mailing labels or envelopes. These main documents have special formatting needs that must be set up before you can add static text.

■ I tell you more about working with envelopes and labels in **Chapter 10**.

Figure 6 A form letter without merge fields.

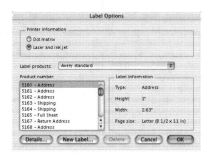

Figure 7 Use the Label Options dialog to set options for a data merge to mailing labels.

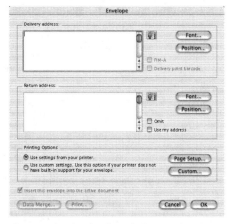

Figure 8 Use the Envelope dialog to set options for a data merge to envelopes.

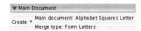

Figure 9 The name and type of the main document appears in the Data Merge Manager.

CREATING A MAIN DOCUMENT

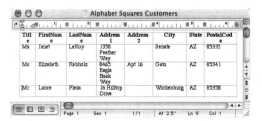

Figure 10 A data source with three records, created within Microsoft Word.

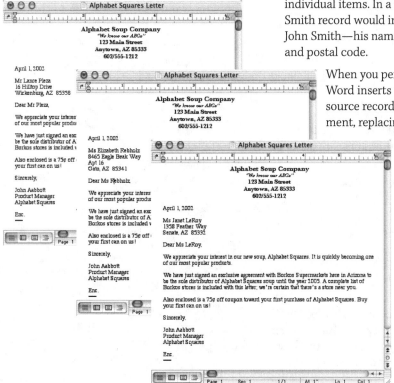

Figure 11 The data source in **Figure 10** merged into the main document in **Figure 5**.

Creating or Opening a Data Source

A data source (**Figure 10**) has two components:

◆ **Fields** are categories of information. In a form letter, for example, *Last Name* and *City* might be two fields. Each field has a unique name which identifies it in both the main document and data source document.

◆ **Records** are collections of information for individual items. In a form letter, the John Smith record would include all fields for John Smith—his name, address, city, state, and postal code.

When you perform a data merge, Word inserts the data from a data source record into a main document, replacing field names with field contents. It repeats the main document for each record in the data source (**Figure 11**).

✔ Tip

■ This chapter explains how to create or open a Word-based data source. You can also use the Office Address Book, a File-Maker Pro database file, or an Excel list as a data source; I tell you more about that in **Chapter 13**.

To create a data source

1. Make sure the main document is the active document window.

2. Choose New Data Source from the Get Data menu on the Data Merge Manager (**Figure 4**) to display the Create Data Source dialog (**Figure 12**). It lists commonly used field names for form letters, mailing labels, and envelopes.

3. Edit the Field names in header row list to include only the field names that you want in your data source document, in the order that you want them to appear:

   ▲ To remove a field name from the list, click to select it, then click the Remove Field Name button.

   ▲ To add a field name, enter it in the Field name text box, then click the Add Field Name button.

   ▲ To move a field name up or down in the list, click to select it, then click one of the Move buttons to the right of the list.

4. When you are finished editing the list, click OK.

5. A Save As dialog appears (**Figure 13**). Use it to name and save the data source file.

6. The Data Form dialog appears next (**Figure 14**). Enter information for a specific record into each of the text boxes. You can press ⎡Tab⎤ to move to the next text box or ⎡Shift⎤⎡Tab⎤ to move to the previous text box.

7. To add another new record, click the Add New button and repeat step 6.

8. When you are finished adding records, click OK.

   Word displays the name of the data source in the Data Merge Manager (**Figure 15**).

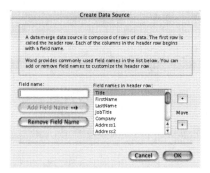

Figure 12 The Create Data Source dialog.

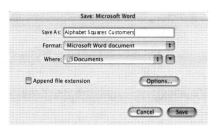

Figure 13 Use a standard Save As dialog to save the data source document.

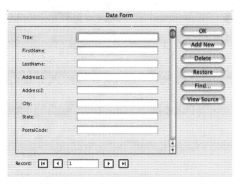

Figure 14 The Data Form dialog.

Figure 15 The name of the data source appears in the Data Merge Manager.

CREATING A DATA SOURCE

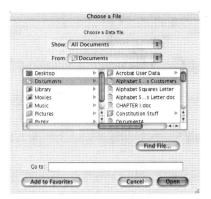

Figure 16 Use the Choose a File dialog to locate and open a data source.

✔ Tips

- Field names cannot include spaces.

- It's a good idea to save the data source in the same folder in which you have saved or will save the main document. This makes it easy to find the data source document when merging the main document.

- You can use other buttons in the Data Form dialog (**Figure 14**) to scroll through, edit, delete, or search for records.

- Clicking the View Source button in the Data Form dialog (**Figure 14**) displays the data source document in a Word document window (**Figure 10**).

- To edit a completed data source, click the Edit Data Source button ⊞ in the Data Source area of the Data Merge Manager (**Figure 15**). This displays the Data Form (**Figure 14**), which you can use to add, modify, or delete records.

To open an existing data source

1. Make sure the main document is the active document window.

2. Choose Open Data Source from the Get Data menu on the Data Merge Manager (**Figure 4**).

3. Use the Choose a File dialog that appears (**Figure 16**) to locate and select the file you want to use as a data source. Click Open.

   Word displays the name of the data source in the Data Merge Manager (**Figure 15**).

✔ Tips

- Use this technique to associate an existing data source with a main document.

- You can also use this technique to change the data source associated with a main document.

Completing a Main Document

Before you can perform a data merge, you must complete the main document by inserting merge fields. How you do this depends on the type of main document you have created.

To complete a form letter or catalog

1. If necessary, open the main document and display the Data Merge Manager (**Figure 17**).

2. Drag a field name from the Merge Field area of the Data Merge Manager into the document window. When the insertion point appears where you want the field (**Figure 18**), release the mouse button. The field appears at the insertion point. As shown in **Figure 19**, it consists of the name of the field surrounded by paired angle brackets («»).

3. Repeat step 2 for each merge field that you want to insert.

    Figure 5 shows an example of a main document with merge fields.

✔ Tips

■ Be sure to include proper spacing and punctuation as necessary between merge fields. To do this, position the insertion point where you want the space or punctuation to appear and press the appropriate keyboard key to insert it.

■ If you drag a field to the wrong place, simply select it and drag it to the correct position within the document window.

■ To remove a field, select it and press Delete.

Figure 17 Display the main document and the Data Merge Manager.

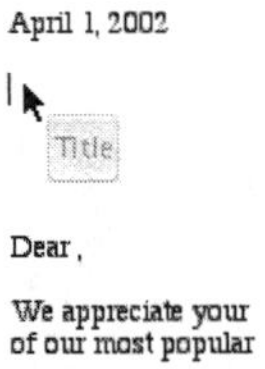

April 1, 2002

Title

Dear,

We appreciate your
of our most popular

Figure 18 When you drag a field into the document window, a tiny document icon appears beside the mouse pointer.

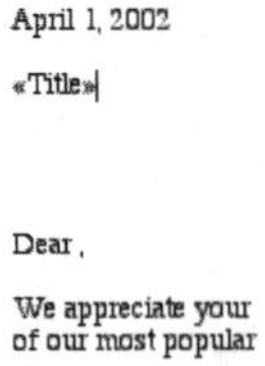

April 1, 2002

«Title»

Dear,

We appreciate your
of our most popular

Figure 19 The field appears at the insertion point.

Figure 20 The Edit Labels dialog.

Figure 21
Use the Insert Merge Field pop-up menu to select merge fields for the label.

Figure 22 The field you select from the Insert Merge Field menu is entered.

Figure 23 Merge fields for a name and address.

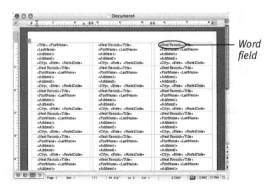

Word field

Figure 24 A mailing labels main document.

To complete mailing labels

1. Create or open a data source for a mailing labels main document as instructed earlier in this chapter. The Edit Labels dialog (**Figure 20**) will appear as part of this process.

2. Choose a merge field from the Insert Merge Field menu (**Figure 21**). The field is inserted in the Sample label box (**Figure 22**).

3. Repeat step 2 for each merge field that you want to include on the label. When you're finished, it might look something like **Figure 23**.

4. Click OK to save your settings. The merge fields appear in the main document window (**Figure 24**).

✔ Tips

- If the Edit Labels dialog does not appear, click the Edit Labels for Data Merge button in the Data Source area of the Data Merge Manager.

- Be sure to include proper spacing and punctuation as necessary between merge fields. To do this, position the insertion point in the Sample label box where you want the space or punctuation to appear and press the appropriate keyboard key to insert it.

- Do not change the Word fields included in the mailing labels main document (**Figure 24**). Altering or removing a field can prevent the mailing labels from merging or printing properly.

COMPLETING A MAILING LABELS DOCUMENT

To complete envelopes

1. If necessary, open the main document and display the Data Merge Manager (**Figure 25**).

2. Drag a field name from the Merge Field area of the Data Merge Manager into the address box in the document window. When the insertion point appears where you want the field (**Figure 26**), release the mouse button. The field appears at the insertion point (**Figure 27**).

3. Repeat step 2 for each merge field that you want to insert.

Figure 28 shows an example of a main document for envelopes with merge fields.

✔ Tip

■ Be sure to include proper spacing and punctuation as necessary between merge fields. To do this, position the insertion point in the document window where you want the space or punctuation to appear and press the appropriate keyboard key to insert it.

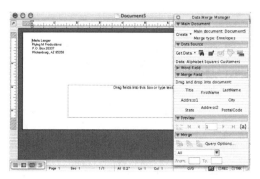

Figure 25 Display the main document and the Data Merge Manager.

Figure 26 When you drag a field into the document window, a tiny document icon appears beside the mouse pointer.

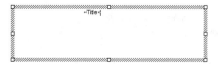

Figure 27 The field appears at the insertion point.

Figure 28 An envelopes main document.

Figure 29
The Data Merge
Manager offers
several options
for merging data.

Merging Documents

The last step in performing a data merge is to merge the main document and data source.

The Data Merge Manager offers several buttons you can use to merge data (**Figure 29**):

◆ **View Merged Data** [icon] displays the merged documents onscreen, enabling you to spot potential problems before actually performing the merge.

◆ **Merge to Printer** [icon] merges the documents directly to paper, labels, or envelopes to create final output.

◆ **Merge to New Document** [icon] creates a file with all of the merged data. The resulting file can be saved, modified, or printed another time.

To view merged data on screen

1. Display the main document and the Data Merge Manager.

2. Click the View Merged Data button [icon] in the Preview area of the Data Merge Manager.

   The merge field names in the main document are replaced with the contents of the first record in the data source (**Figures 11**, **30**, and **31**.)

✔ Tip

■ You can scroll through the records in the data source while viewing merged records by clicking the First Record [icon], Previous Record [icon], Next Record [icon], and Last Record [icon] buttons in the Preview area of the Data Merge Manager.

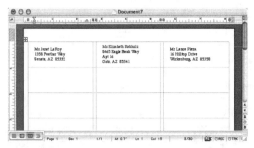

Figure 30 Viewing merged data for a mailing labels main document.

Figure 31 Viewing merged data for an envelopes main document.

MERGING DOCUMENTS

225

To merge to a printer or to a new document

1. Display the main document and the Data Merge Manager.

2. If necessary, choose an option from the pop-up menu in the Merge area of the Data Merge Manager (**Figure 32**):

   ▲ **All** merges all of the records.

   ▲ **Current Record** merges just the record number indicated in the text box in the Preview area of the Data Merge Manager (**Figure 29**).

   ▲ **Custom** enables you to set the starting and ending record number. If you choose this option, enter values in the text boxes beneath the pop-up menu.

3. To merge directly to a printer, click the Merge to Printer button 🖶 in the Merge area.

   or

   To merge to a new document, click the Merge to New Document button 🗋 in the Merge area.

4. If you are merging to a printer, Word displays the Print dialog (**Figure 33**). Set print options as desired and click the Print button.

   or

   If you are merging to a new document, Word creates the new document (**Figure 34**) and displays it as the active window. You can edit, save, or print the document.

✔ Tip

■ I tell you more about printing in **Chapter 6**.

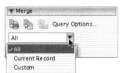

Figure 32 To merge less than all of the records, choose an option from this pop-up menu.

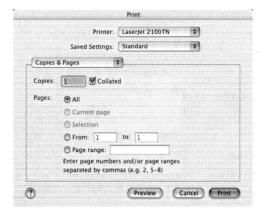

Figure 33 The Print dialog.

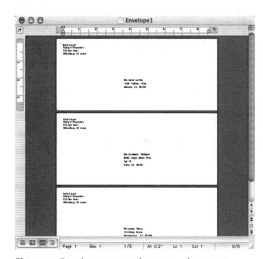

Figure 34 Envelopes merged to a new document.

WORKING WITH OTHERS

Collaboration Features

In office environments, a document is often the work of many people. In the old days, a draft document would be printed and circulated among reviewers. Along the way, it would be marked up with colored ink and covered with sticky notes full of comments. Some poor soul would have to make sense of all the markups and notes to create a clean document. The process was time consuming and was sometimes repeated through several drafts to fine-tune the document for publication.

Microsoft Word, which is widely used in office environments, includes many features that make the collaboration process quicker and easier:

- ◆ **Properties** stores information about the document's creator and contents.

- ◆ **Comments** enables reviewers to enter notes about the document. The notes don't print—unless you want them to.

- ◆ **Versions** enables reviewers to save multiple versions of the same document. At any time, you can revert to a previous version.

- ◆ **Revision Tracking** enables reviewers to edit the document while keeping the original document intact. Changes can be accepted or rejected to finalize the document.

- ◆ **Document Protection** limits how a document can be changed.

Document Properties

The Properties dialog (**Figures 2** and **4**) enables you to store information about a document. This information can be viewed by anyone who opens the document.

✔ Tips

■ The Properties dialog is organized into tabs for storing information. I cover the Summary and Statistics tabs here; explore the other tabs on your own.

■ Information in the Properties dialog is also used by Find File, Word's internal file searching feature. A discussion of Find File is beyond the scope of this book, however, you can explore it on your own by clicking the Find File button in Word's Open dialog (**Figure 3**).

To open the Properties dialog

1. Open the document for which you want to view or edit properties.

2. Choose File > Properties (**Figure 1**).

To enter summary information

1. Open the Properties dialog.

2. If necessary, click the Summary tab to display its options (**Figure 2**).

3. Enter or edit information in each field as desired:

   ▲ **Title** is the title of the document. This does not have to be the same as the file name. This field may already be filled in based on the first line of the document.

   ▲ **Subject** is the subject of the document.

   ▲ **Author** is the person who created the document. This field may already be filled in based on information stored in the User Information pane of the Preferences dialog.

Figure 1
The File menu.

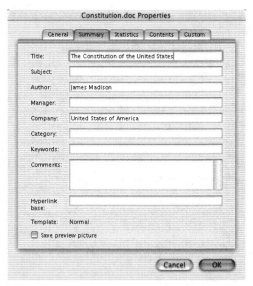

Figure 2 The Summary tab of the Properties dialog offers text boxes for entering information about the document.

DOCUMENT PROPERTIES

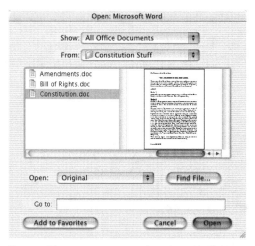

Figure 3 When you create a preview picture in the Summary tab of the Properties dialog, the preview appears in the Open dialog.

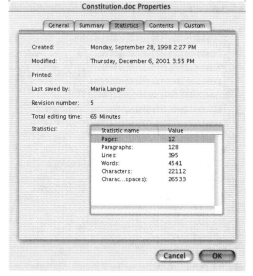

Figure 4 The Statistics tab of the Properties dialog provides additional information about the document.

▲ **Manager** is the person responsible for the document content.

▲ **Company** is the organization for which the author or manager works.

▲ **Category** is a category name assigned to the document. It can be anything you like.

▲ **Keywords** are important words related to the document.

▲ **Comments** are notes about the document.

▲ **Hyperlink base** is an Internet address or path to a folder on a hard disk or network volume. This option works in conjunction with hyperlinks inserted in the document.

4. To create a document preview image that will appear in the Preview area of the Open dialog (**Figure 3**), turn on the Save preview picture check box.

5. Click OK to save your entries.

✔ Tips

■ It is not necessary to enter information in any Summary tab text boxes (**Figure 2**).

■ I tell you about the User Information pane of the Preferences dialog in **Chapter 15** and about Hyperlinks in **Chapter 14**.

To view document statistics

1. Open the Properties dialog.

2. If necessary, click the Statistics tab to display its information (**Figure 4**).

3. When you are finished viewing statistics, click OK to dismiss the dialog.

✔ Tip

■ Information in the Statistics tab (**Figure 4**) is automatically calculated by Word and cannot be changed.

Comments

Comments are annotations that you and other document reviewers can add to a document. These notes can be viewed on screen but don't print unless you want them to.

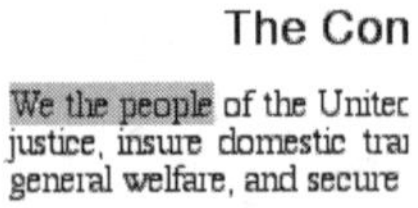

To insert a comment

1. Select the text for which you want to insert a comment (**Figure 5**).

2. Choose Insert > Comment (**Figure 6**).

   A few things happen: A comment marker (your initials and a number within brackets) is inserted after the selected text, the text is highlighted with yellow, the window splits, and the insertion point moves to the bottom pane of the window beside your initials there (**Figure 7**).

3. Type in your comment. It can be as long or as short as you like (**Figure 8**).

✔ Tips

- Word gets your initials from the User Information pane of the Preferences dialog. I tell you more about that in **Chapter 15**.

- The initials, number, and brackets that appear in the document window (**Figure 7**) do not print.

To close the Comment pane

Click the Close button at the top of the Comment pane (**Figure 8**).

The pane closes and the initials disappear. The only indication that a comment exists is the highlighting.

Figure 5 Start by selecting the text you want to enter a comment about.

Figure 6 Choose Comment from the Insert menu.

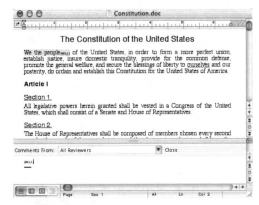

Figure 7 Word prepares to accept your comment.

Figure 8 Enter your comment in the bottom pane of the window.

INSERTING COMMENTS

Figure 9 When you position the mouse pointer over highlighted text, the comment appears in a yellow box.

Figure 10 Choose Comments from the View menu.

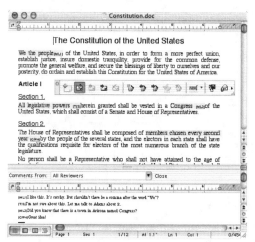

Figure 11 When the Comment pane appears, it shows all comments entered in the document.

Figure 12 Use this pop-up menu to choose the person whose comments you want to see. (I'd choose Jefferson.)

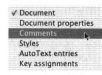

Figure 13 Choose Comments from the Print what pop-up menu in the Print dialog to print document comments.

To view comments

Position the mouse pointer over highlighted text. A yellow box appears containing the name of the person who wrote the comment and the comment itself (**Figure 9**).

or

Choose View > Comments (**Figure 10**). The window splits again. The bottom pane can be scrolled so you can see all comments entered for the document (**Figure 11**).

✔ Tips

- When you display the Comment pane as instructed above, the Reviewing toolbar may appear (**Figure 11**). It includes buttons for Word's Comments and Revisions features.

- To view only those comments made by a specific person, choose the person's name from the Comments From pop-up menu at the top of the Comment pane (**Figure 12**).

To delete a comment

1. If necessary, display the Comment pane (**Figure 11**).

2. In the document window, select the comment marker for the comment that you want to remove.

3. Press Delete or click the Delete Comment button on the Reviewing toolbar.

   All traces of the comment disappear.

To print comments

1. Follow the instructions in **Chapter 6** to prepare the document for printing and open the Print dialog.

2. Choose Microsoft Word from the pop-up menu at the top of the settings area.

3. Choose Comments from the Print what pop-up menu (**Figure 13**).

4. Click Print.

VIEWING, DELETING, & PRINTING COMMENTS

Versions

Word's Versions feature enables you to save multiple versions of a document. You can then revert to any version to undo editing changes made over time.

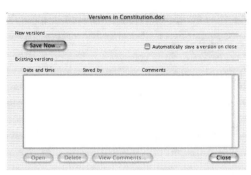

To save a version

1. Choose File > Versions (**Figure 1**).

2. In the Versions dialog that appears (**Figure 14**), click Save Now.

Figure 14 The Versions dialog before any versions have been saved.

3. The Save Version dialog appears (**Figure 15**). If desired, enter comments about the version, then click OK.

    The current state of the document is saved as a version within the document file.

To automatically save a version of the file when you close it

1. Choose File > Versions (**Figure 1**).

2. In the Versions dialog that appears (**Figure 14**), turn on the Automatically save a version on close check box.

3. Click Close.

    From that point forward, every time you close the document, it will be saved as a version.

Figure 15 Use this dialog to enter comments about the version you are saving.

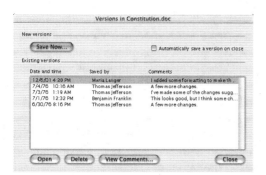

Figure 16 The versions that have been saved are listed in reverse chronological order.

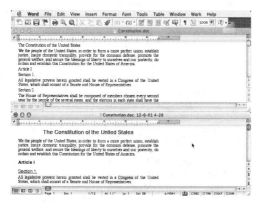

Figure 17 When you open another version of a document, it appears in its own window. Word automatically arranges the windows so you can see them both.

Figure 18 A dialog like this one appears when you delete a version.

To open a version

1. With a document that includes multiple versions open and active, choose File > Versions (**Figure 1**).

2. In the Versions dialog that appears (**Figure 16**), select the version you want to open.

3. Click Open.

   The version of the document that you selected opens. Word arranges both document windows—the one that was open in step 1 and the one that you opened in step 3—so you can see them at the same time (**Figure 17**).

✔ Tips

- You can click the View Comments button in the Versions dialog (**Figure 16**) to see the entire text of a comment. It appears in a dialog like the one in **Figure 15**.

- If you save an opened version of a document, it is saved as a separate document.

To delete a version

1. Choose File > Versions (**Figure 1**).

2. In the Versions dialog that appears (**Figure 16**), select the version you want to delete.

3. Click Delete.

4. A confirmation dialog like the one in **Figure 18** appears. Click Yes.

   The version you deleted is removed from the list in the Versions dialog.

✔ Tip

- Each time you save a file version, you increase the size of the file. If your file becomes too large, you can delete early versions to reduce its size.

Revision Tracking

Word's Revision Tracking feature makes it possible for multiple reviewers to edit a document without actually changing the document. Instead, each reviewer's markups are displayed in color in the document window. At the conclusion of the reviewing process, someone with final say over document contents reviews all of the edits and either accepts or rejects each of them. The end result is a final document that incorporates the accepted changes.

Figure 19
Use commands on the Track Changes submenu to set up and use Word's revision tracking feature.

To turn revision tracking on or off

1. Choose Tools > Track Changes > Highlight Changes (**Figure 19**).

2. In the Highlight Changes dialog that appears (**Figure 20**), toggle check boxes to set up the revision tracking feature:

    ▲ **Track changes while editing** enables the revision tracking feature. Turn on this check box to track the changes you make as you modify the document. Turn off this check box to disable the revision tracking feature.

    ▲ **Highlight changes on screen** displays revision marks in the document window.

    ▲ **Highlight changes in printed document** displays revision marks in document printouts.

3. Click OK.

Figure 20 The Highlight Changes dialog lets you enable and configure the revision tracking feature.

✔ Tip

■ Clicking the Options button in the Highlight Changes dialog (**Figure 20**) displays the Track Changes tab of the Preferences dialog. I tell you more about preferences in **Chapter 15**.

Figure 21 When you edit the document, your changes appear as revision marks.

Figure 22 When you point to a revision mark, a box appears with information about it.

To track changes

1. Turn on revision tracking as instructed on the previous page.

2. Make changes to the document.

   Your changes appear as colored markups and a vertical line appears in the left margin beside each edit (**Figure 21**).

✔ Tip

■ If the document is edited by more than one person, each person's revision marks appear in a different color. This makes it easy to distinguish one editor's changes from another's.

To view revision information

Point to a revision mark. A yellow box with information about the change appears (**Figure 22**).

✔ Tip

■ This is a handy way to see who made a change and when it was made.

To accept or reject revisions

1. Choose Tools > Track Changes > Accept or Reject Changes (**Figure 19**).

2. The Accept or Reject Changes dialog appears (**Figure 23**).

   ▲ To accept all changes, click the Accept All button. A dialog like the one in **Figure 24** appears. Click Yes. All revisions are incorporated into the document and the revision marks disappear. Skip the remaining steps.

   ▲ To reject all changes, click the Reject All button. A dialog like the one in **Figure 25** appears. Click Yes. The revision marks disappear and the document is returned to the way it was before revision tracking was enabled. Skip the remaining steps.

   ▲ To review changes one at a time, click one of the Find buttons. Then continue with step 3 below.

3. Word highlights one of the changes in the document window and displays its information in the Accept or Reject Changes dialog (**Figure 26**).

   ▲ To accept the change, click the Accept button. The change is incorporated into the document and its revision mark disappears.

   ▲ To reject the changes, click the Reject button. The revision mark disappears.

   ▲ To skip over the change for now (to give you time to think about it or to let someone else review it), click the Find button again.

4. Repeat step 3 for each change Word highlights. When it has reached the end of the document, it displays a dialog, telling you.

5. Click Close to dismiss the Accept or Reject Changes dialog.

Figure 23 The Accept or Reject Changes dialog.

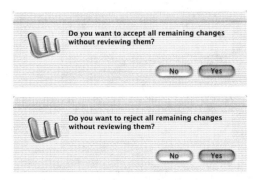

Figures 24 & 25 Word confirms that you want to accept all (top) or reject all (bottom) changes.

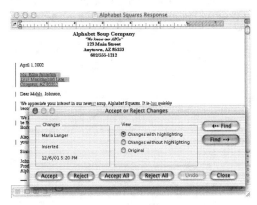

Figure 26 Word highlights the change in the document window and displays its information in the Accept or Reject Changes dialog.

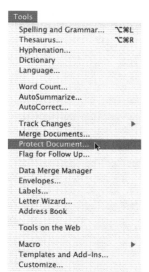

Figure 27
Choose Protect
Document from
the Tools menu.

Figure 28
Use the Protect
Document dialog
to set document
protection options.

Figure 29
Re-enter the
protection pass-
word in the Confirm
Password dialog.

Document Protection

Word's Document Protection feature enables
you to limit the types of changes others can
make to a document. Specifically, you can limit
changes to:

◆ **Tracked changes** enables users to change
the document only with the revision
tracking feature turned on.

◆ **Comments** enables users to add only
comments to the document.

◆ **Forms** enables users to enter information
only into form fields. (This is an advanced
feature of Word that is far beyond the
scope of this book.)

To protect a document

1. Choose Tools > Protect Document
(**Figure 27**).

2. In the Protect Document dialog that
appears (**Figure 28**), select the type of
protection you want.

3. If desired, enter a password in the Password
text box.

4. Click OK.

5. If you entered a password, the Confirm
Password dialog appears (**Figure 29**). Enter
the password again and click OK.

✔ Tips

■ Entering a password in the Protect Document dialog (**Figure 28**) is optional.
However, if you do not use a password
with this feature, the document can be
unprotected by anyone.

■ If you enter a password in the Protect
Document dialog (**Figure 28**), don't forget
it! If you can't remember the password, you
can't unprotect the document!

PROTECTING A DOCUMENT

To work with a protected document

What you can do with a protected document depends on how you protected it:

◆ If you protected the document for revision tracking, the revision tracking feature is enabled. Any change you make to the document appears as revision marks.

◆ If you protected the document for comments, you can only insert comments in the document. If you attempt to edit text, an alert sounds.

To unprotect a document

1. Choose Tools > Unprotect Document (**Figure 30**).

2. If protection is enforced with a password, a dialog like the one in **Figure 31** appears. Enter the password and click OK.

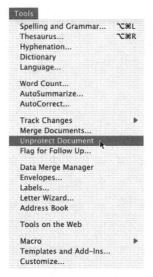

Figure 30
Choose Unprotect Document from the Tools menu.

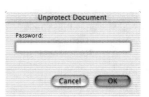

Figure 31 Enter the protection password in this dialog to unprotect the document.

UNPROTECTING A DOCUMENT

USING OTHER APPLICATIONS

Using Word with Other Applications

Word works well with a number of other applications. These programs can expand Word's capabilities:

- ◆ OLE objects created with other Microsoft Office applications can be inserted into Word documents.

- ◆ Word documents can be inserted into documents created with other Microsoft Office applications.

- ◆ Word documents can be e-mailed to others using Entourage.

- ◆ Entourage address book information and FileMaker Pro databases can be used as data sources for a Word data merge.

This chapter explains how you can use Word with some of these other applications.

✔ Tip

- ■ This chapter provides information about applications other than Microsoft Word. To follow instructions for a specific program, that program must be installed on your computer.

OLE Objects

An *object* is all or part of a file created with an OLE-aware application. *OLE*, or *Object Linking and Embedding* is a Microsoft technology that enables you to insert a file as an object within a document (**Figure 1**)—even if the file was created with a different application. Double-clicking the inserted object launches the application that created it so you can modify its contents.

Word's Object command enables you to insert OLE objects in two different ways:

◆ **Create and insert a new OLE object.** This method launches a specific OLE-aware application so you can create an object. When you are finished, you quit the application to insert the new object in your document.

◆ **Insert an existing OLE object.** This method displays the Insert as Object dialog (**Figure 6**) that you can use to locate, select, and insert an existing file as an object.

✔ Tips

■ All Microsoft applications are OLE-aware. Many software applications created by other developers are also OLE-aware; check the documentation that came with a specific software package for details.

■ Microsoft Word comes with a number of OLE-aware applications that can be used to insert objects. The full Microsoft Office package includes even more of these applications.

■ **Chapter 7**, which covered inserting text and multimedia elements, offered a glimpse of OLE objects in its discussion of Microsoft Graph, one of the OLE-aware applications that comes with Word.

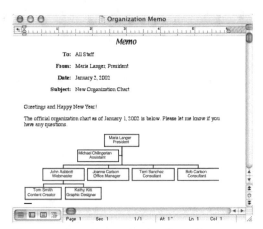

Figure 1 A Microsoft Organization Chart object inserted in a Microsoft Word document.

Figure 2
Choose Object from the Insert menu.

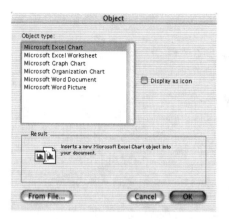

Figure 3 The Object dialog. The options shown here are those that are part of a Microsoft Office X installation.

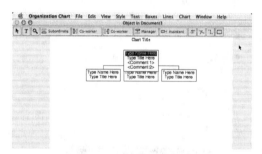

Figure 4 The default Microsoft Organization Chart window.

Figure 5
The Quit command on the Organization Chart menu.

To insert a new object

1. Position the insertion point where you want the object to appear.

2. Choose Insert > Object (**Figure 2**) to display the Object dialog (**Figure 3**).

3. Click to select the type of object that you want to insert.

4. Click OK.

   Word launches the application that you selected. It may take a moment for it to appear. **Figure 4** shows the default Microsoft Organization Chart window and toolbar.

5. Use the application to create the object that you want.

6. When you are finished creating the object, choose the Quit command from the *Application Name* menu (**Figure 5**).

7. If a dialog appears, asking whether you want to update the object in the document, click Update.

   The application closes and the object is inserted in the document (**Figure 1**).

✔ Tips

- The exact wording of the Quit command in step 6 varies depending on the application and the name of the document with which you are working.

- For more information about using one of the OLE-aware applications that comes with Word or Office, use the application's Help menu or Office Assistant.

INSERTING OBJECTS

To insert an existing object

1. Position the insertion point where you want the object to appear.

2. Choose Insert > Object (**Figure 2**) to display the Object dialog (**Figure 3**).

3. Click the From File button to display the Insert as Object dialog (**Figure 6**).

4. Locate and select the file that you want to insert.

5. Click Insert. The file is inserted as an object in the document (**Figure 7**).

✔ Tip

■ To insert a file as an object, the application that created the file must be properly installed on your computer or accessible through a network connection. Word displays a dialog if the application is missing.

To customize an inserted object

Follow the instructions in the previous two sections to create and insert a new object or insert an existing object. In the Object (**Figure 3**) or Insert as Object (**Figure 6**) dialog, turn on check boxes as desired:

◆ **Link to File** creates a link to the object's file so that when it changes, the object inserted within the Word document can change. This is similar to inserting a link, which I tell you about in **Chapter 7**. This option is only available when inserting an existing file as an object.

◆ **Display as icon** (**Figure 8**) displays an icon that represents the object rather than the object itself.

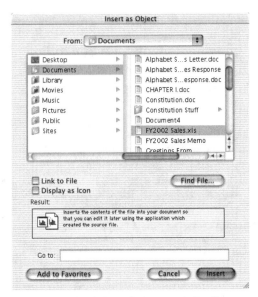

Figure 6 Use this dialog to insert an existing file as an object.

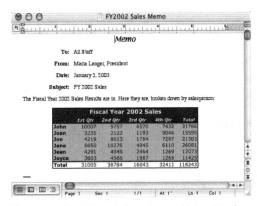

Figure 7 An Excel X worksheet inserted into a Word document.

Figure 8 An Excel X worksheet displayed as an icon.

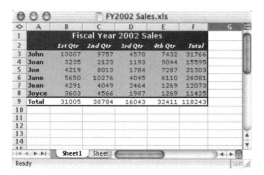

Figure 9 Spreadsheet software like Excel is most often used to create worksheets full of financial information.

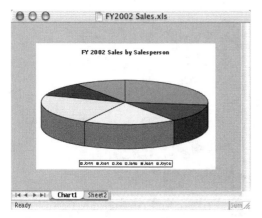

Figure 10 Excel has built-in features for managing lists of information.

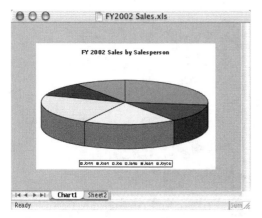

Figure 11 Excel also includes powerful charting capabilities.

Using Excel with Word

Excel is the spreadsheet component of Microsoft Office. A *spreadsheet* is like a computerized accountant's worksheet—you enter information and formulas and the software automatically calculates results (**Figure 9**). Best of all, if you change one of the numbers in the worksheet, the results of calculations automatically change as necessary.

You can use Excel with Word to:

◆ Include information from an Excel document in a Word document (**Figure 7**).

◆ Perform a Word data merge with an Excel list as a data source.

✔ Tips

■ Spreadsheet software is especially handy for financial calculations, but it is often used to maintain lists of data (**Figure 10**).

■ Excel also includes powerful charting capabilities so you can create charts based on spreadsheet information (**Figure 11**).

■ To learn more about using Excel X, pick up a copy of *Excel X for Mac OS X: Visual QuickStart Guide*, a Peachpit Press book by Maria Langer.

To include Excel document content in a Word document

To insert an Excel document as an object in a Word document, consult the section about OLE objects earlier in this chapter.

or

1. In the Excel document, select the cells (**Figure 12**) or chart (**Figure 13**) that you want to include in the Word document.

2. Choose Edit > Copy or press ⌃ ⌘ C (**Figures 14a** and **14b**).

3. Switch to Word and position the insertion point in the Word document where you want the Excel content to appear.

4. Choose Edit > Paste Cells or press ⌃ ⌘ V (**Figure 15**). The selection appears in the Word document at the insertion point (**Figures 16** and **17**).

✔ Tips

- You can also use drag-and-drop editing techniques to drag an Excel document selection into a Word document. I tell you about drag-and-drop in **Chapter 2**.

- Worksheet cells are pasted into Word as a Word table (**Figure 16**). I tell you more about tables in **Chapter 9**.

- An Excel chart is pasted into Word as a picture (**Figure 17**). I tell you more about working with pictures in **Chapter 7**.

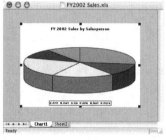

Figure 12
Select the cells...

Figure 13
...or the chart that you want to include.

Figures 14a & 14b
Choosing Copy from Excel's Edit menu when worksheet cells are selected (left) and when a chart is selected (above).

Figure 15
Choosing Paste Cells from Word's Edit menu.

Figure 16 Worksheet cells are pasted into a Word document as a Word table.

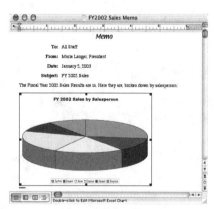

Figure 17 A chart is pasted into a Word document as a picture.

USING EXCEL WITH WORD

Figure 18
Choose Open Data Source from the Get Data pop-up menu.

Figure 19 Use the Choose a File dialog to open the file you want to use as the data source.

Figure 20
Set options in the Open Worksheet dialog to indicate the worksheet and cells where the data resides.

Figure 21
Field names from the Excel list appear in the Merge Field area of the Data Merge Manager.

To use an Excel list as a data source for a data merge

1. Follow the instructions in **Chapter 11** to display the Data Merge Manager and create a main document.

2. Choose Open Data Source from the Get Data pop-up menu in the Data Source area of the Data Merge Manager (**Figure 18**).

3. Use the Choose a File dialog that appears (**Figure 19**) to locate, select, and open the Excel file you want to use for the data merge.

4. Set options in the Open Worksheet dialog (**Figure 20**) to specify which worksheet and cells contain the list you want to use for the merge. Then click OK.

5. Follow the steps in **Chapter 11** to complete the main document with field names that appear in the Merge Field area of the Data Merge Manager (**Figure 21**) and perform the merge.

✔ Tip

■ I explain how to use Word's data merge feature in **Chapter 11**.

Using PowerPoint with Word

PowerPoint is the presentation software component of Microsoft Office. *Presentation software* enables you to create slides for use at meetings and seminars (**Figure 22**). The slides can be printed on paper, output as 35mm slides, saved as a QuickTime movie, or shown directly from the computer.

You can use PowerPoint with Word to:

◆ Create a PowerPoint presentation from a Word outline.

◆ Include a QuickTime movie created with PowerPoint in a Word document.

✔ Tip

■ To learn more about using PowerPoint, consult the documentation that came with the program or its onscreen help feature.

To use a Word outline in a PowerPoint presentation

1. Display the Word outline document you want to use in PowerPoint (**Figure 23**).

2. Choose File > Send To > Microsoft PowerPoint (**Figure 24**).

   The outline is imported into PowerPoint. A new slide is created for each top-level heading (**Figure 22**).

✔ Tip

■ I explain how to use Word's Outline feature in **Chapter 8**.

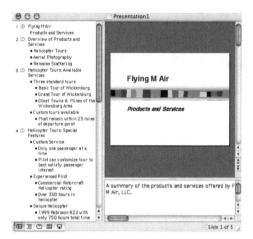

Figure 22 PowerPoint enables you to create slides for presenting information. This is the outline from **Figure 23**, with some formatting applied.

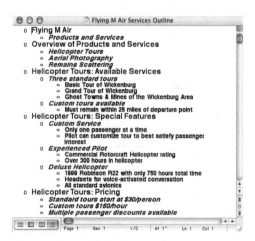

Figure 23 Start with the Word outline that you want to use in PowerPoint.

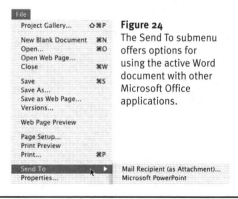

Figure 24
The Send To submenu offers options for using the active Word document with other Microsoft Office applications.

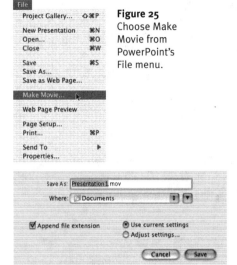

Figure 25
Choose Make
Movie from
PowerPoint's
File menu.

Figure 26 Use this dialog to save the presentation
as a movie.

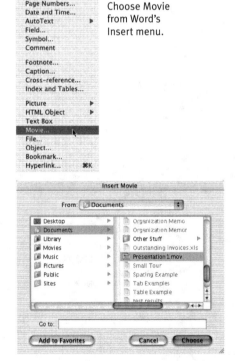

Figure 27
Choose Movie
from Word's
Insert menu.

Figure 28 Select the movie you want to insert.

To insert a PowerPoint QuickTime movie into a Word document

1. Display the PowerPoint presentation that you want to save as a QuickTime movie (**Figure 22**).

2. Choose File > Make Movie (**Figure 25**).

3. Use the dialog that appears (**Figure 26**) to name and save the current presentation as a movie.

4. Switch to Word and position the insertion point where you want the movie to appear.

5. Choose Insert > Movie (**Figure 27**).

6. The Insert Movie dialog appears (**Figure 28**). Use it to locate and choose the movie you created.

   The movie is inserted into the Word document (**Figure 29**).

✔ Tip

- I tell you more about inserting QuickTime movies into Word documents in **Chapter 7**.

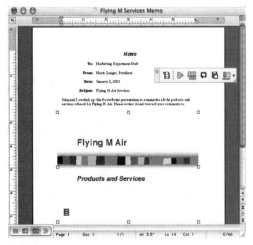

Figure 29 The movie is inserted in the document's drawing layer.

USING POWERPOINT WITH WORD

Using Entourage with Word

Entourage is the e-mail, newsgroup, and personal information management software component of Microsoft Office. *E-mail software* enables you to send and receive electronic mail messages (**Figure 30**). *Newsgroup software* enables you to participate in topical Internet message boards called *newsgroups*. *Personal information management software* enables you to store and organize address book (**Figure 31**) and calendar (**Figure 32**) data.

You can use Entourage with Word to:

◆ E-mail a Word document to a friend, family member, or co-worker.

◆ Perform a Word data merge with an Entourage address book as the data source.

◆ Flag a document for follow up so Entourage reminds you about it.

✔ Tip

■ To learn more about using Entourage, consult the documentation that came with the program or its onscreen help feature.

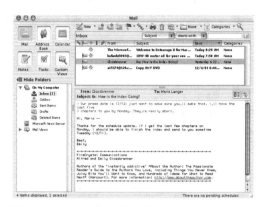

Figure 30 Entourage can handle e-mail, ...

Figure 31 ...address book information, ...

Figure 32 ...and calendar events.

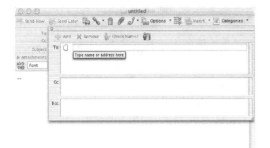

Figure 33 Entourage displays an untitled e-mail form.

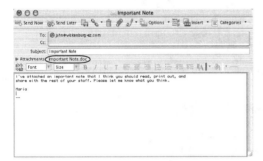

Figure 34 Here's what a finished message might look like. Note that the name of the Word document being sent appears in the Attachments area.

To send a Word document via e-mail

1. Display the Word document you want to send via e-mail.

2. Choose File > Send To > Mail Recipient (as Attachment) (**Figure 24**).

3. Word launches Entourage and displays an empty e-mail window with the To field selected (**Figure 33**). Enter the e-mail address for the person you want to send the document to and press (Return).

4. In the Subject field, enter a subject for the message and press (Tab).

5. In the message body, enter a message to accompany the file. **Figure 34** shows an example.

6. To send the message immediately, click the Send Now button. Entourage connects to the Internet and sends the message.

   or

   To save the message in your outbox so it is sent the next time you send and receive messages, click Send Later.

7. Switch back to Word to continue working with the document or Word.

✔ Tips

- These instructions assume that Entourage is the default e-mail program as set in the Internet preferences pane. If a different program has been set as the default e-mail program, ignore steps 3 through 6 and send the message as you normally would with your e-mail program.

- Entourage (or your default e-mail program) must be properly configured to send and receive e-mail messages. Check the program's documentation or onscreen help if you need assistance with setup.

USING ENTOURAGE WITH WORD

To use an Entourage address book as a data source for a data merge

1. Follow the instructions in **Chapter 11** to display the Data Merge Manager and create a main document.

2. Choose Office Address Book from the Get Data pop-up menu in the Data Source area of the Data Merge Manager (**Figure 35**).

3. Follow the steps in **Chapter 11** to complete the main document with field names that appear in the Merge Field area of the Data Merge Manager (**Figure 36**) and perform the merge.

✔ Tip

■ I explain how to use Word's data merge feature in **Chapter 11**.

To flag a document for follow up

1. Display the Word document you want to flag for follow up.

2. Click the Flag for Follow Up button 🚩 on the Standard toolbar.

3. In the Flag for Follow Up dialog that appears (**Figure 37**), set the date and time that you want to be reminded to work with the document. Then click OK.

   An entry is added to your Entourage Task list. When the date and time you specified approaches, a Reminders window like the one in **Figure 38** appears. You can double-click the name of the document in the Reminders window to open the document.

✔ Tip

■ The Reminders window will only appear at the appropriate time if either Word or Entourage is open.

Figure 35
Choose Office Address Book from the Get Data pop-up menu.

Figure 36
Field names from the Entourage address book appear in the Merge Field area of the Data Merge Manager.

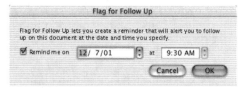

Figure 37 Use this dialog to enter a date and time to be reminded about a document.

Figure 38 Entourage reminds you with a dialog like this.

Figure 39 FileMaker Pro is an excellent program for storing, organizing, and creating reports for all kinds of data.

Figure 40 Choose FileMaker Pro from the Get Data pop-up menu in the Data Merge Manager.

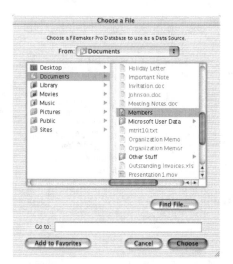

Figure 41 Use the Choose a File dialog to locate and choose the FileMaker Pro file you want to use as a data source.

Using FileMaker Pro with Word

FileMaker Pro is a database application from FileMaker, Inc. *Database software* enables you to store, organize, and create reports for all kinds of data (**Figure 39**). FileMaker Pro is easy to use and extremely flexible—it's no wonder that it's the top-selling database application for Macintosh users.

Word has the ability to use FileMaker Pro database information in a Word data merge. This makes Word more flexible than ever by simplifying the process of merging Word documents with data stored in FileMaker Pro.

✔ Tip

- To learn more about using FileMaker Pro, pick up a copy of *FileMaker Pro 5.5: Visual QuickStart Guide*, a Peachpit Press book by Nolan Hester.

To use a FileMaker Pro database file as a data source for a data merge

1. Follow the instructions in **Chapter 11** to display the Data Merge Manager and create a main document.

2. Choose FileMaker Pro from the Get Data pop-up menu in the Data Source area of the Data Merge Manager (**Figure 40**).

3. Use the Choose a File dialog that appears (**Figure 41**) to locate and choose the FileMaker Pro file you want to use as a data source.

4. The first screen of the FIleMaker Import Wizard appears (**Figure 42**). Use it to select the FileMaker Pro database fields you want to use in the data source:

Continued on next page...

Continued from previous page.

▲ To add a field to the Fields to import list, select it in the Available fields list and click the > button.

▲ To remove a field from the Fields to import list, select it and click the < button.

▲ To change the order of the fields in the Fields to import list, select one of the fields and click one of the triangle buttons to the right of the list.

5. When you are finished selecting fields, click Next.

6. In the next screen of the FileMaker Import Wizard (**Figure 43**), set criteria for selecting the records you want to import.

▲ To set the first criteria, choose options from the two pop-up menus in the Criteria 1 area to set the field and operator, then enter a value in the text box. Repeat this step to add additional criteria; be sure to select the And or Or radio button to specify how the criteria is to be used.

▲ To import all the records, leave the dialog as shown in **Figure 43**.

7. When you are finished setting criteria, click Finish. Word imports the records and displays the names of the fields you selected in the Merge Field area of the Data Merge Manager (**Figure 44**).

8. Follow the steps in **Chapter 11** to complete the main document with fields in the Data Merge Manager and perform the merge.

✔ Tip

■ I explain how to use Word's data merge feature in **Chapter 11**.

Figure 42 The first FileMaker Import Wizard dialog enables you to select the fields you want to import.

Figure 43 The second FileMaker Import Wizard dialog enables you to set criteria for importing records.

Figure 44
The fields you selected appear in the Data Merge Manager window's Merge Field area.

WEB PAGES

Web Pages

The World Wide Web has had a bigger impact on publishing than any other communication medium introduced in the past fifty years. Web pages, which can include text, graphics, and hyperlinks, can be published on the Internet or an intranet, making them available to audiences 24 hours a day, 7 days a week. They can provide information quickly and inexpensively to anyone who needs it.

Microsoft Word has built-in Web page creation, modification, and interaction tools. With Word, you can build Web pages and open links to other Web pages and sites.

✔ Tips

■ This chapter provides enough information to get you started using Word to create Web pages. Complete coverage of Web publishing, however is beyond the scope of this book.

■ To learn more about the World Wide Web and Web publishing, check these Peachpit Press books:

▲ *The Non-Designer's Web Book, Second Edition* by Robin Williams and John Tollett.

▲ *Putting Your Small Business on the Web* by Maria Langer.

Continued on next page...

Continued from previous page.

■ Web pages are normally viewed with a special kind of software called a *Web browser*. Microsoft Internet Explorer, Netscape Navigator, and Netscape Communicator are three examples of Web browsers.

■ To access the Internet, you need an Internet connection, either through a network or dial-up connection. Setting up a connection is beyond the scope of this book; consult the documentation that came with Mac OS or your Internet access software for more information.

■ To publish a Web page, you need access to a Web server. Contact your organization's Network Administrator or *Internet Service Provider* (*ISP*) for more information.

■ A *hyperlink* (or *link*) is text or a graphic that, when clicked, displays other information from the Web.

■ An *intranet* is like the Internet, but it exists only on the internal network of an organization and is usually closed to outsiders.

WEB PAGES

Figure 1
The File menu.

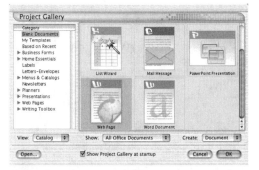

Figure 2 Select the Web Page preview in the Blank Documents category of the Project Gallery dialog.

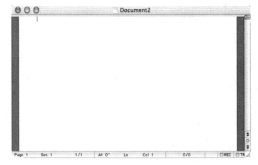

Figure 3 A blank document window for a Web page.

Creating a Web Page

Word offers three ways to create a Web page:

◆ The **Blank Web Page** template lets you create a Web page from scratch, using appropriate formatting options.

◆ **Web Page Templates** let you create Web pages, complete with graphic elements and links, for a specific purpose. Placeholder text helps you organize information on your pages.

◆ The **Save as Web Page** command lets you save a regular Word document as a Web page. This encodes the document and saves it as HTML.

✔ Tips

■ *HTML* (or *HyperText Markup Language*) is a system of codes for defining Web pages.

■ I explain how to save a regular Word document as an HTML file near the end of this chapter.

To use the Blank Web Page template

1. Choose File > Project Gallery (**Figure 1**) or press [Shift][⌃][⌘][P] to display the Project Gallery dialog (**Figure 2**).

2. Select the Blank Documents category.

3. Click the Web Page preview to select it.

4. Click OK. Word creates a blank new Web page and displays it in Online Layout view (**Figure 3**).

5. Enter and format text in the document window as desired to meet your needs.

✔ Tip

■ I explain how to enter and format text for a Web page a little later in this chapter.

To use other Web page templates

1. Choose File > Project Gallery (**Figure 1**) or press (Shift)(⌃)(⌘)(P) to display the Project Gallery dialog (**Figure 2**).

2. Click the Web Pages category to display the subcategories of Web page templates, then click one of the subcategory names to display the template previews (**Figure 4**).

3. Click the preview for the template you want to use.

4. Click OK. Word creates a new Web page document with placeholder text (**Figure 5**).

5. Edit placeholder text as desired to customize the Web page for your needs.

✔ Tips

- Each subcategory under the Web Pages category contains templates designed to be used together on a single Web site. For example, the Cypress subcategory's templates all share the same design elements so they'll look good when used together on a site.

- The colored underlined text that appears on Web pages are hypertext links. I tell you more about hypertext links later in this chapter.

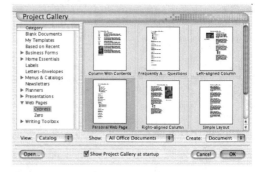

Figure 4 Select a Web Pages subcategory, then select the preview for the page template you want to use.

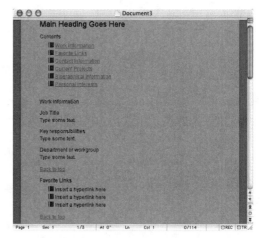

Figure 5 This example shows a Personal Web Page from the Cypress series of Web page templates.

CREATING A WEB PAGE

Figure 6 Select the text that you want to modify.

Figure 7 Whatever you type replaces the selected text.

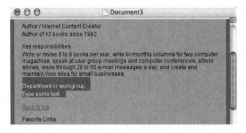

Figure 8 Select the text that you want to delete.

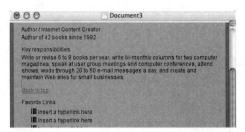

Figure 9 When you press (Delete), the selected text disappears.

Editing Text

You can add, edit, or delete text on a Web page the same way you add, edit, or delete text in a regular Word document.

✔ Tip

- For more detailed instructions about editing text, consult **Chapter 2**.

To add text

1. Position the insertion point where you want to add the text.

2. Type the text that you want to add.

To modify text

1. Select the text that you want to change (**Figure 6**).

2. Type in the replacement text.

    The selected text is deleted and the replacement text is inserted in its place (**Figure 7**).

To delete text

1. Select the text that you want to delete (**Figure 8**).

2. Press (Delete).

    The selected text is deleted (**Figure 9**).

EDITING TEXT

Formatting Text & Pages

You format text on a Web page the same way you format text in any other Word document: by using the Formatting Palette (**Figure 10**), Format menu commands (**Figure 11**) with their related dialogs, and shortcut keys.

Although the font and paragraph formatting techniques are the same for Web pages as they are for regular Word documents, there are two additional options on the Format menu (**Figure 11**) that are especially useful for Web pages:

- **Background** enables you to set the background color, pattern, or image for the page.

- **Theme** enables you to set background patterns, graphic elements, and color schemes for an entire page all at once.

✔ Tips

- For more detailed instructions about formatting text, consult **Chapters 3** and **4**.

- Formatting techniques not specifically covered in this chapter either work exactly as they do for regular Word documents or they do not apply to Web pages.

Figure 10
The Formatting Palette, expanded to display many of the formatting options that can be applied to Web pages and Word documents.

Figure 11
The Format menu offers many commands for formatting a document and its contents.

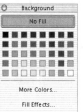

Figure 12
The Background color palette.

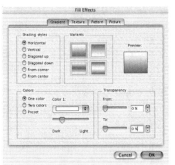

Figure 13
The Fill
Effects dialog
offers options
for Gradient, ...

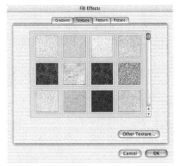

Figure 14
... Texture, ...

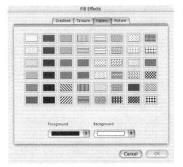

Figure 15
... Pattern, ...

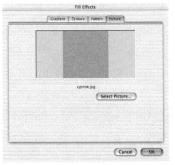

Figure 16
... and Picture
for the
background.

To set the page background color, pattern, or image

1. Choose Format > Background (**Figure 11**) to display the Background color palette (**Figure 12**).

2. To set a background color, click a color button.

   or

   To set a background pattern or texture, click the Fill Effects button. Then set options on one of the four tabs in the Fill Effects dialog that appears:

   ▲ **Gradient** (**Figure 13**) enables you to set a gradient fill pattern for the background. Select a color option and shading style to create the gradient you want. Other options appear in the dialog depending on the options you select.

   ▲ **Texture** (**Figure 14**) enables you to set a texture for the background. Click a texture button to select it.

   ▲ **Pattern** (**Figure 15**) enables you to set a standard fill pattern for the background. Select the pattern you want, then choose Foreground and Background colors from the pop-up menus.

   ▲ **Picture** (**Figure 16**) enables you to use an image as a background. The image is repeated to fill the page. Click the Select Picture button to locate and select a picture file on disk.

   To save the Fill Effects dialog settings, click OK.

   or

   To remove a background color or pattern, click the No Fill button.

3. Click the Background color palette's close button to dismiss it.

SETTING THE PAGE BACKGROUND

To set the page theme

1. Choose Format > Theme (**Figure 11**) to display the Theme dialog (**Figure 17**).

2. In the Theme scrolling list, select the name of the theme you want to apply to the page. The Sample area changes to show what the theme looks like.

3. If desired, in the Color Scheme scrolling list, select the name of the color scheme you want to apply. Again, your selection is applied to the Sample area.

4. Set other options by toggling check boxes near the bottom of the Theme dialog:

   ▲ **Vivid Colors** makes styles and borders a brighter color and changes the document background color.

   ▲ **Active Graphics** displays animated graphics in the Web browser window when the theme includes them.

   ▲ **Background Image** displays the background image for the theme as the page background. Turning off this check box enables you to use a plain background color with a theme.

5. Click OK to save your settings. The page's colors and background change accordingly.

✔ Tip

■ When using themes, make sure there is enough contrast between background patterns or images and the text color. Otherwise, text on your Web page may be difficult to read.

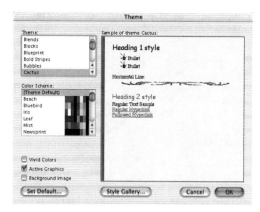

Figure 17 The Theme dialog makes it easy to set an attractive and consistent look for all of your Web pages.

SETTING THE PAGE THEME

Figure 18 Hyperlinks appear as underlined text.

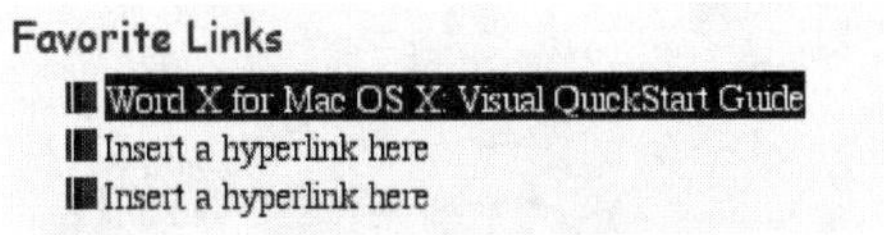

Figure 19 Select the text that you want to use as a hyperlink.

Figure 20
The Insert menu.

Figure 21 The Web Page tab of the Insert Hyperlink dialog.

Hyperlinks

A hyperlink is text or a graphic that, when clicked, displays other information. Word enables you to create two kinds of hyperlinks:

◆ A link to a *URL* (*Uniform Resource Locator*), which is the Internet address of a document or individual. Word makes it easy to create links to two types of URLs:

    ▲ **http://** links to a Web page on a Web server.

    ▲ **mailto:** links to an e-mail address.

◆ A link to a Word document on your hard disk or network.

By default, hyperlinks appear as colored, underlined text (**Figure 18**).

✔ Tip

■ Word can automatically format URLs as hyperlinks. Simply type the complete URL; when you press [Spacebar] or [Return], Word turns the URL into a hyperlink. You can set this option in the AutoFormat dialog, which I tell you about in **Chapter 4**.

To insert a hyperlink

1. Position the insertion point where you want the hyperlink to appear.

   or

   Select the text or picture that you want to convert to a hyperlink (**Figure 19**).

2. Choose Insert > Hyperlink (**Figure 20**) or press ⌃⌘K. The Insert Hyperlink dialog appears (**Figure 21**).

Continued on next page...

INSERTING HYPERLINKS

Continued from previous page.

Figure 22 Type the URL for the link location.

3. To link to a Web page, enter the complete URL of the page in the Link to text box (**Figure 22**).

or

To link to a document on your hard disk or another computer on your network, click the Select button in the Document tab and use the Choose a File dialog that appears (**Figure 23**) to locate and select the document. When you click Open, Word automatically fills in the Link to text box (**Figure 24**).

or

To link to an e-mail address, fill in the To and Subject fields in the E-mail Address tab. Word automatically fills in the Link to text box (**Figure 25**).

4. Click OK to save your settings and dismiss the Insert Hyperlink dialog.

The hyperlink is inserted.

or

The selected text turns into a hyperlink (**Figure 18**).

✔ Tip

■ You can also use the Favorites (**Figure 26**), History, Recent Documents, or Recent Addresses pop-up menu in the Insert Hyperlink dialog to link to a favorite or recently opened item.

Figure 23 Use the Choose a File dialog to locate, select, and open the document you want to link to.

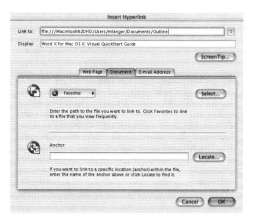

Figure 24 When you select a document to link to, Word fills in the Link to text box for you.

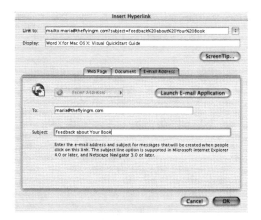

Figure 25 When you fill in the To and Subject text boxes, Word composes the URL to link to the address.

Figure 26 Pop-up menus like this one enable you to link to favorite or recent URLs or documents.

Figure 27 When you point to a link, the mouse pointer turns into a pointing finger and the link location appears in a yellow Screen Tip box above it.

Figure 28 The Web toolbar appears above the document window.

To follow a hyperlink

1. Position the mouse pointer on the hyperlink. The mouse pointer turns into a pointing finger and the link location appears in a yellow box above the hyperlink (**Figure 27**).

2. Click once.

   If the hyperlink points to an Internet URL, Word launches your default Web browser, connects to the Internet, and displays the URL.

   or

   If the hyperlink points to a file on your hard disk or another computer on the network, the file opens.

   or

   If the hyperlink points to an e-mail address, Word launches your default e-mail application and displays a new message form with the address included in the link.

✔ Tip

- The Web toolbar (**Figure 28**) appears above the Word document window when you follow a link. You can use this toolbar to navigate linked pages on your computer, your local area network, or the Web.

To remove a hyperlink

1. Drag to select the hyperlink (**Figure 29**).

2. Choose Insert > Hyperlink (**Figure 20**) or press ⌃ ⌘ K.

3. In the Edit Hyperlink dialog that appears (**Figure 30**), click the Remove Link button.

4. Click OK.

   The link is removed from the text, but the text remains. All hyperlink formatting is removed.

or

1. Drag to select the hyperlink (**Figure 29**).

2. Press Delete.

   Both the text and its hyperlink are removed from the document.

✔ Tip

■ You can also use the Edit Hyperlink dialog (**Figure 30**) to change the Link to text box's contents, as discussed earlier in this section.

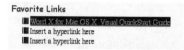

Favorite Links

Figure 29 Select the hyperlink text.

Figure 30 The Edit Hyperlink dialog.

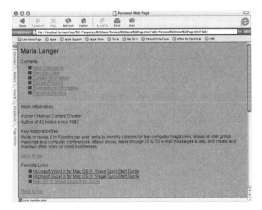

Figure 31 The Web page appears in your default Web browser's window.

Working with Web Page Files

Word offers several options for working with Web page files.

◆ Preview Web pages with your default Web browser.

◆ Save Web pages created with a Web page template.

◆ Save Web page files as regular Word documents.

◆ Save regular Word documents as Web pages.

◆ Open Web pages stored on your computer, another computer on the network, or the World Wide Web.

✔ Tips

■ The name of a Web page file should not contain any spaces and should end with the .htm or .html file name extension to be properly recognized as a Web page file. If you're not sure which extension to use, ask your network administrator or ISP.

■ When copying Web pages to a directory on a Web server, be sure to include the Web page file and its associated image files.

To preview a Web page

Choose File > Web Page Preview (**Figure 1**).

Word launches your default Web browser. The Web page appears in the browser window (**Figure 31**).

✔ Tip

■ Your default Web browser is the one selected in the Web tab of the Internet control panel.

To save a Web page

1. Choose File > Save (**Figure 1**) to display the Save As dialog (**Figure 32**).

2. Use the dialog to enter a name and select a disk location for the file.

3. Make sure Web Page is chosen from the Format pop-up menu (**Figure 33**).

4. Click Save.

   Word saves the file. Each picture within the file is also saved as an individual JPEG or GIF format graphic file in a folder named for the Web page (**Figure 34**).

✔ Tip

- To set advanced options for saving a document as a Web page, click the Web Options button. This displays the Web Options dialog, which is discussed briefly in **Chapter 15**.

To save a Web page as a regular Word document

1. With a Web page open, choose File > Save As (**Figure 1**) to display the Save As dialog (**Figure 32**).

2. Use the dialog to enter a name and select a disk location for the file.

3. Make sure Microsoft Word document is chosen from the Format pop-up menu (**Figure 33**).

4. Click Save.

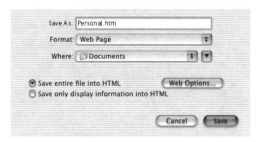

Figure 32 Use this dialog sheet to save a document as a Web page.

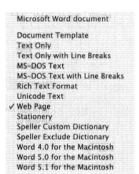

Figure 33
Use the Format pop-up menu in the Save As dialog to choose the format in which you want to save the file.

Figure 34
A saved Web page and image files, viewed in the Finder.

Figure 35 The Open Web Page dialog.

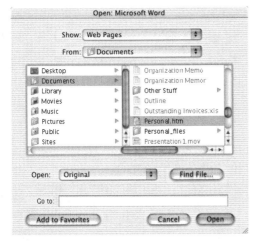

Figure 36 The Open dialog.

To save a regular Word document as a Web page

1. With a Word document open, choose File > Save As Web Page (**Figure 1**) to display the Save As dialog (**Figure 32**).

2. Use the dialog to enter a name and select a disk location for the file.

3. Make sure Web Page is chosen from the Format pop-up menu.

4. Click Save.

   Word saves the document as a Web page. Each picture within the file is saved as a JPEG or GIF format graphic file in a folder named for the Web page (**Figure 34**).

To open a Web page

1. Choose File > Open Web Page (**Figure 1**) to display the Open Web Page dialog (**Figure 35**).

2. Enter the complete URL or pathname for the Web page that you want to open in the text box.

3. Click OK.

   Word opens the Web page you indicated, whether it is on your hard disk, another computer on the network, or the World Wide Web.

✔ Tips

- You can also use the Open command and dialog (**Figure 36**) to open Web page files located on your computer. Be sure to choose Web Pages from the Show pop-up menu so Web pages appear in the list of files.

- Double-clicking the Finder icon for a Web page created with Word will open the document with your default Web browser—*not* Microsoft Word.

SAVING & OPENING WEB PAGE FILES

267

SETTING WORD PREFERENCES

15

The Preferences Dialog

Microsoft Word's Preferences dialog offers ten categories of options that you can set to customize the way Word works for you:

◆ **View** preferences control Word's onscreen appearance.

◆ **General** preferences control general Word operations.

◆ **Edit** preferences control editing.

◆ **Print** preferences control document printing.

◆ **Save** preferences control file saving.

◆ **Spelling and Grammar** preferences control spelling and grammar checker operations.

◆ **Track Changes** preferences control the track changes feature.

◆ **User Information** preferences contain information about the primary user.

◆ **Compatibility** preferences control a document's compatibility with other applications or versions of Word.

◆ **File Locations** preferences specify where certain Word files are stored on disk.

✔ Tip

■ Word's default preference settings are discussed and illustrated throughout this book.

To set preferences

1. Choose Word > Preferences (**Figure 1**) to display the Preferences dialog (**Figure 3**).

2. On the left side of the window, click the name of the category of options you want to set. The dialog changes to display that preferences pane.

3. Set options as desired.

4. Repeat steps 2 and 3 for other categories of options that you want to set.

5. Click OK to save your settings.

✔ Tips

■ I illustrate and discuss all Preferences dialog options throughout this chapter.

■ You can get information about an option by pointing to it; a description of the option appears at the bottom of the Preferences dialog (**Figure 3**).

To restore preferences to the default settings

1. If Word is running, choose Word > Quit Word (**Figure 1**) to quit it.

2. In the Finder, open the folder at this path: ~/Library/Preferences/Microsoft/ (where ~/ represents your home folder).

3. Locate the file named *Word Settings (10)* (**Figure 2**) and drag it to the Trash.

4. Choose Finder > Empty Trash.

5. Launch Word.

✔ Tips

■ When the Word Settings (10) file is deleted, Word automatically creates a new file with the same name, using default preference settings.

■ As you may have guessed, Word creates a Word Settings (10) file for each user.

Figure 1
Both the Preferences and Quit commands were moved to the Word menu in Word X.

Figure 2 Word preferences are stored in the Word Settings (10) file.

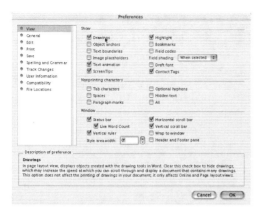

Figure 3 The default options in the View pane of the Preferences dialog in Normal view. Although options are the same in other views, the default settings may differ. Note how the bottom of the dialog displays a description of the option that is being pointed to.

View Preferences

The View tab of the Preferences dialog (**Figure 3**) offers options in three categories: Show, Non-printing characters, and Window.

Show

Show options determine which Word elements appear on screen:

◆ **Drawings** displays objects created with Word's drawing tools. Turning off this option can speed up the display and scrolling of documents with many drawings.

◆ **Object anchors** displays the anchor marker indicating that an object is attached to text. An object's anchor can only appear when the object is selected, this check box is turned on, and nonprinting characters are displayed. You must turn on this option to move an anchor.

◆ **Text boundaries** displays dotted lines around page margins, text columns, and objects.

◆ **Image placeholders** displays graphics as empty boxes. Turning on this option can speed up the display of documents with a lot of graphics.

◆ **Text animation** displays animation applied to text. Turning off this option displays animated text the way it will print.

◆ **ScreenTips** displays comments in yellow boxes when you point to annotated text.

◆ **Highlight** displays text highlighting.

◆ **Bookmarks** displays document bookmarks by enclosing their names in square brackets. If displayed, the bookmarks do not print.

◆ **Field codes** displays field codes instead of results.

Continued on next page...

VIEW PREFERENCES

Continued from previous page.

→   Here's some text to show off all the non-printing characters. ¶

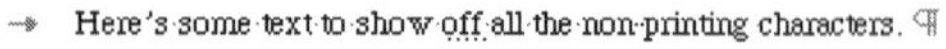

Figure 4 Nonprinting characters revealed!

- **Field shading** enables you to specify how you want fields shaded. The options are:

  ▲ **Never** never shades fields.

  ▲ **Always** always shades fields.

  ▲ **When selected only** shades a field when it is selected.

- **Draft font** displays most character formatting as bold or underlined and displays graphics as empty boxes. Turning on this option can speed up the display of heavily formatted documents.

- **Contact Tags** displays purple dotted underlines beneath information inserted from the Contact toolbar. Clicking one of these contact tags displays a menu you can use to perform certain tasks with the information or its record in Entourage's contact database.

Nonprinting characters

Nonprinting character options determine which (if any) nonprinting characters appear on screen (**Figure 4**).

- **Tab characters** displays gray right-pointing arrows for tab characters.

- **Spaces** displays tiny gray dots for space characters.

- **Paragraph marks** displays gray backwards Ps for return characters.

- **Optional hyphens** displays black dots for optional hyphen characters.

- **Hidden text** displays text formatted as hidden with a dotted underline.

- **All** displays all hidden characters. Turning on this option is the same as turning on the Show/Hide ¶ button ¶ on the Standard toolbar.

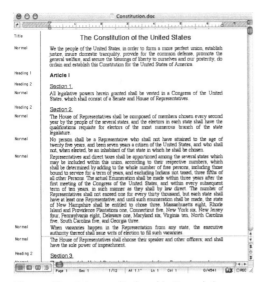

Figure 5 The style area displayed in Normal view.

Window

Window options determine which window elements are displayed.

◆ **Status bar** displays the status bar at the bottom of the window.

◆ **Live Word Count** displays the current word number and total word count in the status bar. The Status bar option must be turned on to turn on this option.

◆ **Vertical ruler** displays a ruler down the left side of the window.

◆ **Style area width** enables you to specify a width for the style area. When set to a value greater than 0, the style area appears along the left side of the window and indicates the style applied to each paragraph in the document (**Figure 5**). You may find this feature useful if you use styles in your documents.

◆ **Horizontal scroll bar** displays a scroll bar along the bottom of the window.

◆ **Vertical scroll bar** displays a scroll bar along the right side of the window.

◆ **Wrap to window** wraps text to the width of the window rather than to the right indent or margin.

◆ **Header and Footer pane** displays the document's header and footer in a separate pane of the document window when the document is in Normal view.

VIEW PREFERENCES

General Preferences

General preferences (**Figure 6**) control the general operation of Word:

◆ **Background repagination** paginates documents automatically as you work. (This option cannot be turned off in Page Layout view.)

◆ **Include formatted text in Clipboard** includes text formatting for any text placed on the Clipboard with the Copy or Cut commands. This makes it possible to paste formatted text with the Paste command.

◆ **Blue background, white text** displays the document as white text on a blue background—like the old WordPerfect software.

◆ **Provide feedback with sound** plays sound effects at the conclusion of certain actions or with the appearance of alerts.

◆ **Provide feedback with animation** displays special animated cursors while waiting for certain actions to complete.

◆ **Confirm conversion at Open** displays a dialog that you can use to select a converter when you open a file created with another application.

◆ **Update automatic links at Open** automatically updates linked information when you open a document containing links to other files.

◆ **Recently used file list** enables you to specify the number of recently opened files that should appear near the bottom of the File menu. This feature is handy for quickly reopening recently accessed files.

◆ **Macro virus protection** displays a warning dialog every time you open a Word document that might contain a macro virus. The dialog lets you decide whether you want to open the file with or without its macros. Use this feature if you share Word files with others.

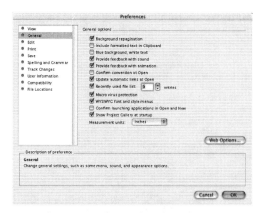

Figure 6 The default options in the General pane of the Preferences dialog.

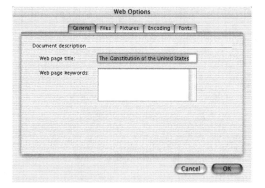

Figure 7 The General tab of the Web Options dialog.

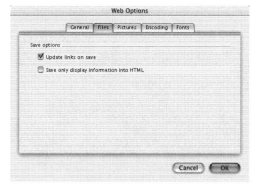

Figure 8 The Files tab of the Web Options dialog.

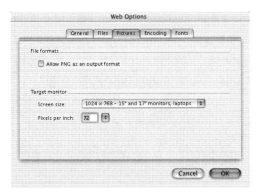

Figure 9 The Pictures tab of the Web Options dialog.

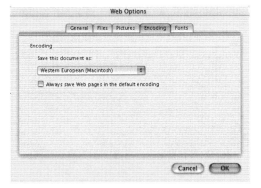

Figure 10 The Encoding tab of the Web Options dialog.

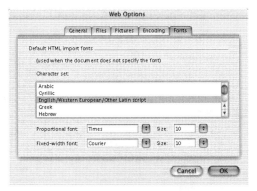

Figure 11 The Fonts tab of the Web options dialog.

◆ **WYSIWYG font and style menus** displays font names in the Font menu in their actual typefaces and style names in the Style menu with their actual formatting. This helps you see what these fonts and styles look like before you apply them.

◆ **Confirm launching applications in Open and New** displays a confirmation dialog when you use the Open dialog or Project Gallery to open or create a non-Word document.

◆ **Show Project Gallery at startup** displays the Project Gallery window when you launch Word by opening its application icon.

◆ **Measurement units** enables you to select the measurement unit used throughout Word. Options are Inches, Centimeters, Points, and Picas.

Web Options

Clicking the Web Options button displays the Web Options dialog (**Figures 7** through **11**), which has five different tabs of options for creating and working with Web pages. Although these options are advanced and far beyond the scope of this book, here's a quick overview of each.

◆ **General** options (**Figure 7**) enable you to specify the name and keywords of the file for use in HTML HEAD tags.

◆ **Files** options (**Figure 8**) enable you to specify how HTML information should be saved for the file.

◆ **Pictures** options (**Figure 9**) enable you to control the file format of images and specify the resolution of the target monitor.

◆ **Encoding** options (**Figure 10**) enable you to control how a Web page is coded when saved.

◆ **Fonts** options (**Figure 11**) enable you to control the character set and default fonts.

Edit Preferences

Edit preferences (**Figure 12**) control the way certain editing tasks work. There are two categories: Editing options and Click and type.

Editing options

Editing options set the way text is edited:

◆ **Typing replaces selection** deletes text when you start typing. If you turn this check box off, Word inserts typed text to the left of any text selected before you began typing.

◆ **Drag-and-drop text editing** allows you to move or copy selected text by dragging it.

◆ **When selecting, automatically select entire word** selects entire words when your selection includes the spaces after words. This feature makes it impossible to use the mouse to select multiple word fragments.

◆ **Use the INS key for paste** enables you to press the ⌐Ins⌐ key to use the Paste command.

◆ **Overtype mode** replaces characters, one at a time, as you type. This is the opposite of Insert mode.

◆ **Use smart cut and paste** adds or removes spaces as necessary when you delete, drag, or paste text. This feature can save time when editing text.

◆ **Tabs and backspace set left indent** increases or decreases the left indent when you press the ⌐Tab⌐ or ⌐Delete⌐ key. This feature can cause undesired paragraph formatting changes.

◆ **Allow accented uppercase in French** enables Word's proofing tools to suggest accent marks for uppercase characters for text formatted as French.

◆ **Match font with keyboard** automatically switches the keyboard layout to match the language of another character set, such as Russian or Greek.

Figure 12 The default options in the Edit pane of the Preferences dialog.

Click and type

Click and type options control the way the click and type feature works:

◆ **Enable click and type** turns on the click and type feature.

◆ **Default Paragraph Style** enables you to select the default style for click and type entries in a document.

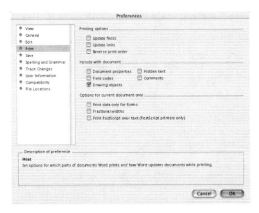

Figure 13 The default options in the Print pane of the Preferences dialog.

Print Preferences

Print preferences (**Figure 13**) control the way documents print. There are three categories: Printing options, Include with document, and Options for current document only.

Printing options

Printing options let you specify how the document content is updated and printed:

- **Update fields** automatically updates Word fields before you print. This feature prevents you from printing a document with outdated field contents.

- **Update links** automatically updates information in linked files before you print. This feature prevents you from printing a file with outdated linked file contents.

- **Reverse print order** prints documents in reverse order—last page first. This might be useful if your printer stacks output face up.

Include with document

Include with document options enable you to print or suppress specific information from the document:

- **Document properties** prints the document's summary information on a separate page after the document. This information is stored in the Summary tab of the Properties dialog (**Figure 15**).

- **Field codes** prints field codes instead of field contents.

- **Drawing objects** prints objects drawn with Word's drawing tools.

- **Hidden text** prints text formatted as hidden.

- **Comments** prints reviewer comments on a separate page after the document.

Options for current document only

As the name implies, options for current document only affect the way the active document prints:

- **Print data only for forms** prints just the information entered in fill-in forms—not the form itself.

- **Fractional widths** adjusts the spacing of proportionally spaced fonts like Helvetica and Times. This may improve the appearance of these fonts when printed.

- **Print PostScript over text** enables Word to print PostScript generated text or graphics over other text and graphics on the document page. This option only works with PostScript printers that support it.

PRINT PREFERENCES

Save Preferences

Save preferences (**Figure 14**) control the way files are saved to disk. There are two categories of Save preferences: Save options and File sharing options for the current file.

Save options

Save options enable you to set file saving preferences for all files that you save.

◆ **Always create backup copy** saves the previous version of a file as a backup copy in the same folder as the original. Each time the file is saved, the new backup copy replaces the old one.

◆ **Allow fast saves** speeds up saving by saving only the changes to an existing file. If you turn off this check box, Word saves the entire file; this takes longer but results in slightly smaller files. This option is not available when the Always create backup copy option is enabled.

◆ **Prompt for document properties** displays the Properties dialog (**Figure 15**) when you save a file for the first time. You can use this dialog to enter and store information about the file.

◆ **Prompt to save Normal template** displays a dialog that enables you to save or discard changes you made to the default settings in the Normal template. With this check box turned off, Word automatically saves changes to the Normal template.

◆ **Save data only for forms** saves the data entered into a form on the current document as a single, tab-delimited record that you can import into a database.

Figure 14 The default options in the Save pane of the Preferences dialog.

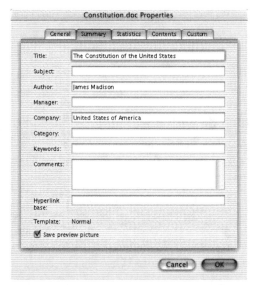

Figure 15 The Summary tab of the Properties dialog.

Figure 16
The Save Word files as pop-up menu in the Save pane of the Preferences dialog.

Figure 17
If a file requires a password to open, this dialog appears when you attempt to open it.

Figure 18 If a file requires a password to modify, this dialog appears when you attempt to open it.

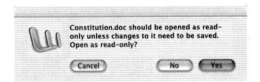

Figure 19 When a file is set to Read-only recommended, Word lets you decide whether you want to open it as read-only.

♦ **Save AutoRecover info every** enables you to set a frequency for automatically saving a special document recovery file. Word can use the AutoRecover file to recreate the document if your computer crashes or loses power before you get a chance to save changes.

♦ **Save Word files as** enables you to choose a default format for saving Word files. The pop-up menu (**Figure 16**) offers the same options found in the Save As dialog.

File sharing options

The File sharing options affect only the current document.

♦ **Password to open** enables you to specify a password that must be entered to open the file (**Figure 17**).

♦ **Password to modify** enables you to specify a password that must be entered to save modifications to the file (**Figure 18**).

♦ **Read-only recommended** displays a dialog that recommends that the file be opened as a read-only file (**Figure 19**). If the file is opened as read-only, changes to the file must be saved in a file with a different name or in a different disk location.

SAVE PREFERENCES

Spelling and Grammar Preferences

Spelling and Grammar preferences (**Figure 20**) control the way the spelling and grammar checkers work. There are two categories of preferences: Spelling and Grammar.

Spelling

Spelling options control the way the spelling checker works:

◆ **Check spelling as you type** turns on the automatic spelling check feature.

◆ **Hide spelling errors in this document** hides the red wavy lines that Word uses to identify possible spelling errors when the automatic spelling check feature is turned on. This option is only available when the Check spelling as you type option is enabled.

◆ **Always suggest corrections** tells Word to automatically display a list of suggested replacements for a misspelled word during a manual spelling check.

◆ **Suggest from main dictionary only** tells Word to suggest replacement words from the main dictionary—not from your custom dictionaries.

◆ **Ignore words in UPPERCASE** tells Word not to check words in all uppercase characters, such as acronyms.

◆ **Ignore words with numbers** tells Word not to check words that include numbers, such as *MariaL1*.

◆ **Ignore Internet and file addresses** tells Word not to check any words that appear to be URLs, e-mail addresses, file names, or file pathnames.

◆ **Use German post-reform rules** tells Word to use German post-reform rules rather than traditional rules when the language is set to German.

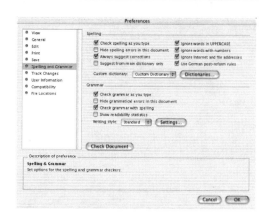

Figure 20 The default options in the Spelling and Grammar pane of the Preferences dialog.

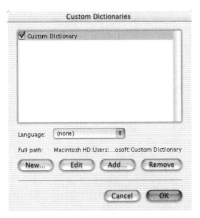

Figure 21 The Custom Dictionaries dialog.

◆ **Custom dictionary** displays the name of the currently selected custom dictionary. This is the dictionary file to which words are added when you add words to the dictionary during a spelling check. You can use the pop-up menu to select a different custom dictionary if desired.

◆ **Dictionaries** enables you to create, edit, add, and remove custom dictionaries. Click this button to display the Custom Dictionaries dialog (**Figure 21**), which lists all the dictionary files open in Word. Then:

▲ To activate a dictionary file so it can be used by the spelling checker, turn on the check box to the left of its name in the Custom dictionaries list.

▲ To change the language of the selected dictionary file, choose a language from the Language pop-up menu.

▲ To create a new custom dictionary, click the New button and use the dialog that appears to name and save the new dictionary file.

▲ To edit the selected dictionary, click the Edit button to open it in Word. Then make changes and save it.

▲ To add a dictionary to the Custom dictionaries list, click the Add button and use the dialog that appears to locate and open the dictionary file. This feature makes it possible to share dictionary files that contain company- or industry-specific terms with other Word users in your workplace.

▲ To remove a dictionary from Word, select the dictionary and click the Remove button. This does not delete the dictionary file from disk.

Grammar

Grammar options control the way the grammar checker works:

◆ **Check grammar as you type** turns on the automatic grammar check feature.

◆ **Hide grammatical errors in this document** hides the green wavy lines that Word uses to identify possible grammar errors when the automatic grammar check feature is turned on. This option is only available when the Check grammar as you type option is enabled.

◆ **Check grammar with spelling** performs a grammar check as part of a manual spelling check.

◆ **Show readability statistics** displays readability statistics (**Figure 22**) for a document at the conclusion of a manual spelling and grammar check. This option is only available when the Check grammar with spelling option is enabled.

◆ **Writing style** enables you to select a set of rules for the grammar checker. Use the pop-up menu to select one of five options (**Figure 23**).

◆ **Settings** enables you to customize the rules for the grammar checker. Click this button to display the Grammar Settings dialog (**Figure 24**). Choose the set of rules that you want to modify from the Writing style pop-up menu (**Figure 23**), then use the options in the dialog to set the style's rules. You can use the Reset All button to reset all writing style rule sets to the default settings.

✔ Tip

■ The Check Document button at the bottom of the Spelling and Grammar pane of the Preferences dialog enables you to clear the list of ignored problems and recheck a document for errors.

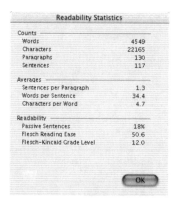

Figure 22 Readability statistics for the Constitution of the United States.

Figure 23
The Writing style pop-up menu offers five different predefined sets of rules.

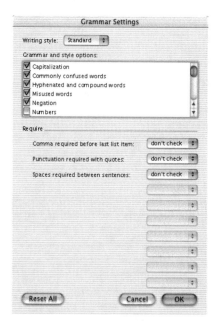

Figure 24 The Grammar Settings dialog lets you fine-tune the settings for different writing style rule sets. The unlabeled pop-up menus may offer a variety of options for languages other than English.

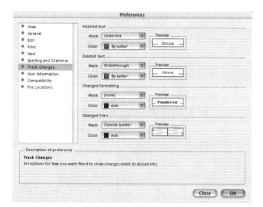

Figure 25 The default options in the Track Changes pane of the Preferences dialog.

Figure 26 The User Information pane of the Preferences dialog.

Track Changes Preferences

The Track Changes preferences (**Figure 25**) control the way the Track Changes feature works. For each option, you can change the mark and color that Word uses to display document changes. The Preview areas show formatting samples.

◆ **Inserted text** controls the appearance of text that is inserted into the document.

◆ **Deleted text** controls the appearance of text that is deleted from the document.

◆ **Changed formatting** controls the appearance of text which has been reformatted.

◆ **Changed lines** controls the appearance and location of margin marks beside changed lines of text.

User Information Preferences

The User Information preferences (**Figure 26**) store information about the primary user of that copy of Word. This information is used by a variety of features throughout Word. The fields of information here are self-explanatory so I won't go into them in detail.

If you click the More button, Word displays an address book form that you can use to enter and edit additional information about yourself.

Compatibility Preferences

Compatibility preferences (**Figure 27**) control the internal formatting of the current Word document for compatibility with other applications or versions of Word.

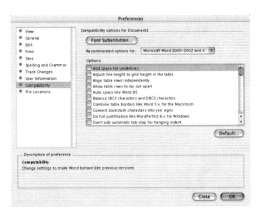

Figure 27 The default options in the Compatibility pane of the Preferences dialog.

◆ **Font Substitution** enables you to specify a font to be used in place of a font applied in the document but not installed on your computer. (This happens most often when you open a file that was created on someone else's computer.) Click this button to display the Font Substitution dialog (**Figure 28**). You can then select the missing font name and choose a substitution font from the Substituted font pop-up menu. The menu will include all fonts installed on your computer. To actually reformat text by applying the substituted font, click the Convert Permanently button. If the document does not contain any missing fonts, Word does not display the Font Substitution dialog.

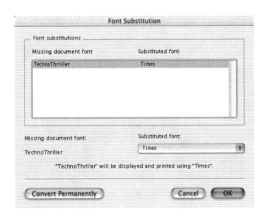

Figure 28 The Font Substitution dialog.

◆ **Recommended options for** enables you to select a collection of compatibility rules for a specific application. Choose an option from the pop-up menu (**Figure 29**).

◆ **Options** enables you to toggle check boxes for a variety of internal formatting options. These options are automatically set when you choose one of the rule sets from the Recommended options for pop-up menu, but you can override them as desired.

◆ **Default** applies the current dialog settings to all documents created with the current template from that point forward.

| • Microsoft Word 2000–2002 and X |
| Microsoft Word 97–98 |
| Microsoft Word 6.0/95 |
| Word for Windows 1.0 |
| Word for Windows 2.0 |
| Word for the Macintosh 5.x |
| Word for MS-DOS |
| WordPerfect 5.x |
| WordPerfect 6.x for Windows |
| WordPerfect 6.0 for DOS |
| Custom |

Figure 29
The Recommended options for pop-up menu.

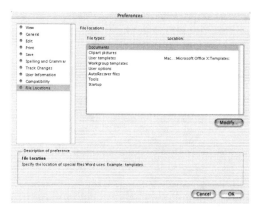

Figure 30 The default settings in the File Locations pane of the Preferences dialog.

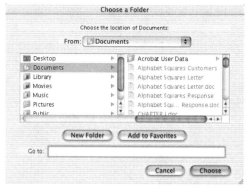

Figure 31 Use this dialog to set the location of a specific type of file.

Figure 32 The pathname for the folder you set appears in the dialog.

File Locations Preferences

File Locations preferences (**Figure 30**) enable you to set the default disk location for certain types of files. This makes it easier for Word (and you) to locate these files.

To set or change a default file location

1. Click to select the name of the file type for which you want to set or change the file location (**Figure 30**).

2. Click the Modify button.

3. Use the Choose a Folder dialog that appears (**Figure 31**) to locate and select the folder in which the files are or will be stored.

4. Click the Choose button.

   The pathname for the location appears to the right of the name of the file type (**Figure 32**).

285

MENUS & SHORTCUT KEYS

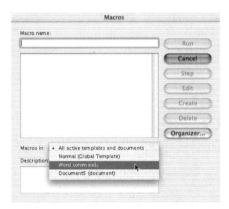

Figure 1 Choose Word commands from the Macros in pop-up menu in the Macros dialog.

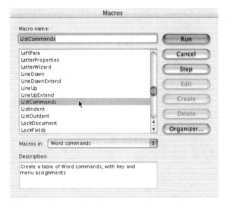

Figure 2 Select ListCommands in the Macro name list.

Figure 3
Use this dialog to specify which commands you want to include in the list.

Menus & Shortcut Keys

This appendix illustrates all of Word's standard menus and provides a list of shortcut keys—including some that don't appear on menus.

To use a shortcut key, hold down the modifier key (usually ⌃ ⌘) and press the keyboard key corresponding to the command. For example, to use the Save command's shortcut key, hold down ⌃ ⌘ and press S.

✔ Tip

■ I tell you all about using menus and shortcut keys in **Chapter 1**.

To create a list of menu commands & shortcut keys

1. Choose Tools > Macro > Macros.

2. In the Macros dialog that appears, choose Word commands from the Macros in pop-up menu (**Figure 1**).

3. Select ListCommands in the Macro name list (**Figure 2**).

4. Click Run.

5. In the List Commands dialog that appears, select the Current menu and keyboard settings radio button (**Figure 3**).

6. Click OK.

   Word creates a new document with a table of all commands and their shortcut keys and menus.

Edit	
Undo Paste	⌘Z
Repeat Copy	⌘Y
Cut	⌘X
Copy	⌘C
Paste	⌘V
Paste Special...	
Paste as Hyperlink	
Clear	▶
Select All	⌘A
Find...	⌘F
Replace...	⇧⌘H
Go To...	⌘G
Links...	
Object	

Word Menu

⌘H	Hide Word
⌘Q	Quit Word

File Menu

Shift ⌘P	Project Gallery
⌘N	New Blank Document
⌘O	Open
⌘W	Close
Option ⌘W	Close All
⌘S	Save
F12	Save As
⌘P	Print

Mail Recipient (as Attachment)...
Microsoft PowerPoint

Send To submenu

(no shortcut keys)

Edit Menu

⌘Z	Undo
⌘Y	Repeat
Option Return	Repeat
⌘X	Cut
⌘C	Copy
⌘V	Paste
⌘A	Select All
⌘F	Find
⌘F	Find
Shift ⌘H	Replace
F5	Go To

Formats
Contents

Clear submenu

Clear	Clear Contents
Delete	Clear Contents

WORD, FILE, & EDIT MENUS

View Menu

Control 5   Word 5 Menus

Insert Menu

Option ⌃ ⌘ A   Comment

Shift ⌃ ⌘ F5   Bookmark

⌃ ⌘ K   Hyperlink

Toolbars submenu
(no shortcut keys)

Break submenu

Shift ←Enter   Page Break

Shift ⌃ ⌘ Return   Column Break

AutoText submenu

Option F3   New

Clip Art...
From File...

Horizontal Line...
AutoShapes
WordArt...
From Scanner or Camera...
Chart

Picture submenu
(no shortcut keys)

Background Sound...
Scrolling Text...

Checkbox...
Option Button...
List Box...
Textbox...
Submit...
Reset...
Hidden...

HTML Object submenu
(no shortcut keys)

Format Menu

⌃ ⌘ D	Font
Option ⌃ ⌘ M	Paragraph
Shift F3	Change Case
Option ⌃ ⌘ K	AutoFormat
Shift ⌃ ⌘ S	Style

Font Menu

(no shortcut keys)

Tools Menu

Option ⌃ ⌘ L	Spelling and Grammar
Option ⌃ ⌘ R	Thesaurus

Track Changes submenu

(no shortcut keys)

Macro submenu

(no shortcut keys)

Table
Draw Table
Insert ▶
Delete ▶
Select ▶
Merge Cells
Split Cells...
Split Table
Table AutoFormat...
AutoFit ▶
Heading Rows Repeat
Convert ▶
Sort...
Formula...
✓ Gridlines
Table Properties...

Window
Zoom Window
Minimize Window ⌘M
Bring All to Front
New Window
Arrange All
Split
1 Alphabet Squares Letter
2 CHAPTER I.doc
✓ 3 Document5
4 Johnson.doc

Table Menu

(no shortcut keys)

Window Menu

⌃ ⌘ M   Minimize

Option ⌃ ⌘ S Split

Table...
Columns to the Left
Columns to the Right
Rows Above
Rows Below
Cells...

Insert submenu

(no shortcut keys)

AutoFit to Contents
AutoFit to Window
Fixed Column Width
Distribute Rows Evenly
Distribute Columns Evenly

AutoFit submenu

(no shortcut keys)

Table
Columns
Rows
Cells...

Delete submenu

(no shortcut keys)

AutoFit to Contents
AutoFit to Window
Fixed Column Width
Distribute Rows Evenly
Distribute Columns Evenly

Convert submenu

(no shortcut keys)

Table
Column
Row
Cell

Select submenu

(no shortcut keys)

TABLE & WINDOW MENUS

Add to Work Menu

Work Menu

(no shortcut keys)

Help

Search Word Help
Word Help Contents
Additional Help Resources

✓ Use the Office Assistant

Downloads and Updates
Visit the Mactopia Web Site
Send Feedback on Word

Help Menu

⌃ ⌘ ?   Search Word
             Help

WORK & HELP MENUS

INDEX

35mm slides, 246
... (ellipsis), in menus, 5
<< >> (paired angle brackets), in form letters, 222
¶ button, 36, 186, 273

A

accented characters, 276
Accept or Reject Changes dialog, 236
Acrobat Reader, 139
Active Graphics option, Theme, 260
active window, 18
address books, 239, 248, 250
address labels. *See* labels
Address Position dialog, 208
Adjust Table Row area, 198
Adobe Acrobat Reader, 139
Align buttons, 65, 191
alignment
    table, 191
    text, 63, 65, 67, 71, 74
all caps, 59, 61, 80
anchor markers, 271
angle brackets (<< >>), in form letters, 222
animated text, 271
annotations, document, 149, 230–231
antonyms, finding, 120
Apple Web site, 163
Aqua interface, xi, xii, 3
Arrange All command, 18
Art menu, 88
AutoComplete feature, 142, 143–144
AutoCorrect feature
    adding/deleting entries, 118
    and AutoComplete options, 143
    and AutoFormat As You Type options, 102
    and AutoText entries, 142–143
    converting characters to symbols with, 101
    setting options for, 117
    and spelling/typing errors, 111, 114, 116, 117
AutoFit options, Table, 182, 200–201
AutoFormat As You Type feature, 99, 102
AutoFormat feature, 75, 99–102, 183, 203
AutoNumber option, footnote/ endnote, 151
AutoRecover options, 279
AutoShapes toolbar, 159
AutoText feature, 109, 141, 142–144, 289

B

Background color palette, 258, 259
Background Image option, 260
background repagination, 274
backups, file, 278
balloon help, 21
barcodes, 208, 212
Based on Recent category, Project Gallery, 32
baseline, 76
Blank Web Page template, 255
blinking insertion point. *See* insertion point
Body Text style, 101
Bold button, 61
bold font style, 60, 101
bookmarks, document, 272
Border Color button, 85
Border Type button/menu, 85
borders
    page, 84, 88–89
    table, 186
    text, 75, 84–87, 102
Borders and Shading dialog, 86–90
boundaries
    cell, 186, 189
    column/row, 186
    text, 271
Break submenu, 289
breaks
    column, 75, 103–104, 106
    line, 25, 35
    page, 75, 103–104
    paragraph, 25, 35
    section, 75, 103–104, 105
brochure template, 31
Browse Object buttons, 3, 15, 16
browsers. *See* Web browsers
bulleted lists, 81–82, 83, 101
Bullets and Numbering dialog, 81–82
Bullets button, 81, 82
button menus, 9
buttons, 8, 9, 12. *See also* specific buttons

C

calendars, 248
Cancel button, 12
capitalization
    all caps, 59, 61
    changing case, 75, 80
    correcting errors in, 117

INDEX

INDEX

OS X

Watch for these titles:

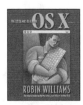

PEACHPIT PRESS

Quality How-to Computer Books

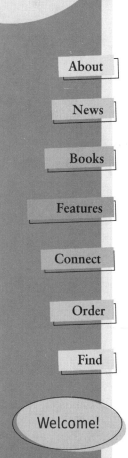

About

News

Books

Features

Connect

Order

Find

Welcome!

Visit Peachpit Press on the Web at www.peachpit.com

- Check out new feature articles each Monday: excerpts, interviews, tips, and plenty of how-tos

- Find any Peachpit book by title, series, author, or topic on the Books page

- See what our authors are up to on the News page: signings, chats, appearances, and more

- Meet the Peachpit staff and authors in the About section: bios, profiles, and candid shots

- Use Connect to reach our academic, sales, customer service, and tech support areas and find out how to become a Peachpit author or join the staff

- Click Order to enter the online store; order books or find out how to find Peachpit books anywhere in the world

Peachpit.com is also the place to:

- Chat with our authors online
- Take advantage of special Web-only offers
- Get the latest info on new books